The Rise, Decline and Future of
the British Commonwealth

The Rise, Decline and Future of the British Commonwealth

Krishnan Srinivasan

First published in 2005 by
PALGRAVE MACMILLAN
Houndmills, Basingstoke, Hampshire RG21 6XS and
175 Fifth Avenue, New York, N.Y. 10010
Companies and representatives throughout the world.

PALGRAVE MACMILLAN is the global academic imprint of the Palgrave
Macmillan division of St. Martin's Press, LLC and of Palgrave Macmillan Ltd.
Macmillan® is a registered trademark in the United States, United Kingdom
and other countries. Palgrave is a registered trademark in the European
Union and other countries.

ISBN-13: 978–1–4039–8715–0 hardback
ISBN-10: 1–4039–8715–7   hardback

This book is printed on paper suitable for recycling and made from fully
managed and sustained forest sources.

A catalogue record for this book is available from the British Library.

Library of Congress Cataloging-in-Publication Data

Srinivasan, Krishnan, 1937–
      The rise, decline and future of the British Commonwealth /
   Krishnan Srinivasan.
          p. cm.
      Includes bibliographical references and index.
      ISBN 1–4039–8715–7
      1. Commonwealth countries – History. I. Title.

DA16.S74 2005
909'.0971241—dc22   2005051552

10 9 8 7 6 5 4 3 2 1
14 13 12 11 10 09 08 07 06 05

Printed and bound in Great Britain by
Antony Rowe Ltd, Chippenham and Eastbourne

I come to talk of Commonwealth affairs.

Shakespeare *Henry VI* Part 2, Act I, Scene 3

My purpose is … to speak about the little-mentioned or noticed, to consider subjects which are neglected; to be critical, not for the sake of casting stones or scoring points but because universities must test from one generation to the next, ideas which may once have been accepted but are no longer in their full vigour, or which may be derided by fashion but worthy of a kinder fate.

Dilks, *Communications, the Commonwealth and the Future* p. 3

India's decision [to remain associated with Britain by joining the Commonwealth] strengthened the Whiggish view of the Empire's progress and purpose including the belief that British rule had been designed originally to allow dependent peoples to advance towards self-government and to reach fulfilment in the Commonwealth … the Commonwealth according to [the] counter-interpretation was not intended to end the Empire, but to continue it by other means.

Brown and Louis, *The Twentieth Century* p. xii

The rise and fall of the British Empire has often been chronicled: its aftermath less so. Perhaps the main reason for this relative neglect lies in an almost natural aversion to anticlimax.

Mayall and Payne, *The Fallacies of Hope* p. 1

What is the Commonwealth but the ghost of the British Empire come to haunt the present troubled state of international relations?

Austin, *The Round Table*, vol. 75 (297) Jan. 1986, p. 16

Contents

List of Abbreviations

ACCT	Agence de Coopération Culturelle et Technique
AIF	Agence Intergouvernmentale de la Francophonie
ANZAM	Australia, New Zealand and Malaya
ANZUS	Australia, New Zealand and the United States
APODOTI	Timorese Popular Democratic Association
BBC	British Broadcasting Corporation
CBC	Commonwealth Business Council
CENTO	Central Treaty Organization aka The Baghdad Pact
CFTC	Commonwealth Fund for Technical Cooperation
CPLP	Comunidade dos Países de Língua Portuguesa
CPP	Convention People's Party
CPSU	Communist Party of the Soviet Union
CRO	Commonwealth Relations Office
ECOSOC	United Nations Economic and Social Council
EEC	European Economic and Community
Enosis	Union of Cyprus with Greece sought by Greek Cypriots
EU	European Union
FCO	Foreign and Commonwealth Office
FLNA	Frente Nacional de Libertação de Angola
FRELIMO	Frente de Libertação de Moçambique
FRETILIN	Revolutionary Front of Independent East Timor
G7	Group of Seven major industrial democracies
G8	Group of Eight major industrial democracies (G7 plus Russia)
GATT	General Agreement on Tariffs and Trade
GDP	Gross Domestic Product
IMF	International Monetary Fund
MFN	Most Favoured Nation
MPLA	Movimento Popular de Libertação de Angola
NATO	North Atlantic Treaty Organization
NGO	Non-Governmental Organization
NIBMAR	No independence before majority African rule
OAS	Organisation Armée Secrète
OCAM	Organization of the African and Malagasy Community
ODA	Official Development Assistance
OEI	Organización de Estados Iberoamericanos

OIF	International Organization de la Francophonie
SEATO	South East Asian Treaty Organization
UDI	Unilateral Declaration of Independence
UDT	Timor Democratic Union
UK	United Kingdom of Great Britain and Northern Ireland
UN	United Nations
UNEF	United Nations Emergency Force
UNITA	União Nacional para a Independência Total de Angola
USA	United States of America
USSR	Union of Soviet Socialist Republics aka The Soviet Union
WTO	World Trade Organization
ZANU-PF	Zimbabwe African National Union-Patriotic Front

Acknowledgements

The author's grateful thanks are due to

The Netherlands Institute for Advanced Study, Wassenaar

The Institute of Commonwealth Studies, London

The Centre of International Studies, Cambridge

Wolfson College, Cambridge

Foreword

The historiography of the Commonwealth (but *not* that of the British Empire) is currently in a curious state of limbo or neglect.

Up until about thirty or forty years ago there was a stream of books and pamphlets about the Commonwealth, some of them (such as the Chatham House Surveys by Hancock, Mansergh and J.D.B. Miller) of real distinction. In the 1950s and 1960s there was much writing about the Commonwealth, which was optimistically teleological, Whiggish or progressivist in its general cast (see e.g. Patrick Gordon-Walker's book *Commonwealth* published in 1962). And within Whitehall there was much behind the scenes discussion, especially in the 1960s, by those mandarins charged with plotting the future for Britain's many remaining colonies and dependencies, several of them mini-polities with small populations.

Within Whitehall, as well, in these years there were some strong-minded empiricists contemptuous of mere rhetoric (heirs in this respect of Edmund Burke, who claimed that 'conduct is the only language that rarely lies'). A somewhat extreme but intentionally private statement of the 'empiricist's' point of view was penned, for internal Whitehall purposes only, in August 1959, by Andrew Snelling, then assistant under-secretary in the Commonwealth Relations Office, in a note sent to a colleague in the Colonial Office.

Snelling remarked that newly independent countries felt a 'psychological necessity' to demonstrate their independence to the world. Canada and South Africa had shown this in the 1920s and 1930s. If the rest of the colonies were now lumped in with these senior Dominions then the older members might believe that this detracted from their status. And then, in a classic sentence of Whitehallese, Snelling said he did 'not despair of our being able to fudge up something when the time comes ... but I do not believe we should bring down hard and fast rules in advance. This is a situation in which we can best play by ear as we go along ... let us continue with our admirable and efficient *ad-hoc-ery*'.

In the first half of the twentieth century to at least the late 1950s there were few, if any, studies of quality which advocated an end to the Commonwealth. In the early twenty-first century there have been few, if any, serious and well-informed studies of the overall Commonwealth at all. Here, however, is a challenging and lucid book on the Commonwealth, whose title indicates its main thrust and argument. It is a measure of Krishnan Srinivasan's intellectual integrity that he should in this book have commented so fully and so emphatically on what he regards as the persisting shortcomings of the contemporary Commonwealth.

As a former senior member of the Commonwealth Secretariat himself, after a distinguished career in India's diplomatic service, Mr Srinivasan understandably touches only lightly on the role of specific individuals in the substantive conduct of Commonwealth affairs. But he does not shrink from criticism of the performance at times of both the Commonwealth and of CMAG – the Commonwealth's Ministerial Action Group. Some of his comments on these matters need to be pondered by those who should want to see the Commonwealth to be a significant force in the immediate future.

Krishnan Srinivasan well knows that the association he is discussing in this challenging book has not been labelled officially as 'The British Commonwealth' since the 1960s. But it is central to his argument that it was a British-run Commonwealth at least until the mid-1960s, and perhaps later, and his conjectures as to whether this could conceivably become an appropriate designation again are of considerable interest. Furthermore, it is worth bearing in mind the ambiguous point that today in the United States and in a number of other countries it is usual to refer anachronistically to 'The British Commonwealth'. Might this be a reference to the future as well as to the past?

Commentary on the Commonwealth in recent years too often has been characterized by utopian boosterism or, even more, by cynical dismissal. Both of these extremes can be controverted by argument and by practical-minded observation of facts; and Krishnan Srinivasan's book provides its readers with plenty of relevant facts.

Mr Srinivasan's book is thus a welcome, short, but reasonably up to date history of the Commonwealth from 1947 to today. It is not teleological history; but then Whig historians have had more than their say in earlier years. And Krishnan Srinivasan is no myopic empiricist advocating *ad-hoc-ery*. He is a practical man and an experienced diplomat; but he does look beyond the present to speculate intelligently – and invariably controversially – about likely futures. Readers will want to consider carefully whether they agree that today's Commonwealth is 'Nobody's Commonwealth' and to think about the contrasts between the Commonwealth and other post-imperial clubs (see especially Chapter 3 below).

Mr Srinivasan makes extensive, some might say excessive, use of *The Round Table* journal to illustrate and mark many of his points. The writer of this foreword, as a former editor of *The Round Table*, should declare an interest here. But *The Round Table* has always been a non-governmental affair whose diverse articles are the responsibility and reflect the views of their individual authors. Jealous guardianship of their archives has made access to official papers difficult for would be scrutineers and surveyors of material inside the 30-year rule for access. These 'thirty-year rules' are the most generous terms currently available for consultation on Commonwealth matters – and these are not as generous as the availability of some American materials released or available under the permissive practices of their Freedom of Information Act. And many Commonwealth member-governments, either out of inefficiency or endemic secrecy do not make their archives available to outsiders at all.

This then is a book which provides, in relatively short compass, an overview of a rather complex institution, in language of lucidity and simplicity. The Commonwealth is a perplexing and persistent phenomenon, not only today and in recent history, but perhaps also for some considerable time to come.

In the immediate future, two sources will need to be trawled extensively by historians of the Commonwealth. The first are the British documents on the End of Empire project (conveniently known and referred to as BDEEP) whose overall editor with the help of particular specialist co-editors is Stephen Ashton from the Institute of Commonwealth Studies in the University of London. This splendid project already has produced, by the end of 2004, 13 volumes of documents, though in the preferred terminology of this enterprise a 'volume' may well consist of two, three or four parts which in binding and presentation, are each volumes in their own right.

The second major source needing to be used is the Archive of the Commonwealth Secretariat, which might cast much light on the doings of the Marlborough House mandarins (of which august company, it is worth repeating, Krishnan Srinivasan was a senior member for a number of years) from 1965 onwards – though this will not obviate the need for a critical scrutiny and comment from outsiders.

The Commonwealth is not widely understood in England, or elsewhere, nowadays. Reading and thinking about '*The Rise, Decline and Future of the British Commonwealth*' should help to lessen rudimentary ignorance and prompt further appraisal.

Peter Lyon
May 2005

Dr Peter H. Lyon, OBE, is Reader Emeritus in International Relations at the Institute of Commonwealth Studies, University of London, and was Editor of *The Round Table: The Commonwealth Journal of International Affairs* from 1983 to 2004. He is a life Vice-President of the Royal Commonwealth Society.

Introduction

The modern post-Second World War Commonwealth was designed by the British political leadership to comfort those in Britain who keenly felt the loss of Empire, and to provide a surrogate for colonial rule: an instrument to replace the Empire with a British sphere of influence covering a quarter of the world's surface. The legacy at least in terms of nomenclature is enduring. The Commonwealth ceased to be 'the British Commonwealth' with the incorporation after the Second World War of sovereign, independent states that were members of the United Nations, and even more so with the establishment in 1965 of a multilateral Secretariat. But the organization continued to have a pronounced British stamp, Britain was the adhesive that held the membership together, and 'the British Commonwealth' became the customary appellation by which the body was known to people in countries outside the Commonwealth, and to many within it as well.

The story of the Commonwealth does not want for historians, some of whom have traced the decline of this 'last Empire' from the initial heady promise of the accession of India, Pakistan and Ceylon, through Britain's descent from the moral heights as a result of Suez, followed by the combination of international circumstances that dramatically foreshortened the decolonization process in Africa and elevated the issue of racism to the highest levels of agenda-setting. The rising tide of African nationalism did not end with independence; it expressed itself vociferously in the councils of the Commonwealth and sought to influence, and even coerce, the mother country in a manner that would have been unthinkable and unacceptable for the architects of the modern Commonwealth, who took as their model the comfortable and cooperative informality of the erstwhile club of white Dominions which had existed before the Second World War. The former British

1

colonies from Africa and Asia made common cause on opposition to white racism, and the influence of the United Kingdom in the organization diminished as the British government tried to come to grips with first, a colonial rebellion in self-governing Rhodesia, and later, the pressure for sanctions against the independent minority-dominated apartheid-based Republic of South Africa. When majority rule in South Africa was imminent, the Commonwealth tried to regenerate itself into a post-Cold War organization with a platform of democracy and human rights that it could enforce through peer-pressure. This values-based approach has proved not to be implementable. Racism in Southern Africa continues to pose a challenge not only to the Commonwealth but even more so to Britain, because it was during its period as a Crown Colony that the main part of Zimbabwe's agricultural land had been alienated to the white settlers, and this inequality was allowed to fester, with the current serious consequences for good governance and the 'Harare principles' in that country.

The Commonwealth survives, its membership swollen to 53 excluding Zimbabwe, while the Dutch-Indonesian Union and the French Union and Community, all of which used precedents from the Commonwealth's experience, went under. The Commonwealth's loyalists are apt to portray their organization as unique, but it shares many common features with the other post-imperial institutions to which it gave a stimulus. The Organization de la Francophonie and the Community of Portuguese-speaking Countries, whose founding fathers drew inspiration from the Commonwealth, are far more recent, post-decolonization organizations which see none of the heated debates on Europe, imperialism and racism that took such a toll of the energies of the Commonwealth and its reputation among the British people.

During the early years when it commanded affection and admiration, and the larger number of years of its declining significance, both for Britain and for the international community, the Commonwealth left an imprint on the policies and attitudes of the British Government and public. Many of these effects were reflected in the venerable Commonwealth periodical *The Round Table*, which had been established as the journal of an intellectual pro-Empire brains-trust in 1910, and in observations in the British media. Declining British influence in the association inevitably led to diminishing British interest. The Commonwealth may have departed from centre-stage in the British public's consciousness but it still has its faithful adherents, not only from a sense of nostalgia for a London-centred past history, but also because of a deeply felt opinion among them that the principles on which the association was based would be swiftly abandoned by many of its member-states if the association itself was to crumble away. There is also particular value placed by these circles on the many non-official people-to-people ties fostered by the Commonwealth civil society links over numerous decades, which often even pre-date the modern Commonwealth, and doubts are expressed whether such bonds could continue if the Commonwealth as an organization was to disappear.

This book studies the impact of the Commonwealth since the Second World War on the process of Britain adjusting to a world without an Empire, a process which affected its view of itself as a major power, as a participant in the evolving European architecture and as a partner in a special relationship with the increasingly assertive United States of America. Economic pressures and vulnerability led to the de-emphasis of Commonwealth ties, even with the old Dominions, and a new orientation towards a Franco-German dominated Europe. This adjustment also affected the vision of national identity; how the British people saw themselves in the post-imperial mode, and how they reacted to immigration flows from the former Empire. The term 'migration' had always been earlier associated with emigration from Britain to the colonies or to the United States. The immigration factor brought racism, an issue never successfully resolved overseas in the Empire, into Britain's heartland and resulted in fresh attitudes to citizenship and nationality that were not always enlightened. Immigration made Britain a multicultural society which would have been unrecognizable even just after the Second World War.

Whither the Commonwealth now? What is its record of achievement, shorn of the habitual self-satisfaction to be found in its documentation and promoted by its Secretariat? What are the benefits of membership to countries in terms of collective political influence and in respect of trade, investment, aid, travel and education? There is no shortage of would-be pall-bearers for the association, including several who have not subjected the Commonwealth's professed qualities to any searching analysis.

Britain, of all member countries, would have to deliberate long and hard before abandoning its present ambivalent attitude of benevolent indifference combined with sporadic bursts of attention, usually brought about for ceremonial or patriotic reasons. The Commonwealth enjoys support from the political parties and especially from those in opposition. It is held in high esteem by Her Majesty the Queen, for the very sound reason that it undoubtedly renders lustre to the British monarchy. But can any practical good be summoned forth from this nearly moribund post-colonial organization, now that the great debates over decolonization are concluded?

My book, which is based on secondary sources to which I am indebted and whose references are given wherever possible, seeks to examine these and other propositions. The historical background makes no claim to great originality but its presentation is necessary to set the context for a consideration of the Commonwealth in the present and to speculate on its future.

And as to all the current discourse on neo-Empires and pseudo-Empires, it might be worth being reminded that any would-be shadow Empire based on smoke and mirrors is a delusion which will sooner rather than later prove unsustainable, simply because it is impossible to maintain a system of post-imperial influence once the reality of physical power is withdrawn.

1
The Nehru Commonwealth

The immediate post-war period

Towards the end of the Second World War, British politicians of all parties reflected on how Britain and the settler-based Dominions, with a combined population of 80 million, might be able to hold their own with the obvious rising power of the United States of America and the Union of Soviet Socialist Republics. They concluded that the possible answer lay in united Commonwealth action on major questions of foreign policy, and it was the degree of imperial cooperation displayed during the war that had made such a concept imaginable. 'It was the scale and solidarity of support from overseas which for a time made it possible to think of the Commonwealth as a power which might speak on level terms to the USA on the one side and the USSR on the other.'[1] During the war, five million servicemen had been enlisted by the Empire, and the 14th Army in Burma was the largest in the world operating as a single unit with one million men, of whom nearly three-quarters were Indian.[2] It was as a global Empire that Britain liked to project itself – wartime Prime Minister Winston Churchill played on the old patriotic themes and used the imperial idiom. But in reality, the Second World War had accelerated the progress of the Dominions to international maturity and propelled the South Asian national movements towards self-government. The attention of the Dominions after 1941 centred on Washington and not London, because they wanted access to the fulcrum of power, and they were no longer willing to accept Britain's leadership automatically on all matters. Lord Halifax, British Ambassador in the United States, had said in a speech in 1944 in Toronto that 'the British Commonwealth and Empire must be the fourth power in that group from which, under Providence, the peace of the world will henceforth depend'[3] – a view that infuriated MacKenzie King, Prime Minister of Canada, who regarded it as revealing a hidden design to revive imperialism. Despite whatever implications might be read into Halifax's remarks, there was no intention on the part of Britain to create a Commonwealth of highly centralized control or exclusive economic union, and even if there had been any such ambition among the die-hard imperialists, it was soon to be dispelled by the attitude of the Dominions themselves.

There were early indications of centrifugal forces. In 1943 and 1944 Australia made proposals for one Dominion to represent the Commonwealth as a whole in a particular region, and the Prime Minister of South Africa, Jan Smuts, proposed that a Dominion could assume some responsibility for colonies in its vicinity. Such decentralizing proposals did not find much favour in Whitehall. While there were certain tendencies common to the self-governing Dominions, there was however no such thing as a joint Dominion point of view, and each country was increasingly asserting its separate national identity. MacKenzie King disagreed that the United Kingdom had to be confident of the unswerving backing of the Dominions if it was to maintain an equal balance with the United States and the Soviet Union; his position was that no formal unity or automatic compliance was needed; only a loose understanding and association based on consent and the general will to act together. At the Dumbarton Oaks and San Francisco negotiations, the Dominions showed their independence from Britain on a number of points of substance, such as on the role and veto power given to the Great Powers in the United Nations Charter. Proposals for greater unity and cooperation were periodically projected by the United Kingdom in its search for continued world prominence, but Australia and New Zealand were seeking more attention for security in the Pacific – and the Pacific had been a distant theatre for Europe. At the 1946 Prime Ministers Meeting, Australia and New Zealand made suggestions for defence cooperation on a regional basis, but were rebuffed.

After the war, the British government had an agenda for the Commonwealth. It felt that Britain could only match its two other big partners in world affairs by creating a Commonwealth third force. Britain was to be positioned at the hub of three interlocking circles; the Commonwealth, the Atlantic Alliance and Europe. Empire and the Commonwealth raised optimistic hopes of the same vitality in peace as recently shown during the war, and of providing a basis for Britain's future international influence. War-time cooperation with the Dominions had led to expectations of Commonwealth solidarity, and the challenge of the time was to make the Commonwealth a close-knit unit with shared foreign policy objectives and an integrated defence system, thereby transforming the hitherto informal partnership into a more coherent association of like-minded states. There was also the need to reconcile the position of the Crown and the question of allegiance, so far the entrenched principle, with the desire of some of the dependencies approaching independence to acquire republican status, and there was the task of absorbing these new members without breaking up the tradition of informal consultation and cooperation.

Britain had emerged from the war as a great power relative to all but the two super-powers. It produced nearly one third of the industrial output of non-communist Europe. In 1952, it was still contributing more than 40 per cent of the defence spending of the European members of the North Atlantic Treaty Organization, was the only nuclear power besides the United States and the Union of Soviet Socialist Republics, and in the early 1950s its production was 50 per cent greater than West Germany's and 250 per cent greater than that of France.[4] Senior figures in the post-war Labour Government had worked in the war-time coalition and none of them was opposed in principle either to the continuation of the Empire or to an international status based on Britain's pre-war influence outside Europe. Prime Minister Clement Attlee intended to maintain Britain's position as a major player, and envisaged the Empire and Commonwealth as having an essential role to this end. So did other theorists; *The Round Table's* editor wrote in 1946, 'The United Kingdom of Great Britain and Northern Ireland is by itself no longer a world power. It can only remain a participant in world power by virtue of its partnership in the British Commonwealth of Nations.'[5] By no means were the colonies regarded at that time as an inheritance to trouble the conscience but rather as an opportunity for planned redevelopment, and Britain proposed to preside over the rebirth of the imperial system rather than over its dissolution. There was a political conviction that Britain owed its unique character to its maritime and imperial connections worldwide and the economic and political benefits derived from them. The victory and sacrifices of the Second World War were looked upon as entitling Britain to great power status as one of the big Three, and since the Empire and Commonwealth had been instrumental in Britain's victories in both World Wars, they were seen as obvious adjuncts to British power and status. Even among the ideological opponents of the Empire, there was little opposition to the continuation of the imperial links which had manifested their value through unity in war-time. Both the Labour and the Conservative Parties were of a mind that without the Empire, Britain would become a mere pawn in United States' diplomacy, besides leaving a vacuum which the Soviet Union and communism were likely to fill. Some Labour politicians held confused convictions; some believed that the Empire was a class phenomenon, an extension of capitalism and opposed to equality – Foreign Secretary Jack Straw recently echoed Stafford Cripps, Labour Party minister during and after the Second World War, in saying, 'There's a lot wrong with imperialism ... you have only got to look at the pages of British Imperial history to hide your head in shame that you are British.'[6] Nevertheless the post-war Labour Cabinet firmly believed that Britain was, and was entitled to be, a world power, and wanted no helter-skelter withdrawals from its overseas possessions.

The Empire raised several issues, including the kith and kin factor that always caused an emotional reaction in Britain while other colonial matters of greater consequence hardly stirred any ripples of interest. The government's preoccupation with British prestige and authority owed much to its perception of the requirements of public opinion at home, or at least the articulate section thereof. Therefore there was in evidence a strong sense of *amour propre* and a disinclination to accept any insult or the prospect of defeat. There was a perceived need to foster the notion that Britain remained a great power, a manager in world politics, and a protector of the kith and kin factor.[7] Colonial rule was to be projected as benevolent and non-coercive and the Commonwealth was to be the new vehicle of British influence when colonial rule became difficult, controversial and less acceptable. Influence was to be retained despite the transfer of power, and the transformation from the Empire to the Commonwealth, the shift in gear from a 'formal to informal empire in a spirit of partnership'[8] was the means by which to mollify domestic disapproval, appease US anti-imperialism, contain Afro-Asian national-ism, prevent communist penetration and maintain worldwide status on the cheap.

The first phase of the modern Commonwealth began when the British Raj departed from South Asia and the three successor states of India, Pakistan and Ceylon became full members of what had until then been an exclusively white-members club of settler Dominions organized and administered by Britain. This previously choate association of loyalists had been managed by Whitehall as the British Commonwealth, in a dis-tinctly monarchical mode, and its solidarities had been amply demon-strated during the recent war. This small club held to the opinion that it proceeded best through intimate and collegial family ways. For the post-Second World War newcomers also, the Commonwealth was not without its uses: it fostered economic and cultural links, it heightened international and diplomatic profile, and the Sterling Area helped their slender resources in foreign trade. Importantly, Sterling Area policy was determined democratically by the prime ministers themselves.

Colonial systems of influence which called for holding of territory necessarily depended upon political quiescence among the subject peoples and on the control of political developments in the dependencies. By the end of the war, these were impossible conditions to fulfill in South Asia where the war had destroyed the old patterns of politics in the Indian sub-continent and Burma. The United Kingdom could no longer reassert its power through garrisons and administrators due to its acute shortage of manpower, the need to curtail foreign expenditure, and crises elsewhere such as in Palestine. As a result London had neither the will nor the means to prevent an accelerated withdrawal with arrangements on the ground hastily arrived at. Viceroy of India Lord Curzon had written in 1901; 'As long as we rule India, we are the greatest power in the world. If we lose it we shall drop straight away to a third rate power.'[9] With the transfer of power to India and Pakistan, the strategic core of the Empire, along with three quarters of its population, were gone.

India and Pakistan

The road-map leading to the independence of India was in effect a contradiction of British policy before the war because the world conflict had broken the previous pattern of close cooperation between Britain and the Congress Party. Civil disobedience organized by the Congress in India, and the fact that the Indian muslim population had been generally loyal during the war, led to sympathy in Britain for opponents of Congress such as the Muslim League, and consequently for the creation of Pakistan. This trend towards confrontation with the Congress, together with the necessity of a large measure of Indianization, inexorably led to the weakening of the steel frame of British Indian administration. Even as late as 1947, some British Ministers wanted to stand firm in India and avoid the impression of a 'scuttle'; but the Labour Party concluded that there had to be early political change in India, though they did not then anticipate that India would prove both unable and unwilling to contribute to any Commonwealth system of security in Asia and the Middle East. India had ended the war as Britain's creditor, and influenced by the grave damage to Britain's prestige from the Anglo-Japanese conflict, the government of independent India saw little reason to enter into a strategic partnership with the former imperial power. So any British aspirations of presiding benignly over the emergence of a single, friendly, new Dominion did not materialize, and after the transfer of power to India and Pakistan, Britain had to make do without the expected Indian contribution, as an integrated, united Dominion, to the validity and strength of its global ambitions.[10] Nevertheless, Peter Lyon claimed that 'Nehru's conception of what India's government and society should be like was not notably different from that of Attlee,'[11] and if India had opted to stay outside the Commonwealth, as Burma had anticipated, it would have been problematic for Pakistan and Ceylon to accept Commonwealth membership; nor would it have been easy for Ghana, Malaya and the rest of the long procession over the years to follow suit.

In 1947 the Dominions Office and the India Office in London were brought together as a new Commonwealth Relations Office, and the old Imperial Conferences, which had not been convened since 1937, were dropped. The British government was conscious that its Commonwealth partners would be of greater value to its proposed scheme of things if the newly independent states were recognized by the United Nations, Moscow and Washington, but at the same time, the British leadership still wanted to continue its privileged special relationship with its Empire, and in order to preserve that, a new international alignment had to be forged to promote Britain's national and global interests. Within a month of his arrival in India, Viceroy Lord Mountbatten, who evidently regarded the Commonwealth as a continuation of British imperialism at its best by other means, told his staff that keeping India in the Commonwealth was the 'most important single problem'.[12] Before independence, Jawaharlal Nehru was disconcerted by sundry importunate British proposals about Privy Council appeals, designs for a flag, and so forth, and before he became India's first Prime Minister, told Mountbatten that emotionally and psychologically, India could not remain in the Commonwealth.[13] Nehru's reluctance before 1947 to join the Commonwealth reflected the displeasure of many members of his Congress Party at any continuing connection with Britain because of London's plans for partition. Pleas by Attlee and Mountbatten to steer Nehru away from a republican path were unavailing, and the British Cabinet had to fight resistance from the government's own legal and Foreign Office officials who persisted in insisting on the traditional principle of allegiance to the Crown. But India was always to be an exception because of the emotional factor of the Anglo-Indian relationship, added to the fact that relatively few concessions were needed to preserve it. Britain feared that an India outside the Commonwealth might turn away from Britain to build an anti-western bloc of Asian States, whereas in the association there was the asset of India as a large creditor, as a trading partner and as a zone of stability in a continent where communism was seen as threatening alarming incursions. In March 1948 Attlee wrote to Nehru arguing that joining the Commonwealth would mean adherence to certain values, democratic institutions, the rule of law and toleration, making up a 'way of life', which, despite whatever differences might exist, gave a sense of community.[14] Such a philosophical approach appealed to Nehru though his specific ideas of the value of the Commonwealth connection were naturally rather different; to offset the factor of the Soviet Union which was unpredictable and initially hostile, to counter-balance growing dependence on the United States and to deny Pakistan the advantage of an Indian withdrawal. Nehru's friendship with Lady Mountbatten may also have played a part in his final decision. Within his Congress Party Nehru argued that there were advantages for India in membership; that it would promote world peace, and that it did not imply alignment with any world bloc or any sacrifice of full independence. In 1949 the Soviet Union detonated its first atomic device and Mao Zedong proclaimed the People's Republic of China. The Cold War was looming. The world was starting to coalesce into two major competing spheres; militarily, politically and ideologically. In the new Commonwealth, India was the odd man out; the only country that was not aligned with the west. A new British–Indian partnership would have been welcomed by London as a possible substitute for the old Raj, but even in its early years of independence, India could not be persuaded into any such anachronistic role.

The 1949 London Declaration of the Commonwealth Prime Ministers, consisting of one printed page – there was, unlike the verbosity of today, commendable brevity in those times – referred to India's intention to become a sovereign independent republic, to continue its full membership of the Commonwealth, and its acceptance of the King as the symbol of the free association of the member nations and as such the Head of the Commonwealth. Cooperation between Attlee and Nehru had produced a splendidly ironic solution to the vexed issue of allegiance and the Imperial Crown, which was not lost on George VI, who quipped to Nehru during a State banquet, 'Mr Nehru, you have reduced me to an *as such*'. He also confided privately to Attlee that he hoped there would not be many more republics in the Commonwealth. *The Times* was equally sceptical about republicanism in the association: 'How many republics, it is asked, can the Commonwealth contain without altering its character?'[15]

To Britain's relief, despite recurrent tensions between the South Asian members, both India and Pakistan chose to remain in the Commonwealth, and Britain's special links with them were safeguarded. 'It was India, the pioneer of modern Asian nationalism,' wrote *The Round Table*, 'who established the *bona fides* of the new Commonwealth based less on blood than on will.'[16] Nehru steadily emerged as a true 'Commonwealth man', and encouraged Britain to sponsor the same formula of self-government within the Commonwealth elsewhere in the Empire. And Pakistan's first prime minister Liaquat Ali Khan, for his part, received a confidential assurance that future requests for republican status on the lines of the Indian precedent would be viewed with similar accommodation.

While the decision of India and Pakistan to accede to the Commonwealth as Dominions was balm to the self-esteem of the British government and public opinion, their bilateral disputes were contrary to everything the Commonwealth was then thought to stand for. Nevertheless, relations between the old and the new members, with the exception of South Africa, were generally conducted in an atmosphere of friendship and goodwill. The greater discord was between the Asian members themselves. Pakistan pressed for a Commonwealth tribunal, and the Indians and the Ceylonese had their differences over Tamil immigration and voting rights. As early as 1947, a Pakistani request for a Commonwealth investigation into the Punjab partition calamity met with little enthusiasm from India, which in turn in the same year brought Pakistan's behaviour on Kashmir to the notice of the UN. *The Round Table* shrewdly remarked in the following year that 'the emergence within the Commonwealth of a dispute so dangerous and bitter ... was a sharp reminder that to uphold the old ideal ... will be far more difficult in the new circumstances,'[17] and by 1948, the Kashmir question was already described by the journal as a 'running sore'.[18] From the very start Pakistan had an equivocal relationship with the Commonwealth. In 1949 Liaquat Ali Khan said that Pakistan's Constituent Assembly would be free to decide whether to leave the Commonwealth for he sensed that his country's public opinion was swinging against the British connection, and in his view, there were no practical benefits to Pakistan from the Commonwealth because there was too great a degree of appeasement of India. Liaquat announced a visit to Moscow – the first prime minister from the new Commonwealth to do so – but then did not go. He gave praise to the Commonwealth in 1950, saying it possessed the potential for great opportunities for raising the hopes of mankind; but he refused to attend the 1951 summit unless Kashmir was discussed. As an ally in the South East Asian Treaty Organization (SEATO) and the Central Treaty Organization aka The Baghdad Pact (CENTO), Pakistan felt it was owed some greater degree of reciprocal loyalty from the London-centred Commonwealth than was forthcoming. Throughout its Commonwealth membership Pakistan would feel hard done by *vis à vis* India, and held Britain largely responsible for the lack of support from the organization. In 1951 Liaquat was the first Commonwealth prime minister to be assassinated. Pakistan was the second Commonwealth country to become a republic in 1956; and in 1958, the first to suffer a coup d'état and military take-over.[19]

Burma

In return for abandoning its original constitutional programme in preference for the grant of early independence, and for prevailing on the hill states to amalgamate in a union with Burma, the British government hoped that Aung San, leader of the Burmese nationalist movement, would choose to join the Commonwealth and embark on a new defence and economic relationship with Britain. London realized that Burma would have a difficult decision to make in respect of the Commonwealth and Attlee in 1946 said

> we do not desire to retain within the Commonwealth and Empire any unwilling peoples ... but we are certain that it will be to their interest, as it will be to ours, if they decide to remain within the Commonwealth and we sincerely hope that they will arrive at such a decision. ... Membership of the Commonwealth ... is not a derogation from independence but an addition to it.[20]

But an impasse developed. Demands for a Burmese Republic were declared, in 1947, to be incompatible with Commonwealth member-ship, and Burma was informed that its decision to become a republic would mean that it would have to remain outside the Commonwealth. Governor-General of Malaya Malcolm MacDonald warned that the situation might develop thus: if Burma left, India might take the cue and follow, and this would spark a decline in Britain's influence in South East Asia. But if Burma was to recognize the King as Head of the Commonwealth, the Crown as head of an increasingly large and varied family of free peoples would achieve 'a position of unexampled glory'.[21] But Burma, for its part, after contemplating some sort of Irish-style external association, rejected any continuance of Britain's influence and finally opted for a complete break. Rangoon's decision was not based solely on matters concerned with a republic. Burma was beset with obsessions about parity with India and mistook India's intentions, assuming that the Indian government would choose to be a republic right away and decline to join the Commonwealth. In addition, it was Burmese paranoia about the weight of British commercial interests, and distaste for the Indian moneylender and the Indian migrant worker who had dominated the Burmese agricultural economy before the war. The Burmese decision, which reflected the country's traditional zenophobia, was a blow to Britain's prestige in South East Asia.[22] It was both an economic set-back and a symbolic loss. British rule, through the Second World War; and British influence, through rejection of the Commonwealth, were thus both brought to an end in Burma, though the British retained a largely ineffective British Services Mission in Burma for some years to come.

Ceylon

Ceylon was an unusual case because it was the first Crown Colony to seek independence. In those times, admission to the Commonwealth was seen as a privilege not available to any country that had not grown into eligibility for membership by the normal slow process of representative and responsible government, eventually ripening into dominion status. The concept was a three stage process; from Protectorate or Crown Colony to Dominion status and thence in the fullness of time to full sovereignty. There was in Whitehall at first some reluctance to allow other than a selected few to traverse this route, and that too, only after a prolonged period of self-government. 'There was … no case for launching ill-prepared independent states prematurely into a dangerous world.'[23] So in return for the concession of short-circuiting this time-table, Ceylon was made to adopt and follow the resolutions of past Imperial Conferences, which it had not attended, and to observe the principles and practices of the Commonwealth in regard to external affairs, information and consultation. No new member other than Ceylon was asked for any such undertakings and the Ceylon precedent was subsequently never followed. The fact that Ceylon was then considered an exception to the rule was not lost on the British officials responsible for dealing with its transfer of power. Lord Soulbury, heading the second Royal Commission on Ceylon, was conscious in his report in 1945 that his recommendations on Dominion status would bring 'nearer the ultimate ideal of British statesmanship, the fusion of the Empire and the Commonwealth.'[24]

Ceylon was blessed with several favourable circumstances. The country had neither Indian-style agitational methods nor communal politics. Though some groups in opposition did declare themselves in favour of full national independence outside the Commonwealth, Ceylon's Sinhala politicians were by and large conservative, and nearly all were from the rich landowning classes, fearful of Indian domination, hostile to communism and wary of non-alignment, and regarded close ties with Britain as the best insurance for safeguarding the country's independence. Britain came to two agreements with the nationalists that guaranteed cooperation in defence, including the use of bases at Trincomalee and Katunayake; and also cooperation in external relations, which, together with Commonwealth membership, was a pattern of decolonization that was highly satisfactory to Whitehall's way of thinking. Ceylon achieved independence within the Commonwealth in 1948 and an official in the Colonial Office was moved to say that the conception of the evolving Commonwealth was 'the boldest stroke of political idealism which the world has yet witnessed, and on by far the grandest scale.'[25]

Due to the prevailing Soviet–American cold war impasse in the United Nations, Ceylon was unable to gain admission to the global organization before 1955, and until that time the Commonwealth was the main forum for its exercise of multilateral diplomacy. In 1956, there was an upsurge of Sinhala nationalism, Buddhist populism, the end of elitist politics, ethnic problems with the Tamils, and the election victory of Prime Minister Solomon Bandaranaike and his Sri Lanka Freedom Party. One of his first acts was to abrogate the defence pact with Britain. Bandaranaike was assassinated in 1959 and was succeeded by his wife Sirimavo, who became the first woman prime minister in the world.

Malaya

British Malaya after the war was in three parts – the Straits settlements (a Crown Colony); four federated Malay States under Sultans (a Protectorate); and five un-federated Malay States with traditional rulers (a Protectorate). There were also outlying possessions on Borneo. The original British government plan was to have a Malay Union including Singapore, but the Sultans of the Malay States wanted to exclude Singapore in order to avoid a Chinese majority. The British government showed no inclination to cut and run, though it declared its intention to grant independence at some unspecified date, and in 1948 it brought into being a new Federation of Malaya comprising the previously federated and un-federated states. With its hard currency earnings from tin and rubber exports, and not least as a base to guard the eastern sea routes, Malaya was at that time considered even more important to British economic and strategic interests than New Zealand.[26]

The Malay leaders were conservative, fearful of Indonesian-type extremism and Chinese domination. A communist insurrection broke out in 1948 and the British government's response was a State of Emergency that lasted till 1960, that is, even after independence. The guerillas held the upper hand for the first couple of years, but by 1954 the situation had been brought reasonably under control. The United States was starting to press its view that resisting communism in Vietnam needed the rapid abolition of colonialism in South East Asia, and this served to bring forward the grant of independence to Malaya in 1957. Britain promised to help with internal and external security and Malaya remained in the Sterling Area, depositing its dollar receipts in London. In 1958 came a constitution for Singapore, by which Britain controlled its defence and foreign policy. Singapore was strongly anti-communist and joined the Malaysian Federation comprising Malaya, Singapore, Sarawak and North Borneo in 1963, but it parted from its Malaysian partner after the 1964 Malay–Chinese inter-communal riots in Singapore, ending in 1965 yet one more of the several unsuccessful federation experiments of the British Empire. Whitehall had hoped that the creation of Malaysia would be a bulwark against communism in South East Asia and blunt any opposition to its base in Singapore. With the separation of Singapore from Malaysia, the base became untenable in the long term, and this was to have its effect on Britain's east of Suez policy. The Protectorate of Brunei took a different course, having decided to remain a British dependency and not join the Federation.

British troops were to stay on, fighting in Malaya and later in Borneo against Indonesian *'konfrontasi'* (confrontation) until 1966, having been joined in 1964 by Australia and New Zealand. During this struggle, Britain, Australia and New Zealand called with some success upon the whole Commonwealth to show support for Malaysia, even at the expense of bilateral relations with Indonesia, and despite Malaysian Prime Minister Tunku Abdul Rahman's less than whole-hearted support for African causes which had by then advanced to the centre of the international stage.

Britain, the Commonwealth and Asian independence

The Empire was an amalgam of independent, semi-independent, and dependent territories held together by economic, strategic, political, demographic and cultural ties with Britain that varied greatly in strength and character from one dependency to the other.[27] In the heyday of Empire, the British government was ready to concede almost total autonomy to the white settler colonies, reflecting the two guiding principles of twentieth century imperialism – 'the freedom of the parts and the united action of the whole.'[28] When countries like Burma and Ireland seceded from Britain's sphere of influence, this was looked upon with relative equanimity provided the rest of the system was safely preserved. After the transfer of power to the South Asian nationalist movements, the British government hoped that with London's assistance in the form of economic aid, capital investment and military and diplomatic support, the mutual benefits of continuing cooperation would be cemented. The concept was that of a Commonwealth founded and nurtured by the basically supportive nationalism of the likes of Canada and South Africa into which the newly independent nations would be admitted, and the Commonwealth Relations Office was established in 1947 to superintend this new incarnation.

The preservation of Britain's interests as a mercantile nation backed by its military might required the resources of global influence and assumptions in the British political establishment about Britain's place in the world were important in giving shape and form to the modern Commonwealth. The special relationship with the pre-war self-governing Commonwealth, namely the old Dominions, which was an indispensable component of Britain's claim to great power influence and status, was expected to withstand the strain of the new constitutional diversity and strategic re-alignment when tradition and sentiment alone were no longer able to represent the main foundations of the association. Thus, in the 1948 Prime Ministers Meeting, – 'Meetings' had a more informal ring to them than 'Conferences' – the three new Asian Dominions took their places. The process, wrote J.D.B. Miller, was eased by the Commonwealth being a 'sufficiently loose organization to satisfy even such "anti-colonialists" as the prime ministers of the Asian Dominions.' Membership involved no special responsibilities, was based on consent, and the Asians were committed only to informal and unspecific consultations. 'The essence of Commonwealth institutions ... is that they have a very high permissive quality and almost no obligation about them.'[29]

There were not only comings; there were also goings. In 1949 the self-governing Dominion of Newfoundland, Britain's oldest colony, voted to merge with Canada as its tenth province, and Ireland also formally departed from the association though it had not participated in any Commonwealth meetings over the previous ten years.[30] In that same year, the laconic text of the London Declaration had referred variously to the British Commonwealth of Nations, the Commonwealth of Nations and the Commonwealth, and Attlee a month later in the House of Commons confirmed that people could use whatever expression they liked best; the British Empire, the British Commonwealth, or just the Commonwealth. One month later still, it was noted that the King, when opening the Colonial Month, referred only to 'the Commonwealth and not "the Empire" '.[31] The term 'Dominion' was increasingly, perhaps to assuage India's sensitivities, being substituted by the term 'fully independent member of the Commonwealth', and Canada and New Zealand dropped the appellation from their titles on joining the United Nations.

In the immediate post-war period, the British government held certain views on re-shaping South Asia in ways that would preserve British influence. Dominion status for India, Pakistan and Ceylon was seen as a means to retain these countries in the Commonwealth club while they wrote up their new constitutions. Positive developments after 1948 gave Whitehall some encouragement that Britain's position as the world's third power was safe for an indefinite period. Britain was popularly believed to have propagated parliamentary democracy in the Westminster model, land tenure systems, the rule of law, and the importance of individual rights, and there was considerable satisfaction when the leaders of the new Asian Commonwealth members by and large initially remained faithful to this inheritance. Elites had moved into colonial positions of authority, displaying nationalism with liberalism, and had acceded to independence with high optimism and a healthy bank balance. Decolonization could therefore be presented as proof that civilized and progressive values had become embedded not only in western society but also successfully exported across the Empire; and in a process moreover, that did not in any sense weaken Europe. Attlee in 1948 declared, 'we are not solely a European Power but a member of a great Commonwealth and Empire',[32] and the Conservative and Unionist Office in 1949 echoed the Prime Minister's views, saying, 'It is sometimes forgotten that the potential strength of the British Empire and Commonwealth is greater than that of either the USA or the USSR'[33] – an argument to be used again in later years to juxtapose against western Europe's efforts to unify. Anti-colonial sentiments in Britain and abroad were blunted by the blurring of distinctions between the Commonwealth and the Empire, the most noteworthy argument being that India of its own accord had joined the Commonwealth. Attlee in 1948 was able confidently to say, 'The Commonwealth nations are our closest friends.'[34]

As a serviceable instrument in the immediate post-war climate, the new modern Commonwealth was accordingly considered by the British leadership to be a considerable success and a major international triumph, even though the three South Asian members were not overly enthusiastic about Britain's great power ambitions, were firmly opposed to South African apartheid, and the existence of Indo-Pakistani disputes had already greatly reduced the Commonwealth's intimacy. The Commonwealth was no longer a club or even an especially convivial association; it had no natural cohesion and existed through bilateral ties with Britain alone. 'The old structural unity ... has gone', lamented Australian Prime Minister Robert Menzies, 'it has been replaced by structural variety'.[35] A contributor wrote in *The Round Table* in 1956, 'Conferences of more than half a dozen or so members soon become too unwieldy to do good work, at least in a short period.'[36] The unity of action demonstrated so impressively during the war conspicuously failed to be replicated by unity in peacetime. For example, as early as November 1947, the United Kingdom abstained, India and Pakistan voted against, and the four old Dominions voted for, a UN General Assembly resolution on Palestine. Within the Commonwealth there was unrelieved tension between India and South Africa due to the latter's racialist policies. South Africa violated human rights, Malaya had its own monarch, India was the first republic, and Pakistan was to be the first Commonwealth military dictatorship. A commentator ascribed the original sin to India for having impaired the traditional foundations of the Commonwealth in the first place.[37]

The new Commonwealth was very much a British creation for British interests. It was not the natural successor to the pre-war Commonwealth which had been held together by ties of kith and kin, a common value-system, democracy and partnership, but instead a device to protect old spheres of interest from new influences, including from that of the United States, to offer to the new members some off-the-shelf international status and prestige, certain benefits in trade and military assistance, and to prevent the spread of communism. Acceptance of India's republican status in the association was a self-conscious and deliberate concession for the preservation of British influence. At that stage, the Commonwealth depended wholly on Britain's capacity to play its economic and strategic role of the past:[38] the question of a full racial partnership was neither specifically raised nor was especially appealing to the old Dominions. Cabinet Secretary Norman Brook summarized the old Dominions' attitude as 'uneasiness' at the prospect of the new Asian members, with support for the efforts made to draw them into the

Commonwealth fold, but reluctance to make any adjustments that might disrupt the existing close relations between the 'central' membership.[39] Menzies was at first in support of a two-tier association, and liked to draw a distinction between the 'Crown Commonwealth' and the Republics. The existence of the Empire in the 1950s 'still enhanced rather than detracted from Britain's prestige in the eyes of those who ruled Australia', and Menzies was deeply shocked when in 1961, Prime Minister Harold Macmillan asked Nehru, rather than Menzies, to take the chair during a temporary absence.[40] The connection between the Commonwealth and colonial policy was a constant preoccupation for the British Cabinet, along with the desire to reinforce the Sterling Area, contain hostile influences in the Empire, provide a multiracial bridge and enhance Britain's standing, especially with the United States.[41] Of significance also was the fact that the Commonwealth protected the British Empire from the condemnation of the colonies themselves, and the post-war anti-imperial sensitivities of countries like the United States and Canada. The demission of British power and authority from South Asia in the late 1940s did not immediately presage a phase when steps towards further decolonization was to be the dominant motif.

'There were considerable outpourings of praise', wrote Lyon, 'for this new greater Commonwealth which had, by Britain's enlightened disimperialism, thrown diplomatic bridges across the continents ... while helping to show, in Jawaharlal Nehru's happy phrase, that membership could mean "independence plus".'[42] Attlee had presented Indian independence as a victory rather than as a defeat – the end of Empire was to be the fulfillment of Britain's imperial vision, the 'maintenance of an imperial role as opposed to imperial rule' and the continuation of 'global authority without colonial responsibility.'[43] The British leadership hoped to consolidate Britain's great power status by a gradual modification of colonial relationships, and was more than willing to work with moderate and responsible nationalists. The relative smoothness of the South Asian transition fostered a sense of popular detachment at home towards Empire that was both welcome and convenient for the government of the day. A period of post-colonial cooperation existed from 1945 to 1960 between Britain and the old Dominions with India, Pakistan and Ceylon, and later also embraced Ghana and Malaya. The Commonwealth as a body acquired an international dimension; a grouping to which the remaining British colonies could aspire. In 1949, global cooperation in a multiracial Commonwealth looked more attractive to Britain than cooperation within Europe, and the British government regarded access to the resources of the Empire as underlining the country's status as the premier power in Western Europe. After the watershed 1949 Commonwealth Prime Ministers Meeting, there followed in the 1950s, 'despite differences in the attitudes of newer and older members to world politics, some brief and retrospectively golden years of hope in a multiracial Commonwealth and its potential contribution to human understanding'.[44] Macmillan was able to assure his Cabinet colleagues that 'The Empire is not breaking up, it is growing up',[45] and *The Round Table* pronounced solemnly that like the Roman Empire which neither declined nor fell, 'the British Empire has likewise not ended, but its children have grown into adult nations, preserving family ties without family discipline'.[46]

Through the early 1950s the optimistic sentiment continued. The Commonwealth cushioned the process of decolonization for Britain, and promised some enhanced status to the former colonies. Of greatest importance was the fact that one of the world's most populous and prominent anti-colonial countries, India, was of its own volition, a leading member of the Commonwealth. To the British authorities' great satisfaction as being within the spirit of the 1949 London Declaration, India decided to continue the practice of describing its envoys to other Commonwealth countries as high commissioners, a practice that established a precedent and continues to this day. The new association generated hope because India, despite various reservations, remained in it and preserved Westminster-style democracy as well. The membership of the independent South Asian nations embellished the image of the Commonwealth in the eyes of the rest of Asia and Africa. 'The positive approach of the Asian Prime Ministers was from the first a source of encouragement', opined *The Round Table*.[47]

But Britain without doubt remained the most essential member, because without the mother country there would be no Commonwealth. Britain extended the privileges of Commonwealth membership in order to retain linkages in a special sort of relationship, which were based on each member's relations with the United Kingdom and not with each other. No other colonial power was on such good terms with its former colonies. Attlee through his quiet leadership and effective chairmanship had achieved a permanent change in British history. Within three years of the end of the Second World War, Britain had given freedom to India, Pakistan, Ceylon and Burma, and had invited them to join an association previously the exclusive preserve of white settler colonies, smoothly and instantly and as full and equal members. There were no threats to remove the trade preferences or Sterling Area membership, which in fact the recusants, Ireland and Burma, continued to enjoy. This association with Britain gave the new Commonwealth members some added value to their limited diplomatic resources, and Britain also gained in stature; it was the principal military power in the Commonwealth and to the outside world the Commonwealth appeared to all intents and purposes as a British-controlled group.[48] 'Primarily the Commonwealth is a British interest' and 'a concert of convenience',[49] wrote one commentator, and in 1960, the Australian High Commissioner in London reported that there was 'a view often held here that Britain must dominate the Commonwealth in order to sustain her own position.'[50] Up to 1965, the Commonwealth had a strong 'British tinge' and showed 'marked British characteristics'.[51]

The Commonwealth eased the way towards independence for the remaining dependencies and also made the decolonizing process easier for Whitehall. It set a finishing line for others to aim at. No other colonial power had such a device at hand and non-Commonwealth newly independent states such as Tunisia, Vietnam and Indonesia, tended to be either hostile or at least to keep their distance from the west. The Commonwealth smoothened Britain's transition from an Empire-builder to an Empire-dismantler, and politicians in London chose not to damp down the proprietorial tone used by the public and the media about a Commonwealth 'dependent upon British wisdom and direction'.[52] Prime Minister Alec Douglas-Home claimed in his autobiography that Britain's word in 1955 counted for all the rest of the membership put together, and Britain was expected to assume the lead and to enjoy support from the other members despite the fig-leaf of equality.[53] The Commonwealth was a body that the British government and the British public instinctively expected would follow London's lead. So its early successes fostered unfounded expectations, and the overselling of the Commonwealth in the 1950s by British politicians and commentators alike caused disillusion and dismay a decade later when it came to be realized that Britain was only one among equals in the association.

By 1952 the challenges in overseas policy in the form of the Korean War had eased, the vast bulk of the Empire still remained intact and there was no challenge to Britain's imperial position. It was the wish of British policy makers to hang on and hold on, to maintain a distance from Europe and to consolidate the Commonwealth connection. Britain needed Asian cooperation to uphold its sphere of influence as well as to maintain a sound economy at home and colonial peace abroad. One concrete expression of such cooperation was the Colombo Plan that started in 1950 as the outcome of the first-ever meeting of Commonwealth foreign ministers and the first-ever Commonwealth ministerial meeting in Asia. Its programme of multilateral official development aid to South and East Asia, which was not confined to Commonwealth countries, displayed a laudable largeness of vision, both political and developmental. It was neither directed nor administered by Britain, and came to be described as a Marshall Plan for Asia. It was a practical expression of Western aid and Commonwealth cohesion, of collaboration between the United Kingdom and the Asian leaders, and provided a useful instrument through which the United States could become a large contributor to Asian development and thereby allay to some extent Asian apprehensions of 'American imperialism'.

The Commonwealth survived the strains of the inclusion of the new Asian members, 'but it was not the "British Commonwealth of Nations" so cherished by the close-knit, cooperating, elite membership up until the 1940s'[54] – after all, it was not until the 1980s that the Canadian, Australian and New Zealand legislatures would complete the constitutional process of gaining their complete autonomy from the British Parliament. Prime Minister Peter Fraser of New Zealand regretted a 'watered down ... flabby ... kingless' Commonwealth,[55] and there were many loyalists in the old Dominions who shared Foreign Secretary Ernest Bevin's doubts whether the admission of reluctant or half-hearted new members would prove to be any asset, since it would only impose liabilities on Britain with few countervailing benefits. Canada, Australia, New Zealand and, of course, South Africa, all felt various degrees of misgiving about the companionship of the three Asian Dominions with whom they had no shared history or sentiment, but they realized that the Commonwealth's influence would sharply decline if India departed. This did not prevent the discreet consideration of various stratagems to retain the old order of things. The 'Core Commonwealth' or 'Crown Commonwealth' scheme put forward in 1956 by Sir Eric Harrison, Australia's high commissioner in London, was that those in allegiance to the Crown and the colonies of settlement should constitute a permanent coordination committee or secretariat. This proposal reflected the nostalgia of people of British descent who felt uncomfortable at the changes in the Empire and British Commonwealth, and ignored the fact that some of the most British of the dependencies had by then become Britain's greatest embarrassments, such as Kenya and the Central African Federation. There was also the 'Commonwealth Expansion' scheme, proposed by Patrick Maitland, a Conservative MP, whereby the Commonwealth could be expanded to consolidate Britain's power and make it more influential as a world system. This expanded

Commonwealth would include Sweden, France, Germany, Benelux, Turkey and Indonesia, first as associates, and then as full members if they wished.[56] All these schemes came to nothing. But in reality a *de facto* two-tier system on racial lines operated in the wings of the Commonwealth and at the pre-meeting consultations, in which only the old Dominions engaged. Before 1954 there was still some degree of consultation and discussion even on issues on which there was little prospect of agreement, but after American military assistance to Pakistan and the establishment of the South East Asia Treaty Organization (SEATO), faith in the informal Commonwealth consultative system quickly dissipated. Military intelligence was shared only between Britain and the old Dominions, and discussions on defence took place in meetings to which not all were invited.

In the 1950s the British political establishment was able to congratulate itself on the ease of overcoming potentially difficult problems at Prime Ministers Meetings and establishing close contacts with the new Asian members. In the age of two superpowers, 'Britain was still wanted, it could still lead and its beliefs and institutions remained of value to countries brought to independence in its traditions.'[57] In 1952 Macmillan wrote, 'This is the choice – the slide into a shoddy and slushy Socialism, or the march to the third British Empire'.[58] Though Pakistan did make repeated efforts to bring up Kashmir, India and Pakistan had not used Commonwealth meetings to put any great pressure on Britain; they were prepared to observe the gentlemanly conventions. The Kashmir dispute did not therefore affect Commonwealth harmony. Nor did racism in South Africa, because India did not raise in Commonwealth meetings what it did so energetically at the United Nations. India was in a key position because it was in the best position to destabilize the association, and it chose not to do so. In that sense, Nehru, who as Indian prime minister attended every single Commonwealth Prime Ministers Meeting in his lifetime, personified the spirit of the new Commonwealth and its informal collegial ways. 'It was perhaps in the Commonwealth setting', recalled senior British civil servant Joe Garner, 'that Nehru performed at his best'.[59] Despite obvious and unchallenged British preeminence, and Nehru's disinclination to be assertive, the presence of the Indian prime minister in its forums held the modern Commonwealth together and gave it credibility in its early years. Every member other than India at that time was a realm, with the Queen as its Head of State. Neither this nor Nehru's non-alignment policy was a considerable problem, and even proved helpful at the 1954 Geneva Conference on Korea and Indo-China. India enjoyed considerable influence on the British government's foreign policy due to Nehru's perceptive assessments, as was shown when China became a People's Republic in 1949, upon which Britain's recognition of the new regime was in marked contrast to Canada, Australia, New Zealand and South Africa, who all preferred to follow the United States lead. For its part, Britain sought to minimize confrontation with India over colonial issues, not only because of India's importance as a member of the Commonwealth but on account of the substantial Indian communities in the colonies. In 1959 author W.H. Morris-Jones wrote, 'just as Athens was the school for Hellas, New Delhi has become the school for Asia'.[60] It suited Britain to cite the Commonwealth as reinforcement for its foreign policy, and in arguments with the United States on the Korean ceasefire and Indo-China, Prime Minister Anthony Eden was able at times to show that he spoke for the Asian Commonwealth as well. To have the support or even just acquiescence from the Commonwealth gave Britain some bargaining power, and India was used for approaches to China, as Pakistan was to the Middle East. *The Round Table* was to write in 1955, 'Sir Anthony Eden, if none else, must know how useful India's contacts with the communist world have been to Britain in helping her shape a more realistic policy to China than can be said for the USA.'[61] But with SEATO, the Baghdad Pact and arms supplies from the United States to Pakistan, India's relations with the West came under increasing strain. Then came the Afro-Asian Conference at Bandung, in which the three Commonwealth South Asian countries took widely differing positions, and thereafter gave more priority to the development of closer bilateral ties with the new emerging Afro-Asian states.

Attlee had declared, 'it will be our aim to maintain the British Commonwealth as an international entity, recognized as such by foreign countries, in particular by the United States and the Soviet Union',[62] and Churchill had warmly referred to his last Commonwealth summit in 1955 as a 'fraternal association',[63] but the concept of the new Commonwealth as a third force could not ultimately be sustained by London in the face of the growing might of the United States and the Soviet Union, added to which were the exhaustion and bankruptcy of Britain itself, the collapse in the East of its reputation for invincibility, post-war doubts about the legitimacy of Empire, and the fresh challenges which arose with the independence of new nations in Asia and Africa. Increasing international multi-polarity contributed towards diminishing the Commonwealth's value. The Commonwealth became less united and largely bilateral in respect of each member's ties with Britain. Only Britain had Commonwealth-wide contacts, and there was soon no identifiable Commonwealth consensus on major political issues. British power declined, sterling became weak, and the British government was obliged to concentrate more on Europe and less on the Commonwealth. Whitehall came up sharply against the limits of its ability to shape international developments. In the Congo crisis, Ghana, Malaysia, Nigeria, Canada and India on the one hand, and Britain on the other, took different positions. India's take-over of Goa, criticized in the west, was acclaimed by the Afro-Asians. Despite the prevailing discord and disillusion, it was still felt by the politically aware section of the British public that the Commonwealth should yet stand for something, such as the values of freedom, democracy, and racial equality. But any sense of the imperial mission had waned and the Commonwealth lost its attraction for most British people.[64] 'The old Commonwealth did see things through British eyes, because ... of people of British stock', said *The Round Table*. 'With the new members ... it is a schoolmaster–pupil relationship rather than a close family link, and as former pupils acquire adult responsibilities they tend no longer to look to Mr Chips for guidance'.[65]

From 1959 to 1964, dramatic global changes took place which reduced Britain to merely a regional power, whose overseas possessions were more often an embarrassment rather than a strength, and whose connections with the Commonwealth weakened with its intention to join the European Economic Community which was then under French leadership.[66] The British government hoped that the Commonwealth, where it still enjoyed a predominant influence, would remain closely aligned with London in foreign and defence policies, but to evoke such an attachment, Britain had to offer concrete benefits in trade and security: sentimental ties alone without a solid material base were unlikely to provide sufficient links on which the loose-knit decentralized Commonwealth could depend. Before the war, no country other than Britain could provide such attractive benefits, but after it, Britain's erstwhile economic magnetism had failed in line with its loss of power. In the period 1960–65, Britain lost the ability to insulate the Commonwealth and Empire from the pressure of external forces and events, and there was the rapid decline of Commonwealth solidarity as the former colonies found new interests, friends and sponsors.[67]

Defence

Without the Empire's support Britain could not have survived the Second World War, and after the war, it was unable to defend the Empire single-handed, being very much the junior partner in the post-war Grand Alliance. After the transfer of power in South Asia, Britain placed great store on securing its strategic interests in the sub-continent by means of defence treaties or failing that, by a continuing Commonwealth link. Pakistan was of special interest; it was seen as a potential ally and there was the attractive prospect of bases in the North-West Province, and of a conduit to relations with the Islamic Middle East. In 1948 Pakistan broached the idea of a military pact with Britain, but when London made it clear that defence cooperation would not cover threats from other Commonwealth countries but be confined to global con-flicts, nothing came of it. Britain's other objective was to persuade India and the other newly independent Commonwealth countries to accept only British military equipment and training. The prospect of the old Dominions, who had won considerable freedom of action during the war, relying increasingly on the United States, was already becoming a matter of concern in London, where such dependence on America was regarded as being yet another distressing symptom of Commonwealth disunity. Beginning with the Ogdensburg pact of 1940, Canada con-cluded various defence agreements covering the north half of the west-ern hemisphere with the United States during Second World War, which were extended thereafter. And while the existence of Empire 'helped both to express and to underwrite Britain's larger world role, something Australia still valued highly even as it looked increasingly to the United States for global leadership,'[68] Australia and New Zealand followed with the Australia, New Zealand and the United States (ANZUS) Treaty in 1951, the first military alliance by those two countries with a foreign power. At that stage, Britain and the Commonwealth were recognized as valuable allies for Washington's defence and foreign policy objectives, and the two Pacific Commonwealth countries could not have envisaged any situation where British and American policies might substantially diverge. Interestingly, from an Australian and New Zealand perspective, ANZUS was the price the United States had to pay for antipodean approval of the peace treaty with Japan, though ANZUS had to be pushed through by the US administration over the initial reservations of the Pentagon, which was reluctant to take on any extra commitments in the Pacific. ANZUS eventually led to Australia and New Zealand's par-ticipation with the Americans in the Vietnam War, while Britain stayed away.

Nehru opposed ANZUS and kept India out of the Korean theatre; he was to be described by *The Round Table* in 1960 as having apathy towards Australia and New Zealand, and antipathy towards Pakistan and

South Africa.[69] By the end of 1951, the United States was on the point of starting negotiations on defence arrangements with Pakistan, which thereafter became a partner in the strategic interests of a superpower. Pakistan then joined SEATO, which was set up in 1954 after the French *débâcle* in Indo-China, and the Baghdad Pact in 1955, while India veered towards non-alignment, which was originally much resented by both superpowers, though much less so in the post-Stalin period of the Soviet Union. Cold War issues erupted in the sub-continent, which polarized India and Pakistan as antagonists on Kashmir and in the US–Soviet conflict, and reduced Britain's leverage further. Both SEATO and the Baghdad Pact angered Nehru, which he said reminded him of the spheres of influence of the Great Powers of the past century. Nehru, incidentally, opposed the North Atlantic Treaty Organization (NATO) partly because of its support to Portugal over Goa, while Pakistan also had reservations about it because of French repressive policy in North Africa.

The development of the Cold War in Europe served to underline the importance of imperial defence commitments. In the post-war period, the British government's aims were to make Britain's economic ends meet, to consolidate the Commonwealth as a third force in world affairs, and to repair or restore its worldwide network of imperial and Commonwealth defence arrangements. In 1950 Attlee had asked his advisers if Britain could place any reliance on colonial manpower in the Western Alliance's Cold War effort, and was given the unwelcome answer that it could not, though colonial governments could make some contributions against internal disorder.[70] By the end of that year, Whitehall also had to rule out the inclusion of India and Pakistan in any formal system of Commonwealth defence, but the British government still continued to hope that its longer-term burdens of defence could be shared with the United States and the Empire/Commonwealth. *The Round Table*, observing that Britain had pledged troops for permanent duty on the European continent in a reversal of the policy between the two world wars, noted in 1954 that 'Britain has accepted in Europe a far-reaching commitment which has hitherto been thought incompatible with its role in the Commonwealth.'[71] The new Commonwealth was ideally to comprise an array of states which Britain hoped could prove to be the vehicle for continuing British influence in the world beyond NATO in the 'pursuit of imperialism by other means'.[72] A British official 'Future Policy Study 1960–70' accordingly stated in 1959, 'United Kingdom power will thus be founded on United States partnership, buttressed by Western European solidarity (we hope), and usable through the instrument of the Commonwealth.'[73] The implicit theme was that

Britain would keep its troops on the Rhine while the Empire and Commonwealth, backed by the United States, would secure large regions of the Middle East, Africa and South East Asia. But Canada rejected any idea of centralization of defence and foreign policy, and South Africa and Australia were reticent on the subject. The Dominions looked outside the Commonwealth for their security and ANZUS did not even include Britain. In the 1950s, South Africa had become Britain's closest strategic Commonwealth partner: the two nations enjoyed a mutually advantageous economic relationship and shared an anxiety about UN interference in colonial questions.

There was a Commonwealth presence in Korea in the form of a brigade that included an Indian ambulance team, but the escalation of the war, to which Britain had dispatched air and ground forces, divided the Commonwealth. The Asian Commonwealth had initially supported the United Nations action in Korea, but came to regard the war negatively as one between imperial powers on Asian soil with little regard to Asian suffering, whereas the western group saw it as collective resistance to aggression. In Indo-China, Nehru advised against the recognition of the French puppet Emperor Bao Dai, – an advice ignored by Britain, Australia and New Zealand, – and extended *de facto* recognition to Ho Chi Minh instead. In 1954 Nehru became the first foreign dignitary to visit Hanoi after the Geneva Agreement. After 1954, Vietnam became the priority overseas preoccupation for the United States, and in 1965 American ground troops in Vietnam were joined by contingents from Australia and New Zealand, – the first time the two Pacific Dominions were to go into action without the United Kingdom.

The main security concern for the British government in Asia had involved keeping the peace in Malaya, where it could not bear to contemplate any repetition of the humiliations of 1941–42. The Australia, New Zealand and Malaya (ANZAM) agreement of 1948 provided the coordination framework for Britain, Australia and New Zealand to work together in South East Asia. From 1955 all three countries participated in the Commonwealth strategic reserve in Malaya. From 1948 to 1960 British troops were engaged in the struggle against communist guerillas in Malaya, and to protect the Malayan tin and rubber's substantial dollar earnings that sustained the Sterling Area's efforts to finance dollar purchases. Due to Nehru's anti-communist inclinations, India voiced no objections to the British military role in Malaya even though it strongly disapproved of SEATO. In the 1950s British defence spokesmen continued to emphasize the 'Commonwealth' aspect of overseas operations but there were in reality few defence agreements concluded between

Britain and its former colonies, many of which had already turned to other countries for training and equipment. But some old illusions remained. *The Times* spoke of 'the pledge ... by the soldiers of the United Kingdom' to Commonwealth countries. 'It is the assurance that no single member of the Commonwealth will be left to stand unaided in face of danger. No military pact, no matter how precise, has stronger force than that abiding assurance.'[74]

Having lost the services of the Indian army, Britain's auxiliary source of military power east of Suez rested on national service conscripts, and austerity at home was required to support the conscript army needed abroad for imperial purposes. Defence spending was the main aspect in which the burden of Empire imposed itself on the British economy and living standards, and public opinion was severely tested. Colonial problems for Britain in the 1950s were described as 'Commonwealth' matters though they were really the consequences of the winding-up of the Empire, especially in the Federations, and there was little Commonwealth unity in defence matters in action or concept. In 1956 the Bandaranaike government had come into power in Ceylon and abrogated the defence agreement with Britain. An agreement with independent Nigeria lasted only one year and it soon became clear that the newly independent former colonies did not wish to be associated with any formal arrangements that implied support for the American-led anti-communist campaign. These and other setbacks led *The Round Table* to express itself strongly in 1963: 'There are those who still hanker after a united front ... who cannot rid themselves of the idea that somehow or other the Commonwealth can be a power structure matching its will against that of the super powers. They are unable to shake themselves free of pre-nuclear concepts of power, prestige and influence, vainly imagining that the Commonwealth can boost the British peoples up from second-class to first-class power status.'[75] By 1965 it was clear that it could not be so. There was a fractious Commonwealth Meeting, the aborted Vietnam mission, an unilateral declaration of independence (UDI) in Rhodesia, civil war in Cyprus, ethnic and regional unrest in Nigeria, the break-up of Malaysia, and the Indo-Pakistan war. 'Pakistan', wrote *The Round Table*, 'has emerged with resentments towards all except the Chinese ... Indian opinion is forgiving only towards the Russians ... By any standard, Commonwealth relations have suffered severely.'[76] Even as late as the time of Prime Minister Harold Wilson, Britain was attempting to perform a world role despite its growing preoccupation with Europe: in defending Malaysia, and suppressing mutinies in Uganda, Kenya and Tanzania. From 1952 to 1957 defence spending had been as high as 10 per cent of the country's GNP, and from 1961 the value of fixed bases was being seriously questioned. A balance had to be struck between staying too long and withdrawing too soon. '[I]t would be important to withdraw before being asked to go ... the classic dilemma of decolonisation'.[77] By the mid-1960s, it was accepted that Commonwealth defence and bases overseas were a luxury that Britain could ill afford.

Both Conservative and Labour Governments maintained British commitments east of Suez until the sterling devaluation in 1967 brought about a reappraisal. Successive defence ministers and chiefs of staff had posed stark alternatives – either the Cabinet had to provide resources sufficient for commitments which could underpin Britain's great power status or it must accept reduction of that status. Britain had by then moved to a nuclear-based defence strategy and cut back on conventional forces. Conscription was abolished. Britain's position in the world was not due to the Empire and Commonwealth but rested on nuclear weapons, its special relationship with the United States, and its permanent seat on the UN Security Council. Attempts to maintain global military power and influence had failed, and Wilson decided, in the teeth of American opposition and Washington's appeals for reconsideration, to withdraw British forces from Asia in 1971, leaving no special capability for action east of Suez. This presence, which had sported the 'Commonwealth' label, was reduced without Commonwealth objection, other than from those in the regions directly affected. Criticism of the withdrawal was expressed by the Conservative Leader of the Opposition, Edward Heath, primarily as a matter of party politics. Visiting the Gulf, he assured the local rulers that if elected to power, his party would rescind Wilson's decision. The rulers were sceptical that this would indeed be the case, and rightly so. When Heath and the Conservatives were returned to office in 1970 they attempted to introduce a few modifications but there was to be no restoration of defence commitments. There was otherwise little opposition to the withdrawal within Britain itself – it was at this stage only a matter of stage-lighting. The crucial decisions had long before been taken – to transfer power to South Asia, to retreat from West Africa much earlier than had been foreseen until a very few years before the event, to leave Malaya as soon as the insurgency had been contained, and to withdraw from the Federation of South Arabia (Aden and the South Arabian Protectorates) in 1967.

After the British decision to withdraw from east of Suez, Australia and New Zealand were then also obliged to make a fundamental reassessment of their own security concerns, though ANZUS already gave them a US guarantee. These two countries decided after 1969 to maintain a force at Singapore, the first time they were not part of any big-power formation. Malaysia and Singapore sought a continuation of the British military presence, and the 'Five Power Defence Arrangements' of 1971 between them and Britain, Australia and New Zealand provided for consultations in the event of an attack on either of them. Financial constraints had obliged the British government to cut back its overseas military deployment after nearly thirty years of overspending on defence during a period when West Germany and Japan spent little. It was estimated that Britain was carrying a heavier defence burden than West Germany, France or Italy with the brunt falling on its balance of payments.[78] Every Commonwealth member-country was by now well aware of Britain's declining importance in global security matters in comparison with the United States, the Soviet Union and China. By 1971 Britain had in substance withdrawn its military presence from all of Asia other than Hong Kong and Brunei. In practical and operational terms, despite all the initial hopes and expectations, Britain had shouldered the burden of post-war 'Commonwealth defence' completely alone, with some assistance only from Australia and New Zealand in South East Asia.

The United States of America and Empire

American President Franklin Roosevelt held a strong conviction that the Second World War had sounded the death knell of European colonialism but his sentiments became muted as the war progressed. Until the war, successive governments of the United States had virtually ignored the Indian independence movement and made no official pronouncements on it, because it was in a region off the American radar screen, and regarded as of little political or economic significance. During the war, US interests became inextricably linked with the American-led alliance against the Axis and Britain's survivability against fascism. It was only the prospect of a Japanese advance into India, where the population was less than enthusiastic about the war, that brought about a change of heart in Washington, though its views on the Raj conveyed to Britain were still couched in diplomatic and non-coercive terms. Both the United Kingdom and the United States tacitly agreed to disagree on their respective interpretations of clause three of the 1941 Atlantic Charter.[79]

Australia and New Zealand were extremely perturbed about possible post-war American policies in the Pacific, in particular Washington's contrasting war-time attitudes towards future French President Charles de Gaulle and Nationalist Chinese supremo Chiang Kaishek, but Roosevelt eventually became ambiguous and sought compromise with the European colonial powers. American national interests overcame his theoretical position, and the same caution was in evidence from his successors Harry Truman and Dwight Eisenhower. The United States was too focused on the communist threat to give much attention to the British Empire, and the independence of South Asia was readily accepted as an earnest of Britain's sincerity in decolonization, leading the British Colonial Secretary to say in 1948, 'the United States have largely come round to our point of view ... and are at present too much preoccupied with communism to spare much time for "British imperialism" '.[80] Thus the policy of non-intervention in South Asia continued until the 1950s, in part out of deference to Britain's perceived primacy in South Asia, and by that time the Empire had got its second wind on the back of increasing American wealth and power and the colonial system was patchily buoyed up. There was a firm conviction in the White House that the developing countries were politically immature and in need of extended political and social apprenticeship, and seldom therefore did American policies directly encourage the nationalists, except in the case of Indonesia in 1949 and later of Egypt during the Suez crisis. During the Second World War the United States was, at least in theory, as strongly anti-colonial as the Soviet Union was anti-imperial, and the Americans contributed towards making the post-war debate about colonialism truly global. But when the US government recognized the value of the United Kingdom as an anti-communist ally, it did not impose any significant pressure on Britain. The Empire was seen as playing its supportive part in the containment of communism, and Britain developed its own special relationship with the United States which admitted of differences – Britain recognized the People's Republic of China in 1950, and London was unmoved by Secretary of State John Foster Dulles' arguments that the defence of Malaya against communism necessitated British intervention in Vietnam. Both the American and British governments were reluctant to be drawn too far into the global commitments of the other, and in a contrary twist, the British leadership feared that too close an association with US policy in Korea and Vietnam could affect British standing in Asia.

During the war, Roosevelt and the United States had been opposed to any 'ganging up' by Commonwealth countries, but after 1945 the US government tolerated the closed Sterling Area and showed some deference to British expertise in the Middle East and South Asia. Washington also gave some support to Britain's fight against the Malayan communists in the 12-year emergency from 1948 to 1960, and London for its part was ready to show America that its policies in South East Asia were responsive and realistic in regard to decolonization – in 1952 the British High Commissioner in Malaya General Gerald Templer was given a somewhat public political directive that Malaya should in due course be fully self-governing. Until 1951 America left South Asia to the British, partly because of the latter's greater experience and contacts in the area, and partly because South Asia still came low on the list of American military priorities.

At the end of the Second World War, the United States was not a dominant presence in the Middle East, which was not regarded as vital to its security concerns, though its continuing involvement in Palestine was shaped by domestic politics. Washington had advance knowledge of the 1952 Egyptian coup and its close dealings with future President Gamal Abdel Nasser were to play an important part in informing its attitude to the Suez crisis. After 1953 it perceived that its closeness to London and Paris was making it suspect in its dealings with the third world, and this led to Eisenhower's private warnings to Churchill against the futility of trying to resist the tide of nationalism.[81] Dulles in 1954 told the Senate Foreign Relations Committee,

> we face a very, very fundamental problem. Historically, we are traditionally aligned with the British and the French and the Europeans. We are called Europeans in much of the world ... These are the countries which have been primarily the colonial nations. Wherever we go in the world, if we work in cooperation with the British and the French, we are tarred by the same brush.[82]

Even before the Suez crisis, the US administration had become dissatisfied with what they saw as the British government's preoccupation with Commonwealth unity and regional predominance in the Middle East at a time when the United States regarded combating communism as the main task. The Middle East, with its oil, was an important strategic and economic interest for the United Kingdom – 'without cheap and plentiful supplies of oil ... recovery and prosperity will not be possible for us. ... we must be able to rely upon the friendly cooperation of all the states from which the oil is derived or through which it has to pass.'[83] The US government did not, for fear of a Soviet riposte, support Britain using force to restore control of the Anglo-Iranian Oil Company, though in 1953 it assisted in the overthrow of Iranian Prime Minister Mohammed Mossadeq. It was impatient with Anglo-Egyptian quarrels, and pushed Britain into the 1954 agreement with Nasser. Washington also insisted on a compromise between London and Saudi Arabia on the Buraimi oasis. In South East Asia, Washington deplored as appeasement Whitehall's willingness to accept communist control of part of Indo-China in the Geneva Accords of 1954, and was irked by Britain's refusal to support American military intervention on the ground.[84] In Malaya, however, the White House was prepared to acknowledge that Britain and the Commonwealth were shouldering a relevant defence burden.

By the 1950s American global activism was making its mark. South Asian leaders came to see that the world was not British or even Anglo-American, but an American-dominated one. The British Foreign Office was concerned about the magnetic appeal of the power of the United States: as early as 1950, a memorandum said, 'an attempt to turn the Commonwealth into a Third World Power would only confront its members with a direct choice between London and Washington, and though sentiment might point one way, interest would certainly lead the other'.[85] But neither of the two superpowers yet showed any inclination to penetrate the geographical areas of British interests. So Whitehall was allowed the freedom from interference to persevere with its notions of a system of power and influence based on the Commonwealth, and until 1956, British diplomacy still appeared confident and possibly even complacent. Even after Suez the American government showed some degree of tolerance of London's pretensions to retain an independent world-power stature. Competition between the two superpowers therefore came unwittingly to the rescue of the *status quo* in the Empire. The Commonwealth also served some purpose for Washington because the newly independent colonies, which had a much wider freedom of manoeuvre than at first seemed likely despite their poverty and military weakness, would not pass for want of any suitable alternative into the sphere of the rival superpower. As it actually transpired, not a single British dependency which joined the Commonwealth declared itself to be communist after attaining independence despite many of them espousing various socialist models of society. The US government therefore collaborated with the European colonizers in an effort to foreclose the opportunities for the Soviet Union and communist expansionism. The American administration viewed itself as an honest broker between the European imperial powers and the colonies, but neither of them ever perceived Washington as such, because at various different periods of time, the independence movements, the colonial system and the Commonwealth were considered by the United States to be instruments for security and stability against the communists, and were supported accordingly.

The question of American support to African nationalism was further complicated by the fact that in the early period after the war, official American attitudes to the liberation of Africa were profoundly unsympathetic. There was a deeply held belief in Washington in African political immaturity and that the African nationalists were unready and incapable of governing themselves. Another question in Washington's mind was whether the Cold War was best prosecuted by cooperation with the nationalists or with the Europeans, since communism was considered a more potent threat than colonialism. After 1954 Washington settled on a policy of orderly transition, 'zeal balanced by patience,' and in 1955 Dulles allegedly told Macmillan that the period of British hegemony was the happiest that Africa had ever enjoyed.[86] After Soviet dictator Joseph Stalin's death and the start of Soviet aid to the Middle East and India, the Cold War in the developing world intensified. Chinese political, economic and ideological penetration of Africa also began. America needed friends in Africa and came to the conclusion that political change would not have to await socio-economic development. Events in Congo were an eye-opener, where all Washington's political nightmares came true, and the Americans began to look for cooperation with African leaders on the road to self-government. In East and Central Africa the United States was concerned that Britain was not moving fast enough, but there was still no great pressure brought to bear on London, although in the first focal point, the Central African Federation, the United States was much less sanguine than London about the future of multiracialism. In 1960, the United States initially wanted to support the UN General Assembly resolution on decolonization but was ever-anxious not to upset the European applecart and the NATO alliance through application of undue pressure on the colonizing countries, and characteristically, on the urgings of Macmillan, in the end decided to abstain. But Washington was at last slowly coming round to the view that colonialism was a doctrine that supplied nations with a reason to sympathize with, or support, communism. The US government therefore now made it clear that it wanted the British political leadership to court Afro-Asian nationalism to checkmate Soviet diplomacy, and a factor in decolonization and the new Commonwealth was henceforth to be the American-driven anti-communist agenda. The British in their response were pragmatic and had no wish, unlike the Portuguese, to maintain their colonies to the last ditch. On the contrary, they realized that the building up of the Commonwealth to garner worldwide influence required a more than token acknowledgement of anti-colonial opinion.

In the 1950s and 1960s, both the world and the Commonwealth were changing too fast for the three circles of the two superpowers along with Britain and its Empire/Commonwealth to be convincing. It proved unrealistic to imagine that the 'last empire' could be any basis for policy making, let alone for the achievement of British parity with Moscow and Washington. 'There is a perceptible awareness', wrote *The Round Table*, 'of the American presence in the world.'[87] The Commonwealth was lacking shape and purpose; of what use was a non-regional, non-military, non-economic organization? The geopolitical map had changed, the supremacy of the United States was obvious, and the three circles were now wholly out of proportion. From the end of the Second World War onwards, the Commonwealth had played a 'decreasingly audible second fiddle'[88] to the United States. So much so that in 1965, *The Round Table* proclaimed grimly, 'we find ourselves, in a sense, within the American Commonwealth.'[89]

The West Indies Federation

In 1951 the Conservatives under Churchill were elected to power, and a Cabinet committee was established to consider the eligibility to Commonwealth membership of the dependencies as and when they became independent. This committee concluded in favour of a uniform type of membership, but expressed its preference for applications to be made as wider groupings or federations. If decolonization was to strengthen Britain and secure its world role, the coming into existence of indigent tottering mini-states was to be avoided, and large political units in the Empire in the form of politically and financially sustainable successor states had to be created to enhance the prospects for the continuation of future British influence. 'For divide and rule', wrote Nicholas Mansergh sardonically, 'there was thus substituted an injunction more appropriate to the Commonwealth – unite and abdicate'.[90]

In the Caribbean, the British government accordingly wanted to promote a West Indies Federation rather than to have small insolvent independent Dominions which would prove to be burdensome to London. But the West Indies Federation had one of the weakest federal systems in history – no common currency, no customs union, no unrestricted inter-island migration. The budget was only one tenth of the revenue of either Jamaica or Trinidad. No direct taxation was levied, no postage stamp issued. The only federal responsibilities were for external relations, communications between the islands, a university college and a regiment, with the last two consuming half of the federal budget.

Above all, there was no commitment to the federation by its incompatible components.[91] The ill-fated West Indies Federation therefore lasted only four years, from 1958 to 1962. Jamaica was the first to opt for full independence, then was followed by Trinidad and Tobago, leaving only eight members. Language, sport, the Crown and post-war migration drew the sentiments of the Caribbean islands towards Britain, but local loyalties and the desire for autonomy were too strong to preserve the larger entity.

Unlike the situation which developed later in independent British Africa, in the independent Commonwealth Caribbean, a tendency to move from pluralism to the centralization of power was resisted, leaders adopted various personality cults but were not elevated to an unassailable pedestal, military coups were averted, the abuse of bureaucratic power was contained, regional cooperation sustained, and socialism nominally espoused but with rather less fervour than private enterprise. These positive developments in the West Indies were a counterpoint to the concurrent creation of an emotional British domestic problem; at the same time as several centuries of colonial rule in the West Indies were drawing to a close, the Caribbean connection had become a major political issue in Britain due to immigration and the factor of race.

The Suez crisis and its aftermath

British statesmen like Eden and his predecessors had been unprepared by family background, temperament and upbringing for bringing a closure to Empire[92] and were reluctant to accept the role of junior partners to the United States. Eden had resigned over Munich in 1938 and he wanted to demonstrate during the Suez crisis that he had learned the bitter lessons of appeasement. Lester Pearson, Canada's then Foreign Minister, thought Suez had brought the Commonwealth to the verge of dissolution.[93] His country had split ranks with the rest of the old Commonwealth on this issue, and he claimed that its attitude had assisted to heal Commonwealth divisions, in addition to helping to find a solution by securing a ceasefire and establishing the United Nations Emergency Force (UNEF), resisting the American administration's efforts to humiliate London, and providing Britain with an escape route and a means of retreat. All this was in marked contrast to Menzies' unstinted backing for Eden, which was described by C. Rajagopalachari, the last Governor-General of India, as 'the true voice of British colonialism, speaking from the grave.'[94]

In Britain it was generally felt that after Suez, the Commonwealth would never be the same again, but the Prime Ministers Meeting of

July 1957 resumed some degree of normality. Canada, India and Ceylon had castigated Britain during the crisis, but Canada, along with India, had eventually saved the Commonwealth. Nehru was, 'in its first major crisis, its saviour',[95] though there was considerable recrimination when he did not condemn the Soviet invasion of Hungary in equal measure. In Commonwealth terms, Suez had demonstrated that the age of British colonialism was over, the former colonies could not be coerced, and that Commonwealth members were more influential in world affairs than they had been a decade earlier. Apart from Suez, no other colonial commitment was a comparably prominent and controversial domestic political issue in Britain in the 1950s. For the Conservative Party, the traditional assumption that the Commonwealth was a supportive asset came into question for the first time. As for the Commonwealth, Britain remained the principal and predominant partner, but 'with a leadership less likely than hitherto to secure backing ... in doubtful or disputed issues'.[96] Suez had not been the subject of any prior consultation by Whitehall with any Commonwealth member, but Menzies, a strong advocate of consultation even as late as in June 1956, was not disturbed about this, probably because his conception of the Australian national interest was unfailingly consistent attachment to the British government's position. For the senior partner to break the principle put an end to the practice. Consultation, or the lack of it, ceased to be invoked in the Commonwealth thenceforward and this principle was never again to be seriously resuscitated.

Suez had been a telling blow to British diplomacy, strategy and politics, and brought about a crisis in the Commonwealth. It showed that the post-war redistribution of power had not been fully consolidated in the early 1950s as was hoped for by the British authorities. Britain had perforce to turn to the United States and the International Monetary Fund (IMF) for massive aid, which was facilitated by the American government for fear of driving the Arabs into the Soviet camp, against the condition that Britain withdrew from Egypt. The crisis showed that sterling and British oil supplies were vulnerable to the US administration's policies and laid bare the adverse consequences of future attempts at foreign intervention and colonial repression. With the intensification of the Cold War, the United States emerged as a global power with interests in every region of the world, and any notions that Britain could retain a privileged position in Africa, the Middle East and South Asia were swept away. Yet the British government was still interested in retaining the Commonwealth as a system of status and power, and this 'led to a further inflation of the windy rhetoric about the Commonwealth's uniqueness as a multi-racial association which served, perhaps unconsciously, to veil its defects as a vehicle of British influence'.[97] Some new signposts in British policy emerged; not to allow any major gap to develop between British and American foreign policy, and to avoid being isolated at the United Nations. Doubts about the use of military capacity to protect British overseas interests started to surface, together with an awareness that the domestic repercussions of any assertive foreign policy initiative required close management if critical public opinion was not to be aroused. Of equal significance and relevance was the fact that at the same time as Britain was buckling under Washington's pressure, West Germany and France were deciding to fashion a new Europe.

For a time, the British government's determination to remain a world power remained plausible: the United States and the Soviet Union were both cautious about expanding their influence to new regions until the mid-1950s. But the constitutional arrangements made by Britain in many colonies to appease unrest in fact accelerated political change and activism which could not be settled without repression, which was hard to apply and even harder to sustain. Britain had expected to remain the dominant influence in the former colonies and preserve the special international status that imperial power had brought it. That this was found not to be possible; to give up imperial burdens but not enjoy post-imperial benefits, came as a disagreeable surprise. But the perception began to dawn in London of a new pro-European orientation of British interests, along with the realization that Britain could no longer deal with any major colonial conflict without at least the tacit acquiescence of the United States.

The winds of change started to blow from both Washington and Moscow. Communist Party Secretary Nikita Khruschev and the Twentieth Party Conference of the CPSU in 1956 heralded the Soviet Union's readiness to carry communist influence into the non-European world, and after Suez and Hungary, the USSR became more active in the third world, especially in the matter of arms supplies. The British leadership's reaction was a determination to preserve its influence where possible, and it did not give up its hopes of a close Indo-UK partnership until the mid-1950s when Prime Minister Nicolai Bulganin and Khruschev visited India and praised its independent and non-aligned foreign policy. The United Nations became more important as both east and west vied for the support of the third world. Anti-colonialism became an accepted article of faith. In UN councils, British representatives tried to prevent the establishment of any principle of formal accountability for colonial policy, maintaining this was legally a matter of exclusive domestic jurisdiction, but were hampered by the fact that Suez had damaged British prestige and international legitimacy because of the loss of the country's moral standing. The more competitive international climate after 1960 also served to accelerate the diminution of British power and influence overseas. The end of the Empire was brought about as a result of Britain's desperate search for dollars and economic revival, Soviet advances in the third world, a u-turn in French colonial policy, a new perspective in Washington on decolonization and the Congo crisis which all contributed in wrecking Britain's leisurely East and Central African decolonization timetables. In sum, the British government found it could not distance itself from Europe and concentrate on the Empire. Neither could it achieve a transfer of power to the former colonies that would suitably safeguard its vital strategic and political interests. Indeed, after 1960, any grand design of a remodelled Empire in the form of the Commonwealth disintegrated rapidly. Britain casting about for a new world role was described cuttingly by Jan Morris 'as the aging chatelaine of the increasingly skittish Commonwealth'.[98] In 1961, the former US Secretary of State Dean Acheson remarked that the Commonwealth possessed 'no political structure, or unity or strength',[99] and a year later, that Britain had lost an Empire and had not found a role. This marked two decades of British post-war decline; the former grandeur was fast dissolving into memory, and the end of Empire came in the period between 1960 and 1965, when Britain was unable to exert sufficient influence in economic, strategic and political terms. The new generation of leaders in the former colonies was not prepared to accept satellite status in a British-led Commonwealth as the white Dominion prime ministers had done between the wars in the twentieth century. Britain was no longer a major actor in the world and could not underwrite many benefits that its associates might expect to derive from it. From the late 1950s its ability to operate an informal empire was rapidly declining, which was made evident by Suez, and this change in its status could not be concealed or neutralized by any assertion of influence such as through the Commonwealth connection.[100]

The Middle East and Cyprus

In July 1956 the Suez Canal was nationalized by a local authority which defied and confronted Britain, and London was driven to try to protect its interests by a desperate military gamble with little consequent success. In the years that followed Britain's withdrawal from Suez in

December 1956, Britain's erstwhile supremacy in the region came to an end, and in 1958 the Iraq monarchy, Britain's foremost ally in the region, was overthrown. In 1955 a militant campaign began among Greek Cypriots for *enosis*, meaning the union of Cyprus with Greece, while the Turkish Cypriots agitated for partition. Cyprus was to prove the most intractable colonial problem of the late 1950s, further complicated by several factors. The British military bases on Cyprus were needed for the troops withdrawn from the Canal Zone, and the British government was anxious to keep Turkey in the Baghdad Pact of 1955. After the Suez set-back, the prospect of yet another ignominious British military withdrawal was unthinkable. Even the Labour Party, in a document setting out its colonial policy in 1957, viewed Cyprus as a territory that 'will neither be capable of national sovereignty nor anxious to attain it'.[101] *Enosis* was rejected by London, and eventually abandoned by the Greek Cypriot leader Archbishop Makarios in 1958, but Britain was forced to associate both Greece and Turkey with the future of independent Cyprus, though it secured in perpetuity its two bases covering 99 square miles of the island.[102] It also secured bases in Malta for 15 years after that country's independence in 1964.

Britain was initially not inclined to agree to Commonwealth membership for either Cyprus or Malta, both small island states, and Cyprus in addition being the first colony to aspire to join the association as a republic. As in the case of Ghana in the former decade, the possibility of a two-tier Commonwealth, with the newcomers assigned to the lesser tier, was once again re-examined. Mezzanine status, non-member category, Malta's integration with the United Kingdom – all these variations were considered and rejected or dropped. Cyprus spurned the idea of being part of any second X1 team and a Commonwealth study group under Norman Brook concluded that Commonwealth membership could not be denied to it,[103] though the unwelcome implications of the precedent were obvious, with the likely prospect of independence and membership in the association for other small and micro states, and more disputes and disunity as an inevitable consequence of the larger numbers. Any residual reluctance on the part of the British government to grant full and equal membership of the Commonwealth to all newcomers was finally given up, and the composition of the modern Commonwealth was once again transformed. No guidelines regarding membership were laid down until 1991, and no criteria of territorial size or population had to be satisfied in the future.

2
The African Commonwealth

British Africa

British statesmen were always anxious to portray London's concessions to the colonies in respect of national self-determination in the most favourable light, as a projection of the highest stage of political theory, and to demonstrate how well the Asian and African colonies had absorbed the values of Westminster. Moreover, claimed the British, thanks to their enlightened colonial order, the new leaders in the former colonies could now administer a defined country and not merely a motley aggregation of ethnic groups, tribes, castes and regions. Intellectuals associated with *The Round Table* professed that Britain had a moral duty to disseminate the benefits of the rule of law and free political institutions within the Empire, thereby turning it by gradual stages into a multiracial Commonwealth. Macmillan claimed that self-government had been the intention behind colonial rule from the very beginning, and that independence was only the last installment of a graduated and anticipated advance in the constitutional programme.[1] Meanwhile, the British government was determined to orchestrate the process meticulously and outbreaks like the Mau Mau in Kenya from 1952 to 1956 were firmly suppressed before they were succeeded by the later political transactions towards independence.

The first British withdrawals from the African continent were in 1954–1956 from Egypt and Sudan – neither of which had considered any Commonwealth link and which would have been vetoed by South Africa in any case. The years 1948 to 1957 'had not been notable for new thoughts or even new activities in intra-Commonwealth matters ... There had been the deafening silence of little or no serious discussion of Commonwealth affairs for months at a time for most of the 1950s.'[2]

From 1948 to 1957 the composition of Commonwealth summits had remained static, and the editor of *The Round Table* in 1983 expressed retrospectively critical judgment:

> The Commonwealth has never been regarded as a candidate for super-power status, though the rather idle belief that it did or might at least add substantial cubits to Britain's diplomatic stature caused some distractions from hard thinking and clear sighted planning in the decade after 1947.[3]

At first the British government did not consider African colonial independence as being at all incompatible with its objectives of close strategic and economic cooperation. In Ghana, the pragmatic outlook of the CPP leadership under future Prime Minister and President Kwame Nkrumah, who accepted membership of the Commonwealth, the Sterling Area and the dollar pool, was quite in accord with London's expectations. But Nkrumah's application in 1951 for Dominion status for the Gold Coast had clearly troubled Attlee, who was not seeking to dismantle the Empire and was also anxious about South Africa's likely reaction to the eventual presence of a black African prime minister in the Commonwealth.[4] South African Prime Minister D.F. Malan reminded London that Commonwealth membership was not something exclusively in Britain's gift but required the consent of all existing members, which gave the British leadership pause for speculation as to the nature of the future Commonwealth. Full membership of the Commonwealth for Ghana was accepted somewhat reluctantly because it was obvious that failure to grant it would not only alienate the Asian members but would mean the loss to the Commonwealth of the rest of the British African Empire after independence as well. Semantics were also of consequence; the Cabinet agreed in 1955 that the use of the term 'full self-government' was preferable to 'independence' since the latter might imply a separation from the Commonwealth.[5] In the second half of 1953, *The Round Table*, with commendable prescience, had expressed the view 'that the Commonwealth as an entity, formal or practical, will in the next decade stand or fall by what happens in Africa'.[6] But the Commonwealth Journal of International Affairs was still hopeful that both the new African members and the Commonwealth as a whole would benefit in security from the incorporation of the former in the latter: in 1955 it stated, 'so long as they remain within the British Commonwealth ... we must assume that the Commonwealth, within the NATO system, can protect itself and its members',[7] and a year later, continued to exhibit the same confidence;

> no conceivable organization or connexion other than the Commonwealth can provide the right system within which countries of widely different stages of political and economic advancement and ... vitality ... can proceed and develop, giving each other mutual aid and support. An African continent without a British Commonwealth, one whose territories had always the naked choice between colonialism and a spurious and insecure independence, would be heading for chaos and disaster.[8]

Governor-General Lord Listowel, presenting the Ghana Independence Bill in 1957, declared, 'yet another stage will have been achieved in the journey of this great Commonwealth of Nations towards its destiny',[9] and 1957 also marked the first Prime Ministers Meeting at which an independent African member was present. The communiqué noted Ghana's presence but said nothing more on Africa, a remarkable omission that was never repeated subsequently. Apart from South Africa, Australia was predictably the least enthusiastic about the latest expansion of Commonwealth membership, but the evolution of the Commonwealth had by now become inextricably linked with decolonization in Africa.

In East Africa, Britain was more rigorous, since London did not regard the developments in West Africa as necessarily providing a precedent for its other colonies in Africa to follow. A committee of officials set up by Macmillan to evaluate the profit and loss to Britain of every colony moving towards full self-government felt that the Gold Coast had set too fast a pace for emulation, and 'the thrust of the officials' argument was that withdrawing from colonies might produce some modest financial saving but would be discreditable where it was not dangerous, and not only for strategic reasons ... Where international reputation, strategic requirements or global prestige could not be said to be at stake, the officials raised the objection of "moral abdication." '[10] East Africa had white settlers and Asians, and was of far greater strategic importance for the Middle East and the Indian Ocean; the British government was accordingly less inclined to be generous. In 1959 the Colonial Secretary said in the House of Commons; 'I cannot now foresee a date when it will be possible for any British Government to surrender their ultimate responsibilities for the destiny and well-being of Kenya.'[11] In line with their customary policy of those times, the British leaders were also pursuing the prospect of engineering a Federation within the three East African countries in which a multiracial but European settler-led

Kenya would play the dominant part. In 1959, after Macmillan had won the largest parliamentary majority since the Second World War, Iain Macleod arrived at the Colonial Office as secretary of state. He was described by Macmillan as 'a Minister of great imagination, even genius'.[12] Macleod accepted the inevitability of rapid African political advance, and scrapped the principle of gradualism, although there was no overall master-plan as such and decolonization had not even been an issue at the general election. He was to assert that 'the march of men towards their freedom can be guided, but not halted. Of course there were risks in moving quickly. But the risks of moving slowly were far greater.'[13] Nevertheless, even in 1960, the British Cabinet did not want to pursue a policy that would change the substance of the colonial relationship. It hoped that after independence, influence would yield as much as direct rule had done, though *The Round Table* in 1962 sounded a prophetic warning: 'This lack of common basis is seen most clearly in Africa. ... It certainly seems unlikely that the Commonwealth in ten years time will be the same comfortable club that it was ten years ago.'[14] With de Gaulle offering West and Equatorial Africa full independence in 1960, which had a profound influence on Macmillan, and Congo's independence from Belgium in that same year, fears in Whitehall of a spill-over of the chaos of the Congo led to a complete turn-around in policy, an abandonment of notional time-tables, the break-up of the Central African Federation and the loss of British influence in Africa among the whites and blacks alike. The Congo crisis signalled the possibility that Britain might have to reckon with major military operations if it did not disengage fast from Africa, at a time when British public opinion had lost the desire to dominate others against their will, and even less to fight in Africa to maintain imperial rule. Independence could not much longer be delayed, and it had to be granted swiftly if Britain was to keep some control over the proceedings.

The ensuing period, therefore, saw all of British Africa free except for Rhodesia, the departure of South Africa from the Commonwealth, the establishment of dictatorships, military and otherwise, and the end of the West Indies Federation, the Central African Federation, the Malaysian Federation, the South Arabian Federation, and protracted British humiliation over Rhodesia. The end of Empire was not when the majority of the colonies achieved independence, but when Britain ceased to enjoy primacy which was the situation by the end of the 1960s. In some Commonwealth member-countries, Soviet and Chinese influence started to become evident. Sterling Area unity was broken by greater global prosperity and economic multilateralism. Both the British

Empire and the Commonwealth 'got lost in Africa. ... in Africa the Empire and the Commonwealth met their greatest crises'.[15]

The British people were encouraged to harbour a sense of pride and satisfaction that their country's plans had progressively led to self-government in the Empire, and expected that the democratic parliamentary system would prevail in Africa, with the rule of law and civil liberties believed to have been deeply embedded by the British colonial administration. Thus there was shock and disappointment with the unfolding undemocratic and anti-democratic events in Ghana, Kenya, Uganda, Tanzania, Malawi, Zambia, Lesotho, Sierra Leone and Nigeria. Egypt and Sudan had already established bad precedents a decade earlier, constituting precedents of a type to which most Afro-Asian nations would unhappily become accustomed, but puzzling and unfamiliar to the British.[16] The democratic process often became reduced to a sham electoral competition for a nation's resources, and ethnic, religious and regional rivalries and rampant corruption predominated. The judiciary, police and civil service became intensely politicized. No level of government could control the levels below it. After the first breakdown of the democratic process, the style was for the rule of law to remain suspended indefinitely while military or autocratic regimes succeeded themselves in power. There were three main causes of surprise and resentment over Africa for the British public – stridently condemnatory African anti-colonialism, the rejection of democracy, and racial conflict in Southern Africa. The South Asian independent nations had caused Britain little embarrassment, and were far more critical in the United Nations forums of the French, Dutch and Portuguese colonizers than of the British. But African diplomacy was found to be vigorous and overtly confrontational. The white/black split in the Commonwealth which had been avoided over Suez in 1956 and South Africa in 1961, mainly due to Canada breaking ranks with the other white members, now emerged into the open with full clarity. 'Africa brought a new dimension to Commonwealth relations,' wrote Miller. 'It was not simply a matter of issues; it involved tone, temper and emotion.'[17] The African aggressiveness and clamant tactics were hurtful to Britain, and especially to its overseas aid-workers and civil servants, who felt with some justification that they had laboured hard for African independence and on behalf of the African people. There were threats by Ghana and Tanzania in 1965 to leave the Commonwealth, to break relations with Britain, and to curtail British trade and investment. Garner of the Commonwealth Relations Office claims that in the 1960s there were no fewer than a dozen occasions when requests were made by Commonwealth countries through diplomatic channels for the removal of the resident British high commissioner.[18] This kind of antagonism and acrimony became the unpalatable norm for the Commonwealth's prevailing political climate. When the UN General Assembly rejected the Gibraltar referendum of 1967, declared free and fair by the Commonwealth Secretariat, as many as 10 Commonwealth members voted for the motion or abstained.

South Africa

In 1960 the Sharpeville massacre took place in South Africa. In the councils of the Commonwealth, Nehru continued to raise the question of apartheid but in a low key, and *The Round Table* reported, 'nor is much heard nowadays about India's leaving the Commonwealth'.[19] But in the following year came the 'wind of change' speech, South Africa voted to become a republic and the Commonwealth Prime Ministers were to convene again shortly thereafter. Republican precedents were aplenty; India, Pakistan, Ghana and Cyprus. But as far as South Africa was concerned, matters were coming to a head. Tanganyika was not yet independent, but Julius Nyerere, future prime minister and president, had already announced that his country could not join any association that included a racialist state.

South Africa's policy of apartheid threatened Britain's good relations with the rest of the Commonwealth, and even the hardened Conservatives had to concede that the South African economy would come under severe stress if apartheid continued. Macmillan was influenced strongly by the fact that Canada had led the critics of South Africa, and was disappointed when some Commonwealth members refused to be deflected from discussing South African apartheid policies in the context of its proposed republican status. When the Commonwealth Prime Ministers discussed South Africa's internal affairs, it was the first time the Commonwealth had directly censured any of its own members. South African Prime Minister Hendrik Verwoerd did not help his cause by being combative, and caused offence by a defiant justification of apartheid and his refusal to accept high commissioners from the non-white members. Upon Macmillan's urging, Verwoerd finally withdrew his country's application to remain in the Commonwealth. Only Menzies, on the principle of non-interference in domestic affairs, objected to South Africa being obliged to leave the Commonwealth, and did not agree with the others that the Commonwealth would be better off without it. The views of the prime ministers of the United Kingdom and Australia had accordingly not prevailed in a Commonwealth matter of major importance. Macmillan later wrote to Menzies; 'I now shrink from any Commonwealth meeting because I know how troublesome it will be,'[20] and admitted to being 'weighed down by a sense of grief and foreboding'.[21] South Africa was not however to be penalized by Britain after it left the Commonwealth; it had received assurances about continued bilateral cooperation even before it withdrew.[22] This showed that Commonwealth consensus opinion made no difference to the British government's attitude or its practical arrangements, especially when it came to the old Dominions.

Although Verwoerd had predicted that South Africa's withdrawal would prove to be the 'beginning of the disintegration of the Commonwealth',[23] in fact the departure of South Africa from the Commonwealth seemed at first to heal the rift between the Africans and Britain. But the Rhodesian issue, then the Unilateral Declaration of Independence (UDI), the question of the use of force by Britain against the white minority regime in Rhodesia, arms sales to South Africa and sanctions against the South African apartheid regime arose successively to vitiate the situation. The expectations of a hopeful *Round Table* were belied: it had written rather unctuously on the departure of South Africa that 'perhaps the outstanding mission of the Commonwealth in the latter part of the century is to take the lead in drawing Africa into the mainstream of world civilization'.[24] If there was one foreign policy objective that united the disparate new members, it was the aggressive and vocal opposition to South Africa. The Commonwealth was much valued by them as a forum to pressurize Britain, and indirectly the United States, to apply sanctions. This embarrassed the west and kept the South African issue both alive and high on the international agenda.

The British Empire in Africa had effectively disintegrated by 1971. Whether the Commonwealth itself would survive the challenges it faced in Africa was in some serious doubt before the Singapore Heads of Government Meeting, which was the first regular summit to be held outside Britain. Prime Minister Edward Heath, fearing considerable bit-terness over arms sales to South Africa and the Rhodesian UDI, advised the Queen to stay away. The Conservative government wanted to fulfill its obligations under the Simonstown Agreement of 1955, and Heath's arguments in Singapore about 'maritime equipment' sales (in fact, heli-copters for anti-submarine frigates) to South Africa received support only from Australia and New Zealand. Nyerere threatened once again to withdraw from the Commonwealth. Heath, who 'was impatient with the Commonwealth from the outset, and not a little hostile',[25] nevertheless made it clear that he fully retained the right to take whatever action was needed to give effect to British global defence policy, which included Simonstown as an element, and sales to South Africa was the price which was to be paid for continued use of Simonstown.[26] Having asserted Britain's independence from Commonwealth pressures, and even in the face of threats of withdrawal, he went out sailing rather than participate in informal negotiations to achieve consensus with the other heads of government. But the Singapore outcome, the Declaration, which was based on ideas submitted by Nyerere and Zambian President Kenneth Kaunda, was greeted with general relief. The period of confrontation between the old and the new Commonwealth members appeared to be over, causing Nyerere to say, 'the Commonwealth is stronger than treaties, less selfish than alliances, less restrictive than any other association'.[27] But this was only a lull before the long drawn-out acrimony between Britain and the Commonwealth majority on Rhodesia and South Africa. Heath wanted to postpone the next summit until 1975 but Canadian Prime Minister Pierre Trudeau and Commonwealth Secretary-General Arnold Smith contrived to convene another one two years later.

In 1986 only 13 independent member countries participated in, while as many as 31 member countries boycotted, the Commonwealth Games at Edinburgh, with Nigeria leading the dissent, on the question of Britain's opposition to sanctions against South Africa. The British government under Conservative Prime Ministers Margaret Thatcher, and later John Major, did not hesitate to break with the Commonwealth consensus when it ran counter to British policy. The Thatcher years proved conclusively that the opinions of the Commonwealth either singly or collectively were of scant importance to Britain's political leaders when it came to issues concerning Britain's security or prosperity, and whether Britain was isolated in the organization or any member threatened to walk out mattered not at all to Whitehall. It was also clear that the Commonwealth 'carries no entitlements when it comes to the formation of British policy'[28] and 'consensus without Britain was fast becoming a Commonwealth tradition.'[29] This often left Britain as a lone voice, and at Kuala Lumpur in 1989, Prime Minister Geoffrey Palmer of New Zealand declared sadly that it was 'not a good idea for the Commonwealth to turn into an organization to orchestrate hymns of hate against the United Kingdom'.[30] Mrs Thatcher was determined not to sacrifice Britain's commercial and investment relations with South Africa, and was convinced that sanctions against South Africa would not work. She rejected any view that the United Kingdom was isolated, and instead ridiculed the Secretariat by alleging that the Secretariat fiddled while Ramphal roamed.[31] The South African issue, unlike Rhodesia which was a matter of decolonization, was a different problem of enfranchisement and emancipation, and the campaign against apartheid had become something of a personal crusade for Commonwealth Secretary-General Shridath Ramphal. Apartheid was the policy of a fully self-governing republic with a white minority government over which Britain had no direct control or responsibility. But Britain was trapped by its history. The connecting thread in Southern Africa was racism, and the issue persisted until the establishment of a multiracial South Africa in 1994, only to resurface with President Robert Mugabe's seizure of white-owned farming land in Zimbabwe.

The Central African Federation and Rhodesia

The transfer of power in Africa resulted in multiracialism being adopted as a basic principle in the Commonwealth. Of all the issues pertaining to African nationalist politics, nothing caused more trouble for the British government than white settler nationalism in Central Africa. 'Africans are not the problem in Africa,' declared Macmillan, 'it is the Europeans who are the problem.'[32] Well organized politically and strong economically, Southern Rhodesia had been almost completely internally self-governing since 1923, and in practice Britain had not intervened in the domestic field of its 'native policy'. This stimulated similar demands for self-government from the white settlers in Northern Rhodesia and Nyasaland, and South Africa's proximity encouraged such claims for independence. Whitehall was prepared to be accommodating, not least to check South Africa's influence northwards by keeping Rhodesia from Pretoria's embrace and by constructing the Central African Federation. To these settlers, majority rule was a fanciful concept and in the 1950s such views were not wholly discordant with those held by British politicians and officials, though by the 1960s and 1970s, with the accession of a large number of African States to full independence, opinions of this nature would come to be considered as bigoted and racialist. *The Round Table* expressed the opinion that the independence demand was 'of the gravest importance not only to the three territories concerned, but also to future racial harmony throughout the British Empire, and, indeed throughout the world'.[33] The 1953 Central African Federation fell well short of the independence aspirations of the white minority, but much depended on whether London was prepared to advance the white-ruled Federation towards full Dominion status. The Ghanaian precedent led to representations for Commonwealth membership from the Federation, and Whitehall was inclined to confer a status like Newfoundland's before it was absorbed within Canada, that is, to be invited to sit at the conference table without being self-governing. From 1964 onwards, after the demise of the Federation, the presence of Rhodesia was no longer accepted at Commonwealth summits although it had been an observer at the Imperial Conferences since 1930.[34] From the very start, the term 'partnership' in the Federation had meant very different things to the British government, the blacks and the whites. Black nationalism grew apace with the majority's fears of the settlers and the Federation, and the prime cause of the break-up of the Central African Federation was the strength of African nationalism, which took both the British leadership and the federal authorities by surprise.

It is a matter of irony that since the American War of Independence, the only rebellion which ousted British constitutional authority was by a minority community of settlers of European descent in Africa who always protested their devoted loyalty to the Crown and British institutions. Rhodesia was the rock upon which pessimistic Commonwealth watchers feared that 'the frail Commonwealth bark might split'[35] because the rebellion touched on the kith and kin factor, sensitive racial chords and on raw nerves domestically. After Ian Smith replaced Winston Field in 1964 as Rhodesian Prime Minister, there was little desire in Salisbury for any compromise; the mainly white electorate voted for independence in a referendum, and the unilateral declaration thereof came in November 1965. One year earlier, a Commonwealth collapse on Rhodesia had been predicted at the Prime Ministers Meeting but this did not happen though the Africans pressed for firmer action by Britain, and Douglas-Home described some new members as 'not the easiest of associates'.[36] Canada was sympathetic to the aspirations of the new African members and only Australia supported the white settlers. In that year, the Commonwealth Relations Office List, in describing the Commonwealth, wryly commented that 'there is no legal or formal obstacle to any member pursuing a policy diametrically opposed to that of any other member',[37] and Garner records that 'by 1964 British officials were being placed in an intolerable position at these meetings'.[38]

The leader of the Labour Party, Harold Wilson, was elected into office as prime minister in 1964 with the reputation of being a strong Commonwealth supporter. His party had come to power with the objective of reinvigorating the Commonwealth as a bridge between the old and the new members. After all, the Labour Party under Attlee and independent India under Nehru had cooperated to create the modern Commonwealth, which still retained some powerful elements of symbolism both in Parliament and with British public opinion, and Wilson had served in Attlee's first Cabinet. In 1965 Wilson, with the support of the House of Commons, put forward a proposal at his first Commonwealth Prime Ministers Meeting for a mission to the governments concerned with the Vietnam conflict to discuss a possible international peace conference. The members of that mission were to be the heads of government of Britain, Ceylon, Ghana, Nigeria, and Trinidad and Tobago. Tanzania however objected on the grounds that Britain's closeness to the United States would doom the mission and protested that the Commonwealth was being used for British domestic political purposes. Prime Minister Eric Williams of Trinidad and Tobago complained that British ministers always referred to the mission as 'Mr Wilson's mission'.[39] It also transpired to the annoyance of the majority of members that Wilson had consulted the 'old' Commonwealth members in advance but none of the 'new'. Some Asian and African members wanted Wilson himself replaced by Canadian Prime Minister Lester Pearson as the mission's leader, but Pearson was not interested in undertaking such a role. The Africans felt the mission was a distraction from a discussion on Rhodesia. In any event, the mission ultimately aborted since North Vietnam said it was not interested in it, but this whole sorry episode showed that the African members entertained suspicions that the British authorities still viewed the Commonwealth as a possible instrument of British policy. It was an inauspicious beginning for Wilson and left him sorely disillusioned with the Commonwealth. He came to believe that no previous British government ever had to confront a problem like Rhodesia – 'so complicated or so apparently insoluable'.[40] There was a storm of outrage in Britain in 1965 when Zambia's high commissioner in London called Britain a toothless bulldog, and in the United Nations, Britain was later to be taunted with having put down a rebellion in Anguilla in 1969 but was refusing to act against the white Rhodesians. Kaunda of Zambia spoke of leaving the Commonwealth in 1966 but did not do so. He wanted Uganda, Kenya and Tanzania to leave with him if Britain did not take harsher measures against Rhodesia, but they were reluctant to take such a step.

In an attempt to preserve the unity of the Commonwealth, Britain agreed to two Commonwealth summits in 1966. The special Lagos Summit was the result of a proposal by Nigerian Prime Minister Abubakr Tafewa Balewa as a means to reconcile Britain and the Africans, was the first to be held outside London, and was the first to be organized by the new Secretariat and in which the British prime minister was not the host and chairman. Wilson tried and failed to persuade Canada to host the regular 1966 Prime Ministers Meeting, and when it took place in London, 'after bitter words and frayed tempers',[41] the British government refused to use force in Rhodesia unless there was a breakdown of law and order, refused to ask for mandatory UN sanctions, and refused to go along with the appeal for 'No independence before majority African rule' (NIBMAR). It wanted some elbow room to deal with Smith and was wary of domestic opinion widely sympathetic to the white Rhodesians. This 1966 meeting, called 'a nightmare conference'[42] by Wilson, 'by common consent the worst ever held up to that time',[43] was attended only by 14 Commonwealth heads of government; perhaps because, as admitted by Sierra Leone, it was feared by many that the meeting might impair the African members' bilateral relations with Britain. Despite the stormy gathering, with 5 (Britain, Australia, New Zealand, Malta and Malawi) ranged against 17, the Commonwealth survived, accompanied by 'what had become the normal sighs of relief from the newspapers that the Commonwealth was still intact'.[44] On Rhodesia, Wilson, and later, Heath, both showed a disposition to compromise and seek settlement by negotiation with the rebels, though not at the cost of the sacrifice of any basic principle. Wilson was even ready to contemplate independence before majority rule and his public renunciation of the use of force before the UDI weakened his hand. Only after the failure of his talks with Smith on the Royal Navy warships *Tiger* (1966) and *Fearless* (1968) did he come round to conditional acceptance of NIBMAR and mandatory sanctions – even so, it was not Britain's emphasis on NIBMAR but rather Smith's suspicious nature and reluctance to strike a deal that prevented the prolongation of minority rule for several decades longer. The Commonwealth had survived, but at the expense of its cohesion. Before the next summit, Wilson declared that he recognized that Commonwealth members wanted to assert their independence, but that 'Britain has also achieved her independence' and 'we have a right to ask for ... the support of the whole Commonwealth in this issue'.[45] He did not win that support, though he was somewhat reassured by the next meeting in 1969; calling it 'by far the most successful ever held'.[46] British independence from the Commonwealth was to be asserted in rather similar terms by subsequent British prime ministers.

From 1964 onwards, Rhodesia became almost the only topic of Commonwealth discussion, so much so that *The Guardian* in an editorial in 1965 claimed the Commonwealth 'has the reputation of being a bit of a bore'.[47] When the Rhodesian issue looked intractable, the organization was found wanting not only by the British government but by the African political leaders as well. Without the existence of the newly created Secretariat the association might not have survived the existence of a dispute in which Britain had become the main object of condemnation.

Rhodesia became a republic in March 1970. The territory came to represent a prolonged indignity for Britain, and British policy was pilloried as racist. The Africans were frustrated because they were unable to shift Whitehall from its refusal to use forceful methods against the rebels. As for the Commonwealth, an organization over which Britain had long presided, it had become a watch-dog over Britain on Rhodesia. 'In no previous phase in the process of decolonization', wrote Mansergh, 'had Commonwealth participation in the shaping of British policy been so pronounced, nor British freedom of manoeuvre become so narrowly constricted, nor the limits of British authority been so painfully and so publicly demonstrated over a long period of time'.[48] As for Australia and New Zealand, they began to realize the growing diplomatic importance of the new African states, and in 1971 at the Singapore Commonwealth summit, Britain had to concede that any settlement in Rhodesia would have to be acceptable to the colony's people as a whole.

From 1964 to 1980 Rhodesia, which was described by Labour Government Minister Richard Crossman as 'this appalling liability',[49] proved to be a source of anxiety and periodic humiliation for London, and its effect on British prestige as the leader and main-spring of the Commonwealth was damaging. It also dealt a mortal blow to the hopes for the perpetuation of British influence in Africa. The British public's obvious sympathy for the Rhodesian rebels contrasted with their growing animosity to the predominantly Afro-Asian Commonwealth, even on the part of some who had earlier championed the cause of the preservation of overseas connections. By 1971 the old loyalties to the Commonwealth, which had so divided domestic opinion on the application to join the European Economic Community (EEC) a decade earlier, had all but faded away.

Talks with the rebels in 1966, 1968 and 1971 all proved fruitless, and the Rhodesian issue became internationalized. British policy was ostensibly to replace the Smith regime with one that would be responsive and malleable to Whitehall, but in reality to do the least that was necessary to appease its critics in the United Nations, in Africa and the Commonwealth. Selective mandatory sanctions imposed by the UN Security Council were breached, and the British special representative in East and Central Africa Malcolm MacDonald reported in 1968 'that this British government's word is no longer trusted either in Africa or in some other parts of the world'.[50] Changes finally came about due to the guerilla war led by Mugabe that began in 1973, and the Portuguese coup in 1974 and Lisbon's subsequent withdrawal from Mozambique and Angola, both of whom signed ominous friendship treaties with the Soviet Union. Pretoria then sought a compromise and there was also increasing pressure for a settlement from the United States. The Commonwealth majority was only able to exert influence on the west up to a point, but it made it abundantly clear that it did not concur with Britain's plan to sponsor the international recognition of Bishop Abel Muzorewa who had become Prime Minister after the Rhodesian election of 1979, and Nigeria underlined this stand by threatening to walk out of the Commonwealth. Mrs Thatcher agreed at the Lusaka Commonwealth summit to a conclave of all the parties concerned, which led to the Lancaster House Conference. This was attended, despite misgivings, by Mugabe's Patriotic Front, and resulted in fresh elections with the participation of the Patriotic Front and monitoring by Commonwealth observers. The resulting 1980 election victory by Mugabe's Zanu-PF was described as 'unexpected, unintended and unwelcome'[51] for the British government, but the main issue for most voters in Zimbabwe was evidently the desire to back the party most likely to recover the farmlands alienated to the white settlers.

The Commonwealth is believed by commentators on international affairs to have helped Britain in four ways over Rhodesia. It prevailed on Mrs Thatcher not to recognize Muzorewa, and to convene the Lancaster House Conference; it influenced Zambia and Tanzania to accept the peace plan; and it deployed military observers to check the ceasefire and civil observers to monitor the elections.[52] 'Rarely', noted Mansergh, 'has the Commonwealth ... been seen to better advantage'.[53] But Foreign Secretary Lord Carrington's assessments differed sharply. He viewed the Commonwealth as a basically unsympathetic forum which had to be managed and kept in its place by the British government, and described as nonsense the idea that the Lancaster House Conference was attributable to any Commonwealth initiative; and still less that its successful outcome was due to any interventions by Ramphal.[54] Supporters of the Commonwealth, however, took heart from the transformation of Rhodesia to Zimbabwe, declaring that 'the Commonwealth's most striking recent achievement has undoubtedly been the inspired approach to and solution of the Rhodesian deadlock'.[55] Rhodesia had almost broken the Commonwealth. In the end, it did not, but it reshaped the association and moved it into a new era, which has still not yet come to a close.

Britain, the Commonwealth and Independent Africa

In January 1957, the British colonial Empire in Africa was at its broadest expanse; by December 1967, nothing of it remained except Swaziland and the running sore of rebel Rhodesia. In the British political system the Conservatives were well placed to carry through radical measures – 'it was accordingly without serious domestic opposition that a Conservative Government was able to wind up British colonial responsibilities ... at a pace which had not been contemplated'.[56] Giving up its Empire came to be accepted as British bipartisan national policy, with Commonwealth membership for the newly independent states softening to some extent the finality of the parting of ways. During this protracted process the Commonwealth and the Empire coexisted, and the British government's emphasis was on continuity, assisted by the relative ease with which the transition took place when compared to other European Empires.

British politicians themselves had talked up the Commonwealth as an institution generating both pride and utility. It was a forum in which Britain had a privileged position and acquired additional prestige because the Commonwealth enabled Whitehall to speak on behalf of others as well as for itself. The Commonwealth added stature to Britain and assisted the decolonizing process. Here was an association to which newly independent states could aspire to belong and thereby come under British indirect tutelage. It provided some diplomatic traction and some trade and economic opportunities. In 1955, the Conservative Party manifesto affirmed that the British Commonwealth and Empire were 'the greatest force for peace and progress in the world today',[57] and even as late as Macmillan's tenure of office, and despite the divisions over Suez and recurrent Indo-Pakistan disputes, Britain constantly tried to revive the prospect of unity among Commonwealth members. *The Round Table* described the association as a bridge to the whole uncommitted world, conceding that 'there may be others, but none that will bear so broad a stream of traffic in mutual understanding'.[58] A Conservative party pamphlet in 1960 claimed, 'no political party would now dare to suggest publicly that the Commonwealth has outlived its usefulness. Today every political party is anxious to establish a reputation for unwavering devotion to this great heritage'.[59] It was not easy for the Conservative Party to adjust to the diminution of Britain's imperial power: 'hence the anxiety of the leadership to present the transformation of the old dependent Empire into the new Commonwealth as some kind of new triumph for British statesmanship; the working out of a time-hallowed plan ... for self-government'.[60] But the decline in Britain's position in the Commonwealth and the world at large was becoming progressively quite apparent. By 1961 there was a non-European majority in the Commonwealth summits. Thus Macmillan wrote to Menzies in 1962 in a conciliatory manner about their critics in the Commonwealth; 'I think the real reason for keeping the Commonwealth together is that I believe we can influence it, slowly and gradually, but effectively ... And as the years pass I think it is possible with patience and putting up with a lot of trouble and insults from them that it will be worth doing.'[61]

South Africa's withdrawal had dented right-wing support in Britain for the Commonwealth: then there was non-white immigration, the widespread erosion of democracy in Africa and the problem of Rhodesia. The broad consensus of approval for the Commonwealth among the British public turned first to disinterest and then to disapproval in the 1960s, largely because of Rhodesia and the kith and kin factor. In the late 1960s, 'the collapse of self-confidence amongst erstwhile champions of the Commonwealth seemed swiftly complete',[62] and Britain took a declining interest in the organization in contrast to a growing desire to associate more closely with the highly industrialized countries. 'For the short term', wrote Mansergh, 'the political price of Commonwealth in Africa was seen to be high. Disillusion spread and it was deepened by African disorder.'[63] These events played their part in the process of Britain looking in a spirit of expectation not to the Commonwealth but to Europe. Foreign Secretary Selwyn Lloyd and Douglas-Home attempted to interest the old Dominions in some new ideas to revitalize the association but nothing came of these efforts, and Douglas-Home's own senior colleagues, such as Heath, were much more interested in another approach for admission to the EEC.

Menzies, who was Prime Minister of Australia from 1952 to 1966, and for whom the Empire and Commonwealth belonged to the days when they were for the most part British by name, composition, loyalty and united purpose, had at last retired from politics. He had agonized over the breakdown of his cherished old order and the changing character of the Commonwealth; the appeasement, as he saw it, of the Afro-Asians by Britain, restrictions on Commonwealth immigration, Britain's desire to draw closer to Europe, and its inclination to withdraw its forces from Asia. Similarly, other nostalgic loyalists of the original five-member club 'felt almost overwhelmed by the pace of change and depressed by the periodic spurts of dramatic acceleration'.[64]

In Britain itself, there were feelings of wounded pride, and strong resentment about a perceived lack of gratitude from the former colonies. There was a reversal of roles in that whereas in the past Britain had sought to influence the Commonwealth, now the Commonwealth was seeking to influence Britain, though the instruments used were blunter and lacked finesse. The number of Commonwealth republics now outnumbered the monarchies. 'Crisis succeeded crisis unpredictably', wrote Garner, 'and problems arose in every part of the Commonwealth.'[65] At the same time, the British government was preoccupied with its application for entry into the EEC, difficulties with balance of payments and sterling, non-white immigration, and changes in defence policy. The British could not come to terms with the proposition that their former imperial role could imply and necessitate further continuing obligations. Britain had tried unsuccessfully to re-write history and convert a world order which had turned from influence into rule into one which transformed rule back to influence;[66] in other words, to rearrange matters in such a way that 'colonial rule must die that influence might live: empire must be sacrificed to world power'.[67] In each region of the world Britain found that the effort of moving to a less formal kind of superior status proved unworkable. It required the existence of a worldwide British system, but Britain now lacked the economic and military power to hold its own against the competition of other world powers, quite apart from its other pressing domestic and international compulsions.

To the British politicians and officialdom the Commonwealth was clearly a diminishing asset and the Afro-Asian members for their part were obviously sceptical about any equal partnership. The age of faith in the Commonwealth was drawing to a close. 'The Commonwealth is beginning to be a drag on some of its members,' wrote Hugh Tinker in *The Round Table*. Whereas there had been a 'reasonable balance' in the 1950s, 'it is ... a predominantly African organization ... with, at most, a continental outlook ... The 1960s see not a dialogue but a confrontation.'[68] By 1969 the notion was dispelled that colonial issues could be considered as being a subject only of domestic jurisdiction, or that issues within the Commonwealth (the so-called *inter se* doctrine) were not to be aired in other forums. The most enthusiastic members of the Commonwealth were now the newest and the smallest countries; the older members felt a world-weary sense of lassitude towards it. From 1945 to 1965 the number of people under British colonial rule had shrunk from seven hundred million to five million, three million of whom were in Hong Kong.[69]

During the 1960s and 1970s, the Africans were united, vociferous and emotional and sceptical about any genuine equality in Commonwealth partnership. The Commonwealth Prime Ministers Meetings gave them an international platform and worldwide publicity for the first time. They could not influence Whitehall policy to any great extent but their outspoken attacks served to turn British public opinion decisively against the Commonwealth. The organization had assisted and culminated in the freedom and association of the majority of people who constituted the largest and greatest of the European Empires, but while achieving this, it had lost its *raison d'être*, and now had to find other causes to espouse.[70] The setting up of a permanent Secretariat was entirely consistent with the new African dimension and had been created at their initiative, especially that of Nkrumah and Ugandan Prime Minister Milton Obote, who were supported eagerly by Canada, though India and Australia were cool to the idea. At the 1965 summit it was noticeable that the newer members voiced the strongest opinions, and that the communiqué condemned Portugal, South Africa and Rhodesia. The African and the Caribbean countries now acted as an anti-British pressure-group, and Wilson was disinclined to convene a Commonwealth Prime Ministers Meeting for three years after 1966 to avoid confrontations over Rhodesia; he even tried without success to persuade Pearson to host a meeting in Quebec. This pause enabled the Secretariat to find its feet and establish an identity separate from the British government. The British authorities for their part were glad to rid themselves of an invidious task as they saw it, that of managing Commonwealth meetings in which their policies were constantly under fire.[71]

At the United Nations in the middle 1960s, the gentleman's agreement on the 'Commonwealth seat' on the Security Council and the United Nations Economic and Social Council (ECOSOC) came to an end, and regular meetings of the Commonwealth permanent representatives had stopped because of Rhodesia. For the British government, the desire and opportunity to operate a Commonwealth system had been curtailed. London was no longer even *primus inter pares*. Writing of the Ottawa summit of 1973, *The Round Table* declared, not altogether sadly, 'Britain is no longer, except in purely historical terms, the Mother Country ... That image is now seen to be totally outmoded.'[72] In 1974 Trudeau endorsed this view when he wrote, 'none is senior; none is superior',[73] and a year later it was he, and not the British prime minister, who suggested that the association should observe an annual 'Commonwealth Day', the first being held in 1977. Tanzania and Ghana had drawn a distinction between Britain and the Commonwealth; they suspended diplomatic relations with Britain from 1965 to 1968 but stayed in the association, thereby manifesting their view that it should no longer be considered a British-dominated club. In 1967 James Eayrs asserted in *The Round Table*, 'that the Commonwealth is in disarray, that its future is in doubt, are facts to be stated rather than points to be debated'.[74] In October 1968, the Foreign Office and the Commonwealth Office merged as the Foreign and Commonwealth Office (FCO), just over two years after the Commonwealth Relations Office (CRO) had absorbed the Colonial Office to become the Commonwealth Office, and the Commonwealth ceased to be not-foreign. High commissioners in London and some British high commissioners abroad had resisted these developments for seven years on the grounds that the British government was downgrading the Commonwealth but their appeals only delayed the inevitable outcome. 'With the disappearance of a government department,' wrote Lyon, "exclusively assigned to watch over Commonwealth relations, in Whitehall and throughout British government, the values and relevance of the Commonwealth have become not suddenly but nevertheless drastically diminished.'[75] In 1969, the Duncan Report on Overseas Representation cast the major part of the Commonwealth outside the area of main concentration for the United Kingdom's future diplomatic focus.

In 1969 *The Round Table* in a contribution by Miller gave thought and expression as to how the Commonwealth had changed.

Although it is usual for people in the white Commonwealth countries to contrast today's Commonwealth with that which existed before the Second World War, the real contrast is with the 'Nehru Commonwealth', the relatively cosy arrangement which existed between 1947 and 1960, with the brief interruption of Suez in 1956. This was a Commonwealth in which the principle of respect for domestic jurisdiction was closely preserved (perhaps because of Mr Nehru's sensitivity over Kashmir), in which there was considerable cooperation in economic matters in spite of disagreement over the question of alignment with the USA or USSR, and in which the numbers were small enough to make discussion informal around a relatively small table. The underlying assumptions of this 'Nehru Commonwealth' were knocked away by the unhappy coincidence of rapidly increased African membership and the mishandling of Britain's most difficult colonial problem, that of Rhodesia. Unlike their Asian predecessors, the African leaders had become accustomed to cooperation in agitation: they carried over, after independence, the slogans and procedures which had worked so well in the lobbies of the UN.[76]

The Indian summer of the British Commonwealth, a period from 1947 to about 1965, was finally at an end.

By 1971, 'British sovereignty had ended, imperial defence had waned, common allegiance to the Crown was no more, the primacy of British manufactures and the British market had passed, and common citizenship and common rights of entry into Britain had been curtailed ... A new age of realism had commenced in which the Commonwealth continued, was taken for granted, but did not have too much expected of it'.[77] Dean Acheson reminisced: 'It didn't really strike home to us that the British Empire was gone, the great power of France was gone ... These were countries hardly much more important than Brazil in the world.'[78] The Commonwealth to the British public had become a mainly third world forum with its attendant largely negative features. In Uganda, President Idi Amin's honeymoon period with Britain caused by London's aversion to Obote ended and the military dictator's human rights violations began, leading Heath to contemplate proposing Uganda's expulsion from the Commonwealth. The Secretariat meanwhile tried to promote a new post-colonial Commonwealth system of collectively shared institutions and consensus-based policies without Britain at the hub, and to replace residual but significant anglo-centricity with multilateralism. Relationships independent of Britain were to be the future key, despite the Queen's continuing position as the Head of the Commonwealth. Yet as Kenyan Professor Ali Mazuri asked: 'In the ultimate analysis, what could a New Zealander have in common with a Jamaican or a Zambian if not the bonds of a shared Britishness?'[79]

The 1980s marked yet another wave of disillusion and a growing distance between Britain and the Commonwealth. Mrs Thatcher carried into her government little of the traditional high Tory reverence of Empire or faith in the Commonwealth, though by this time London was only dealing with 'the loose ends'.[80] Equality had been a founding doctrine, but in the British public's mind every Commonwealth member now seemed more equal than Britain, which nevertheless paid the largest bills. Democracy and non-racial attitudes were much admired at home, but military rule, one-party rule and racial antagonisms seemed to be the order of the day in the former colonies, and the Commonwealth was held to have little to commend it. 'An empire of enormous wealth and power has been transformed into an international association whose chief merit lies not in its capacity to act but in its willingness to argue,'[81] wrote Dennis Austin. The end of the Cold War and of apartheid in South Africa and the fall of Mrs Thatcher brought some temporary relief to the Commonwealth, along with hopes that the organization could find a new and meaningful role for itself with a post-Cold War agenda of promoting democracy and development. And with the entry of Namibia and the re-entry of South Africa, and the more borderline-case admissions of Mozambique and Cameroon, it appeared that the number of Commonwealth members would be stabilized for the foreseeable future.

But the problems of Africa are still central to today's Commonwealth and typifying this, out of the five scheduled summit meetings of the organization between 1999 and 2007, three will be hosted in Africa. Of the various regional groupings in the Commonwealth, Africa's is the largest, and whether in the realm of political crises or in the social and economic areas, the greatest challenges to the association's values and programmes continue to lie in Africa.

Economic matters

The Empire was a network of economic relationships of mutual dependence and the wealth generated from it paid for colonial rule and imperial defence. The Port of London's logo proudly proclaimed itself as the Port of Empire. The Empire may have been described as 'men, money and markets', but even at its peak, excluding the Second World War period, Britain's trade with the colonies never reached 50 per cent of its total trade turnover.[82] The Empire, and later the Commonwealth, proved unable to absorb all its products, and no member was prepared to discourage local production in favour of imports from Britain.

Regarding currency, sterling went on the defensive after the First World War. Britain abandoned the Gold Standard in 1931 and developed a sterling bloc, which excluded Canada. Members built up their sterling reserves in London and this sterling group became a Sterling Area in September 1939. With the introduction of strict exchange controls in 1940, it was transformed into a monetary union that pooled gold and dollar reserves for the war effort. The Sterling Area meant that each country might have its own currency, but in carrying out most of their business transactions, the members would draw down sterling accounts with one another, using the British pound as the common unit of currency. The Sterling Area was a binding element in the Commonwealth that had no replica on the political side, and it enhanced Britain's position of leadership in the Commonwealth, and its international prestige, in the 1940s and 1950s.

In 1932 Britain offered imperial preference, being by far the most important trading partner and banker for the Dominions and colonies. Imperial preference was embodied in a series of bilateral trade agreements and was not multilateral in operation. It did not embrace the 'new' members; nor did it cover the principal exports of a number of Commonwealth countries. Preference gave opportunities to specific items such as Indian textiles, Malayan rubber and Australian canned fruits, but the scheme was never revised, had no central control, and no commodity development fund.[83]

In 1939 Britain's international trade was equal to that of the United States's, its industrial base equal to Germany's and stronger than that of Japan.[84] It was the biggest exporter of capital and raised substantial invisible income. During the Second World War, Britain was largely cut off from the European markets and turned to its colonies, where it faced no competition from the Japanese or Europeans, and to the United States. Trade in sterling was preferred to available alternatives, and investment was mainly in countries in the Sterling Area. The war transformed Britain's surpluses into shortages of capital and manpower and the United States emerged from it as the world's most powerful country. During the war Britain borrowed from the United States double what it was able to borrow from the dominions and colonies, and consequently became dependent on US aid, added to which was the burden it bore of its overseas defence spending. Between 1947 and 1987 British defence expenditure was 5.8 per cent of the GDP; one hundred years before it had only been 2.6 per cent.[85] Whereas Britain was once able to finance its deficit in trade by returns on overseas investments, now Britain faced a crushing foreign debt, and in 1947, 1949 and 1951 financial and economic disaster seemed close at hand. In 1945, Britain's own reserves were 15 times less than its liabilities, with India, Ceylon and Pakistan holding the largest credit balances.[86] Nevertheless, at the end of the war, the Sterling Area was still responsible for financing a quarter of the world's trade, and half of British exports went to the Commonwealth and Empire.[87]

The Labour Government in 1945 had pledged itself to build a welfare state, which could only be affordable if overseas commitments were reduced. In 1947 Britain imposed strict controls on foreign exchange, which tied independent members of the Sterling Area to a common trade policy, limited their rights to the credits they had accumulated during the war, and obliged them to source more imports from Britain.

The dollars received by Britain under the Marshall Plan and from exports from Australia, Hong Kong, Malaya and West Africa provided the hard currency the Dominions lacked, and this was the recompense for the blocked sterling balances and foreign exchange controls. The Empire/Commonwealth had an interest in keeping Britain solvent, and for most of the Dominions and dependencies, Britain was still the most important market. Commonwealth membership assured continued access to the advantage of special ties with Britain – its market, investment capability and the strength of sterling as backing for the Area. Additionally, for some countries like Malaya, even access to military support; in this case, Malayan tin and rubber exports for hard currency were important arguments for Britain to commit itself to the anti-communist struggle there from 1948.

For the credibility and success of Britain's role and prospects as a powerful trading nation, a global reach and perspective were necessary, for which the Empire and Commonwealth were essential elements. Therefore, 'on merits', concluded a meeting of British senior officials in 1949, 'there is no attraction for us in long term economic cooperation with Europe'.[88] After the war, Britain wanted food and raw materials that did not have to be paid for in dollars. So it turned to the Empire both to supply Britain and to swell the Sterling Area's dollar pool. The post-war Labour government dreamed of developing the British Empire economically to compensate for the loss of India. 'Without such colonial development', wrote Defence Minister A.V. Alexander, 'there can be no major improvement in the standard of living of our own people at home.'[89] Labour Party economists felt that Africa could produce the required food and minerals, and Bevin claimed 'we could have the United States dependent on us and eating out of our hand in four or five years'.[90] In a last flush of colonial exuberance, the Colonial Development and Welfare Act of 1940 was re-launched in 1945, new British expatriates arrived in Africa, and federation schemes were conceived in Africa, the Caribbean and South East Asia. Though the policy was clothed in progressive rhetoric, there was the expectation that the use of resources pumped into the colonies would produce food as well as provide new markets to serve Britain's economic needs and meet the frantic quest for food and raw materials. There was also the attraction of operating in sheltered areas of the world where British influence could be exercised independently of the United States. But economic recovery was under way in Europe from the mid-1950s, the dollar shortage was being overcome, and inefficient means of production in the colonies were no longer viable. There was little return on this investment and it became clear that the colonies were not going to fuel a European recovery. Between 1950 and 1973 the British GDP per capita rate of growth remained the lowest in Europe[91] and seven years after the War, domestic rationing was still in force for some items.

There was a sterling devaluation in 1949, followed by all members of the Area other than Pakistan, caused by continual problems of balance of payments and shortage of dollars. The need for Commonwealth investment grew too great for Britain alone to satisfy the demand. A balance of payments crisis in 1951 showed how vulnerable Britain was to the economic policies of the United States and to over-extended defence commitments, and in 1952, fearing another devaluation, a Commonwealth economic conference decided to shift from discriminatory policies and a closed economy to multilateralism and convertibility. By 1955 many at home were starting to doubt the merit of overseas possessions and to question whether economic development there need necessarily precede political advance to self-government.

Britain continued to suffer balance of payments crises in the 1950s and 1960s. By 1956 it had become hard to define any positive role for the colonies in assessing Britain's prospects for economic recovery. Britain's industrial and dollar-earning capacity gradually improved, colonial hard currency earnings counted for less, imperial protection and the value of Commonwealth preference were found to be of little importance. While evaluating the benefits of Commonwealth preference, members did not wish to lay themselves open to reprisals from the growing markets in the United States, Japan or Europe, or to take any actions that might prejudice the prospects of their future collaboration with the United States. The creditors of the Sterling Area were at the same time also diversifying their reserves. Though as late as 1958 the near-identity between the Sterling Area and the Commonwealth still gave some distinction to the association and especially to the central role of Britain, the sterling balances held by the Commonwealth and colonies in London were always a mixed blessing – British official commitment to this was mainly concerned with international standing, but the British government knew there were better outlets for capital. Britain's exports had a favoured position over goods to be paid for in dollars, but there were drawbacks – a possible dollar deficit which Britain would have to make up, a deficit in the rest of the Sterling Area which Britain would have to finance and a possible run on the bank if every sterling holder made demands at the same time. The Suez crisis highlighted the fragility of sterling and the reserve position. This increased London's dependence on the United States, though it did not yet wholly restrain Britain from aspiring to retain global standing and an effective strategic presence east of Suez.[92]

Accordingly the British delegation in 1958 at the Commonwealth Trade Conference at Montreal continued to reaffirm its faith in the association as a trading entity. It was felt politically important to maintain the sterling system and up to that time there was no sign that British politicians had come to the conclusion that the imperial economy was redundant. They rejected any plan that would impair their right to buy food from the Commonwealth or maintain preferences. International confidence in sterling seemed to depend on Britain acting as a great imperial power and one of the internal arguments for the 1956 Suez action was that Egyptian 'piracy' on the Canal 'represents a very great danger to sterling'.[93] Commonwealth obligations had been invoked by Eden in 1952 to explain why Britain could not respond to American requests for it to play a role in the creation of the European Community, and again by Macmillan in 1958 in answer to why Britain could not join the EEC at its foundation. Sterling became convertible to non-dollar currencies in 1954 and fully convertible in 1958, and the European Free Trade Agreement came into being in November 1959. By the 1960s Britain had to choose between global ambitions, which it still harboured, and a more secure and prosperous future as part of a European system. Another year of crisis was in 1961 when, despite its application to join the EEC, Britain still hoped to preserve the benefits of Commonwealth trade relations, though by that time British exports to the Commonwealth were static while those to the United States and EEC were growing fast.[94] Menzies' attempts to convene special meetings of the old Commonwealth members to discuss the protection of their trading interests were deflected by Macmillan, who wrote in 1962 that he was shaken by the Commonwealth's attitude, and especially that of the old Dominions.[95] Heath was particularly singled out for trenchant criticism by the Australians. *The Round Table* much later commented retrospectively,

> While the United Kingdom continued to provide assurances throughout the EEC negotiations that Commonwealth interests would be catered for, it became increasingly obvious, not least to the likes of the Australians, Canadians and New Zealanders, that these were shelved once Britain's own interests were threatened ... the proceedings had exposed the fragility of Commonwealth cohesion, the dominance of national interests, the absence of trust on all sides and went a long way towards dispelling the warm glow surrounding old Commonwealth country relations.[96]

On the other side of the Channel, de Gaulle deplored what he saw as collusion between Britain and the United States to uphold the privileged system of exclusive markets, though his reasoning was out of date. He claimed with much greater justification that Britain was not yet ready for Europe, carried too much American and Commonwealth baggage, was unable to choose conclusively between the Commonwealth and Europe, and had extra-European responsibilities and obligations in the wider world. The French veto in 1963 postponed Britain's entry to the EEC by a decade and was sourly ascribed by the British media to the French purpose of constructing a political Europe under French hegemony, which would have been frustrated with British entry.[97] This veto gave rise to renewed talk of the Commonwealth as an alternative force, though the Conservatives sought to play down such theoretical possibilities.

In 1964 Wilson had said that to give up the Sterling Area would be 'a body blow to the Commonwealth and all it stands for',[98] but another fiscal crisis developed with budget deficits, a run on British reserves, and depreciation of the pound against the dollar, leading to another devaluation. It became clear that Britain had neither the capital nor the military muscle to hold together the decentralized Commonwealth as a sphere of influence in pursuit of an 'informal empire'. In 1966 Wilson conceded that he had again to seek EEC membership. In 1967 the pound was devalued by 14 per cent and Britain had to turn to the IMF to persuade sterling holders to retain a minimum of their reserves in pounds, which were guaranteed in dollars against further sterling devaluation. This brought to an end the Sterling Area and London's quest for an imperial role. The British Cabinet accepted that Europe was thenceforward to be the main centre of overseas effort and attention. Sterling devaluation was on this occasion not followed by all other members of the Sterling Area, as had been the case in 1949, and their unease about the strength of sterling and the reality of their wider trading needs caused them increasingly to hold their reserves in gold or dollars. By the end of 1968, sterling as a reserve currency had effectively ended and the Sterling Area disappeared, its official demise being declared in 1972. Most Commonwealth members by that time had insufficient economic strength to hold substantial reserves and were consequently of decreasing importance to British and world trade. The African dimension was economic as well as political; most of the newly independent states needed economic and technical assistance from the very start. The 1960s also marked the diminishing importance of preference, which was of little significance for the new members, and the US administration during and after the Second World War had urged its reduction or abolition. Already by the end of the war, mechanisms were set up to prevent the British Empire being shut up to world trade like an 'oyster shell', as US Secretary of State Cordell Hull put it.[99] The General Agreement on Tariffs and Trade (GATT) from 1947 and trade negotiations such as the Kennedy Round introduced Most Favoured Nation (MFN) clauses in the UK tariff and narrowed the margin of preference for Commonwealth imports. The margin of preference enjoyed was 11 per cent in 1937, about 7 per cent post-war, and by 1959 had reduced to 5 per cent.[100] In exports to its former colonies, the British now faced increasing competition from Europe.

In 1965 Wilson suggested three economic proposals to the Commonwealth members; a meeting of trade ministers; coordination of development programmes and consultations on aircraft requirements. But he was greatly disappointed at the reaction of indifference, which revealed that Commonwealth countries had by then developed strong attachments outside Britain. The pattern of Commonwealth economic cooperation until 1970 was still British-centred overall, but this was being fast replaced by relations with other developed countries, and showed 'the incapacity of the Commonwealth as a sufficient universe for the aims and activities of its members'.[101] From 1950 to 1970, Britain's exports to the Commonwealth (and South Africa) fell from 48 per cent to 24 per cent, and its imports from 42 per cent to 26 per cent of its trade turnover.[102] Meanwhile Europe and the United States were growing increasingly important for British investments as well as trade. By the late 1960s, Britain's largest single trading partner was the United States, which had become the main market for many other Commonwealth countries as well.

New patterns of trade and finance had emerged and Britain's role as a central, managerial focus was weakened by its economic decline, plagued by inflation and a vulnerable currency. Limits had to be set on foreign investment and military spending. By 1967 Wilson had given up on any Commonwealth alternative to Europe and a second application to accede to the Treaty of Rome was made, only to be vetoed again by de Gaulle, on the grounds that expansion would change the EEC's character because Britain was still tied too closely to the United States – 'for the British Isles really to moor themselves alongside the Continent, a very vast and very deep transformation is still required'.[103] The lessening need of Britain for the Commonwealth was mutual; the ex-colonies diversified away from their former dependence on Britain as a market, supplier, investor and financier. Britain took the stand that its entry into Europe would benefit other Commonwealth members since they would take advantage from Britain's increased prosperity, that developing countries had plenty of time to get used to the idea of losing preferences in the United Kingdom, and that special trade agreements between the EEC and certain countries would be facilitated. *The Round Table* also reflected this blithely optimistic view of the future for the Commonwealth with Britain joining Europe: 'It is probable that once the effort of Britain's entry into Europe has been accomplished, there will be a welcome revival of concern for the future of the Commonwealth relationship, both in Britain and in the other countries ... This revival will probably be assisted by the interest in the countries of the Commonwealth that will certainly be shown by Britain's new partners in Europe.'[104] But in reality it was Hobson's choice all round. With the passage of time, the heat had been taken out of the problem and by the year of accession, all Commonwealth members acquiesced. *The Round Table* opined rather cynically,

> various Commonwealth institutions and activities promoted by Britain ... divert attention from the real British objectives of casting off the burden of Empire as fast as possible ... and getting into Europe; they are the rifles left to fire mechanically after the withdrawal has taken place.[105]

The United States favoured Britain's entry into Europe, and domestic antipathy, for diverse reasons, towards the Commonwealth created a climate propitious for entry. There were several areas which had been thought to require special consideration; sugar, New Zealand dairy products, Asian manufactures including textiles, developed country manufactures and their temperate foodstuffs, and jute, rubber, tea, cocoa, copra and palm oil. By 1973, Commonwealth special interests had narrowed to just the first two items, and Commonwealth preference was finally buried in 1977. By 1973 Britain had been economically overtaken by France and West Germany[106] and it was only after EEC entry that British trade was reoriented to Europe, when European tariffs, mainly on agriculture, introduced several far-reaching changes and *inter alia*, spelled the end of the Commonwealth sugar agreement. The 1975 British referendum on EEC membership produced a large majority for staying in. Britain's interests had become less global, less maritime, and exports from 1971 to 1980 to the EEC grew at a rate far faster than the figure for total exports.[107]

Britain's entry to the EEC

In the 1940s and even the 1950s, despite France being the major contributor of NATO ground troops in Europe, Britain had been the premier European member of the Western Alliance. With a dual character as a European state and an Atlantic power on terms of intimacy with the United States, the British Cabinet was even able at times to contemplate the vision of a third force of the Commonwealth and western Europe under British leadership. Throughout the 1950s it was the received wisdom among British political circles that membership of the EEC was incompatible with the Commonwealth, with British global commitments, and its special relationship with the United States. In most of the Empire, the transfer of power was an easy and painless process which public opinion in Britain accepted with 'remarkable nonchalance',[108] especially because the early phases of transfer of power had inducted local political leaders, almost all of whom showed some degree of enthusiasm for continued ties through Commonwealth membership, and the willingness of the smaller countries later on to join the Commonwealth was accompanied by their general orthodoxy and relative restraint in political and economic policies.

The Commonwealth retained British financial and economic links with the former colonies, gave comfort to the British people that the Empire was not breaking up but growing up, and preserved the appearance of British power. In the 1950s all these aspects were valuable but by the 1960s, they were regarded as far less important than hitherto. Even the most rudimentary community of interest with the former Empire had waned during the 1960s with significant pressures on Britain from the African Commonwealth. By the late 1960s, Britain had largely completed the transfers of power. The Rhodesian issue revealed the Commonwealth to the British people not as a supportive asset but rather as an obstacle for Britain in completing its task of decolonization. Nor could the existence of the Commonwealth conceal the fact that Britain was not qualified for the international top table, or that its global influence might be greater if exerted from inside Europe. There was still a requirement to impress and influence the United States, but this could be done more persuasively as part of Europe. In the future, Commonwealth ties would become looser still, and its remaining significance sought through the agency of the Secretariat in mainly non-political terms until 1991, because those areas were the least susceptible to attrition and acrimony.[109]

There was a distressing lack of Commonwealth support for Britain at the United Nations. Military take-overs in member states added to the disillusionment. There were coups in Ghana, Nigeria and Sierra Leone, mutinies in East Africa, repression of opposition in Uganda and one-party states in Zambia and Tanzania. It became accepted slowly in Britain that the Westminster model of parliamentary democracy would seldom prevail, and the one-party state would typify political life in many non-white members of the Commonwealth. Immigration from the new Commonwealth to Britain became a highly charged domestic issue. The multiracialism propagated by Britain in places like Kenya or Malaysia could not be achieved in the Central African Federation or imposed in Rhodesia. For its economic well-being, Britain could no longer set much store by the Commonwealth connection or on American finance and special ties. It turned to the EEC, entry into which meant that Commonwealth obligations, including military ones, had to be curtailed, and a debate began among both civilian and defence officials whether bases and an armed presence outside Europe were needed to sustain and enhance Britain's international position. But the loudest voices were of those who successfully criticized the expense of the overseas bases and wanted Britain to concentrate on the alignment of military forces within Europe.

As London's attempt through the European Free Trade Area to get the best out of both worlds came to nothing, and after an abortive effort to obtain the Commonwealth's consensus of approval, Britain applied to join the EEC in 1961, the moment of 'decisive choice between the global ambitions and imperial commitments of the past and a future as a member country of a united Europe'.[110] The 1961 application was vetoed by de Gaulle in 1963. British policy was checked but not wholly diverted by the French veto. For three years after 1964 the Labour government still clung to the illusion of Britain being an effective military power east of Suez and refused to devalue the currency; but in 1967 the pound had indeed to be devalued. Britain's steep decline in the 1960s set the stamp of failure on its dream-like vision of a post-imperial Commonwealth-centred future. In 1970 the new Conservative Government which came into office under Heath was committed to joining the EEC. In 1971 British forces departed from the bases in Malaysia, Singapore and the Gulf; and the Indian Ocean, the last sphere in which Britain retained world-power status, was given up with Diego Garcia being leased to the United States until 2016. Withdrawal from the east was met largely with domestic indifference; the public felt that the British presence there had mainly been for American convenience because of Vietnam, had yielded no special advantages and was of questionable value. 'There was also agreement,' wrote Stephen Ashton, 'that to a far greater extent than in other theatres, Britain's defence spending in the Far East and South-East Asia was out of all proportion to the extent of British economic interests in the area.'[111] Britain was now to be strategically purely a European power, global aspirations were cast aside, and even the 'shadow empire of influence'[112] was finally discarded. 'For about fourteen years from the first application to join the EEC in 1961 until the British referendum of June 1975, which confirmed our continuing membership,' wrote Lyon, 'there was a near-obsessive concentration on European Community matters.'[113] The Commonwealth had been permanently relegated to a back seat.

The marked decentralization of governance in the Empire reduced the tangible impact of decolonization to a minimum. There was no constitutional crisis in the United Kingdom, no political upheaval such as in France; there was no quick reduction to the rump of a previously potent economic zone.[114] When Britain handed over power to its colonies, it hoped to wield considerable and durable influence on the basis of a special relationship and close alignment in foreign policy. With the promotion and deliberate inflation of the Commonwealth's significance and prestige, stress was laid on the attractions of the Commonwealth to new members. Britain wanted to make accession as easy and attractive as possible. Once ensconced in the club, the new member's links with the former ruling power would be enhanced, communism kept at bay, it would be oriented towards the British/American orbit, and persuaded to maintain an open economy attractive to British business. It was hoped that such ties would be almost as close as those that prevailed with the old Dominions. But in effect the newly independent States did not extend much priority to the Commonwealth, links with Britain were balanced along with the opening of ties to others, and the model constitutions handed down by the British did not usually stand the tests of time and the local circumstances. The Woolsack in the House of Lords may be stuffed with symbolic Commonwealth and not exclusively British, wool, but Westminster-style democracy was very rarely emulated. In many cases the economies of the new members were brought under some degree of state control. Britain was subject to abuse and criticism, and by the early 1970s, the time-honoured historical bonds implied no special obligations or expectations of loyalty or support. Britain had little to offer compared to other major powers like the United States, the Soviet Union or even France and China. These and other industrial and developed countries offered better opportunities and markets than Britain, and the Commonwealth countries, including the old Dominions, sought out new partners like the United States, Japan and the international financial institutions. The former colonies reduced their London balances and cast off the external controls on the administration of their currency. Britain had limited diplomatic leverage outside Europe, was accused of creating post-colonial problems, and its alliance with the United States drew upon itself implied or explicit criticism over such American policies as in Vietnam. Therefore independence in many cases, despite Commonwealth membership, was followed by more disengagement and British-inherited institutions suffered assault. Relations between Britain and the former colonies frequently became a mutual embarrassment.[115] The political landscape of the 1950s and 1960s had enabled the newly independent countries to acquire greater bargaining power with the major nations: for instance, India after 1962 turned increasingly to the Soviet Union as its leading ally against China. When Britain first applied to join the EEC, the Commonwealth was one reason for Britain's initial reluctance and an obstacle to the success of its application; by 1970 all such considerations had practically disappeared.

The Conservative government's White Paper in 1971 titled 'The United Kingdom and the European Communities' stated that the Commonwealth did not 'offer us, or indeed wish to offer us, alternative and comparable opportunities'.[116] Heath admitted in the House of Commons that any idea that the Commonwealth would become 'an effective economic and political, let alone military, bloc, had never been realized',[117] while any impression that the Commonwealth could be an effective trading bloc, according to one observer, 'should by now have been relegated to the limbo of impracticable policies and bad history'.[118] In the Commonwealth, wrote *The Round Table*, the prevailing mood 'as it contemplates the involvement of its senior member in the economic and to some extent necessarily in the political future of Europe, partakes much more of resignation than of enthusiasm'.[119] Indeed, there was no sign or semblance of any collective Commonwealth protest and such continuing debate as persisted was within Britain, and not inside the Commonwealth. Between 1973, when Britain joined the EEC, and 1975, Britain's imperial career had ended, and by the end of that decade it was obvious that Britain did not intend to lead the Commonwealth or endow it with any particular importance in its foreign policy.

Immigration and citizenship

The Empire had always meant settlement. No other country in the world came close to exporting an aggregate of so many of its inhabitants.

Twenty million people left Britain from 1815 to 1914; at least three million had emigrated during Victoria's reign; from 1900 to 1963, six million; from 1946 to 1953, seventy thousand a year on average, 80 per cent of whom went by sea with cheap or assisted passages.[120] South Africa leaving the Commonwealth had not curtailed the flow of migrants to that country; in fact, quite the contrary. A paper posted on Migration Watch UK's internet website explains the situation.

> Britain is a nation of emigrants, not of immigrants. Since the middle ages our people have spread to all the corners of the globe: the country's dominant migration experience has been to send people abroad, rather than to receive them from overseas. The balance did not change until the early 1980s. ... After the second world war migration resumed on a large scale encouraged by government and Commonwealth schemes of various kinds, which did not end until the 1960s. While emigration to the USA never exceeded about 13,000 per year after the mid-1960s, the net loss by emigration to the Old Commonwealth (Australia, Canada, and New Zealand) was 104,000 people as late as 1974. ... Even the very large immigration from the New Commonwealth which got under way in the 1950s and which still continues, was smaller than the net outflow of British citizens until the early 1980s. In the last two decades Britain has become a country of net immigration, thus reversing the historical trend of previous centuries.[121]

Migration had been a unifying factor for the white communities, but movements of non-white peoples across the Empire on the other hand had created racial, citizenship and nationhood tensions – among others, Malay/Chinese, African/Asian, Asian/Polynesian and Tamil/Sinhala. In the demographic sense, the British Empire was not British at all: just over 10 per cent were European, and the most commonly practised religions were Hinduism and Islam. Throughout the Commonwealth there exist many diasporas: one aspect of these family linkages is the estimate of a Commonwealth observer that 'about two-thirds of primary school children in Britain today have at least second cousins in at least one other Commonwealth country.'[122]

In 1946 Canada defined its citizenship. This led to some other countries defining their own citizenships, including the British Nationality Act of 1948 that created the UK and Colonies citizenship, and introduced the concept of separate Commonwealth citizenships together with the myth of an over-arching status as a Commonwealth citizen, and in Britain only, with the rights of a British subject. The Act also said that any person who did not acquire the citizenship of another Commonwealth country would automatically be a UK and Colonies citizen. At that time, it was never anticipated that any need could arise to restrict the entry to Britain of Commonwealth citizens. Curiously, the Ireland Act of 1949 separately gave the Irish special non-foreign status and the same rights as British citizens, well nigh conferring Commonwealth benefits without Commonwealth membership.

Though not without recurrent Cabinet misgivings, Britain was the only Commonwealth country that for some 17 years after the Second World War gave unhindered right of entry and special civil and political rights to all Commonwealth and colonial citizens. It was part of the imperial credo that there should be an open immigration policy: the British Commonwealth was a family whose members were free to travel within it. The image of the 'mother country' depended on this, and it had, previous to the Canadian Nationality Act, been an accepted tradition that there would be a common nationality and that all persons born in the Dominions were British. The 1948 Act had reinforced this principle, and was intended, according to Attorney General Hartley Shawcross, 'to maintain the common status of British nationality and with it the metropolitan tradition that this country is the homeland of the Commonwealth.'[123] But across the Commonwealth this was non-reciprocal; only in Britain was there, till 1962, an open door.

Post-war migration to Britain was a response to the demand for labour in certain sectors of the economy. The new workers were required in the factories in the Midlands, textile mills in the north, the transport sector in major cities, and throughout the health service, generally to occupy the lower-paid jobs avoided by the white working class. From the 1940s onwards, immigration was the aspect of decolonization which had the most long-term bruising effect on political and public opinion at home, and which thoroughly discredited the Commonwealth connection in the minds of the British people.[124] Post-war immigration began in 1948 with the 492 persons from Jamaica on the 'Windrush', and as early as the 1950s, alarm bells started to ring. The US immigration policy in 1952 had the unintended effect of diverting West Indian job-seekers to Britain and the number of these immigrants jumped from 2000 in 1953 to 20,000 in 1955.[125] The government began referring to the inward flow of coloured British subjects as 'Commonwealth immigrants' and the Secretary of State for Commonwealth Relations, Lord Swinton, expressed alarm in 1955 about 'working-class Indians coming here. This is a new development and unless it is checked, it could become a menace.' The Cabinet, while loath to introduce explicit racial immigration controls, wanted to protect 'the racial character of the English people'.[126]

In 1951, there were half a million Irish and 375,000 people from the Commonwealth and Empire in the United Kingdom.[127] From 1946 to 1962 one million entered the United Kingdom, two-thirds of them from Ireland and 100,000 from Australia and New Zealand, but also a growing number from the non-white Commonwealth, to the extent, in the late 1950s, of 36,000 a year.[128] There were race riots in Nottingham and Notting Hill in 1958. The total number of immigrants from the 'new Commonwealth' was 58,000 in 1960, and 136,000 the next year.[129] In 1960, 50,000 of them came from the West Indies; in 1961, 70,000. By this time there were about half a million or one per cent of the British population from the new non-white Commonwealth, and half of them were from the West Indies.[130] But during the 1960s, there was a marked immigration trend away from the Caribbean and towards South Asia, because by the end of that decade West Indians were once again taking up fresh employment opportunities in the United States and Canada.

Emigration from Britain had been officially encouraged, but immigration was deeply disturbing. The Empire had moved people around the globe but now the point of convergence had become the United Kingdom. Social tensions related to housing and education arising out of immigration contributed to the growing disillusionment with the Commonwealth among the British masses, most of whom were not prepared to regard coloured people as acceptable fellow citizens. By the 1960s the word 'migration' to the common man in Britain had come to mean coloured immigration from the Commonwealth and not emigration to the colonies. The Commonwealth connection was thus brought into full and controversial discussion in Britain, though the other Commonwealth governments did not have much to say about it officially.

In 1962 the first Commonwealth Immigration Act was passed to regulate immigration from the Commonwealth and the colonies. It applied to all immigrants, including the old Dominions, in order to avoid the accusation of being racialist, though that was indeed the accusation leveled at Britain. The Act disclosed how much less of a unity the Commonwealth had become in British eyes. The government claimed it was only checking the flow of immigrants rather than setting up barriers, but the privileges attached to common Commonwealth citizenship were largely discontinued. Only those born or naturalized in Britain or with passports issued by the United Kingdom or its diplomatic missions abroad (a measure intended to assist white settlers but which was soon to have unexpected consequences) were allowed entry, which was otherwise limited to students, visitors, dependents and work-voucher holders. Non-UK passport holders seeking to migrate had to possess a work-voucher, which was intended to reduce the number of immigrants to about 40,000 a year, comprising people able to demonstrate their employment plans, skills and qualifications. In 1965 the matter was brought up at a Prime Ministers Meeting by Jamaica and Trinidad, but they too acknowledged that immigration policy was not a 'Commonwealth' matter but one for each individual country to determine.

The 1948 Act defining the citizenship of United Kingdom and Colonies and the power delegated to British high commissions to issue such passports led to problems in East Africa. 'This is only another instance of a policy', wrote senior British civil servant Charles Dixon, 'embarked on as an act of good faith, which has profoundly disappointed our hopes.'[131] The Kenyan Asian question became a bilateral dispute between Britain on the one hand and India and Pakistan on the other, when control by consent was attempted with the countries of origin, but failed. As a result, in 1967, 7000 Asians with UK passports arrived from Kenya. Few of these Asians had opted for local citizenship and used their UK and Colonies passports as an insurance policy when the Kenyan authorities abolished permanent residence certificates, introduced entry permits and embarked on a process of 'Kenyanisation' in the distributive trade. Consequently, in 1968 and 1971, new restrictions had to be devised.

In 1964 Labour had come into power intending to retain and reinforce the immigration controls that they had denounced while in opposition. In 1965 over 40,000 immigrants entered Britain, and Labour's White Paper of that year titled 'Immigration from the Commonwealth' reduced the number of available work-vouchers. In 1968, after the Asians with British passports arrived from East Africa, restrictions were applied by the second Commonwealth Immigrants Act to those with British passports issued overseas by UK diplomatic missions. According to the new Act, only those with citizenship obtained in the United Kingdom or who had one parent or grandparent born or naturalized in the United Kingdom were admitted as 'belongers' or as subsequently re-named, 'patrials'. A patrial was defined as a citizen of the United Kingdom and Colonies by birth, adoption or naturalization, or with a parent or grandparent born, adopted, naturalized or registered in the United Kingdom. Commonwealth citizens with a grandparent born in the United Kingdom enjoyed right of entry and were exempt from work permits. Meanwhile, in April 1968 at Birmingham, a Conservative Member of Parliament and former Minister Enoch Powell fanned the flames of anti-immigrant sentiment with a notorious speech that predicted that immigration would cause a 'total transformation to which there is no parallel in a thousand years of English history'.[132] Though Powell was denounced by both main political parties, they nevertheless embraced his argument to some extent.

The problem of racialism that had never been satisfactorily resolved overseas had now come to haunt Britain at home. By 1970 there were one and a half million immigrants or 2.7 per cent of the British population[133] from the new Commonwealth, and the small permanently resident coloured minority became an unexpected legacy of Empire. The Conservative manifesto in 1970 stated that no large-scale immigration would be allowed and in 1971 the Government passed another Immigration Act with discriminatory immigration provisions. By this Act and the rules of 1973, a patrial with a parent or grandparent born in the United Kingdom enjoyed the right of entry and abode. The 'grandfather clause' was to enable Australians, Canadians and New Zealanders to enter without restrictions, and these ancient connections, as Home Secretary Reginald Maudling assured the House of Commons, would ensure that the vast majority of those entering the United Kingdom would be white. This caused *The Round Table* to write in 1971 that the history of immigration policy had been 'to control after prolonged hesitation while professing not to be really doing so; to intensify control but to represent the process differently to different parties concerned; and finally to throw away all restraint both in language and policy'.[134] Successive British governments were conscious that legislation to control immigration would imperil relations with the sending countries, undermine their attempts to build multiracial communities in East and Central Africa and elsewhere, and fragment the unity of the Commonwealth. But from 1962 onwards the diminishing prospects for the Empire and Commonwealth had clearly also been taken into account by the policy makers and the lawmakers at Westminster.

In 1972, about 28,000 Asians expelled from Amin's Uganda arrived in Britain for settlement. These new Asian arrivals from East Africa, who gravitated towards London and Leicester, were not work-seeking migrants but refugees with substantial skills and some resources, who set up a wide range of businesses. By 1981, 4 per cent of the British population were new-Commonwealth immigrants;[135] and in 1998, they rose to 5.4 per cent. In 1986, visa requirements were introduced for visitors from the Indian sub-continent and West Africa. There also came into being the 'primary purpose' rule, namely, that a husband and wife could be admitted provided it could be proven that the marriage was not entered into primarily for admission to the United Kingdom. This was amended in 1997 to allow some rights of appeal, but proof is still needed to show that the couple would live together and not be a burden on public funds. By the late 1990s Britain had become multiracial, and there were about 3 million people with racial and ethnic origins in India (0.9 million), Pakistan (0.6 million), the Caribbean (0.8 million), Africa (0.4 million) or Bangladesh (0.2 million).

A Briton did not have to travel across the world to meet the new Commonwealth; it was 'usually no further away than just around the corner'.[136] The domestic impact of the erstwhile Empire, with immigrants from the West Indies, South Asia and Africa, the mosques, temples, eating habits, ethnic shops and restaurants, dialects, and the non-white presence in art, pop music, literature, sports and the media, became a part of every day life. Islam rather than the Church of England claimed the largest number of regular worshippers. Racism was transferred to the domestic scene. In 1978 Mrs Thatcher spoke of Britain being 'swamped' by immigrants. The next year she led the Conservatives back into power and in 1981 there was passed into law a new Nationality Act which replaced the term 'patrial', which had fallen foul of the European Human Rights Commission, by 'close connection' with Britain; and defined five groups, the patrials with close connections, those from dependent territories, overseas British citizens, British Protected persons and British subjects. Of these categories, only the patrials had the right of abode and freedom from immigration controls. The retreat from the liberalism of the early post-war years was complete, though there were a few like Paddy Ashdown, then leader of the Liberal Democrats, who stated, 'if we will not take their goods, we will take their people'.[137]

Jan Morris, referring to the Queen's Golden Jubilee internet website's reference to the Commonwealth as 'significant to the development and modern life of the nation', commented acidly that 'everyone knows what that means: that the influx of immigrants from Asia, Africa and the Caribbean has altered the very fabric of Britain, and posed so far insoluable problems of bigotry and instinct'.[138] In 2001, the race riots in the north of England revealed how little attitudes had really changed. The media described the rioters as Asians though many of them had been born and brought up in Britain. There is a serious problem with race, and intolerance is growing even though foreign residents from non-white countries are still a relatively small fraction of the British population.

The immigration debate has always been conducted on the assumption that immigration is a problem and not an opportunity or a necessity. No detailed economic or social studies have been carried out into the need for, or effect of, immigration. Now there is a new problem; that of asylum seekers mainly from conflict-prone areas such as, in the top ten of 2000, Iraq, Sri Lanka, former Yugoslavia, Afghanistan, Iran, Somalia, the former Soviet Union, Turkey, China and Pakistan – only two of them being Commonwealth countries. This aspect has also resulted in a highly charged public debate, though Britain is not the leading European recipient of refugees. The Home Office argues that most of these asylum seekers are not victims of persecution but economic migrants looking for a better life.

The factor of demography adds another ingredient. Western Europe will have a shortage of young workers due to declining and aging populations, and an assessment will need to be made urgently of the benefits of immigration. Ironically, despite all the rhetoric, does Britain, and Europe in general, have the luxury of ending immigration? The working population in the European Union will shrink by 5 per cent in the next 25 years and millions of workers will be needed to keep its economy growing. With the largest single expansion the EU has ever experienced, 73 million people from ten countries have joined it in 2004, with an average income only one-eighth of that in Britain, and with the presumed right to live and work in the United Kingdom, which has the strongest labour market in the G7. Jack Straw said it would be in Britain's economic interest, and Prime Minister Tony Blair agreed that the benefits brought to the United Kingdom by immigration had never been greater, since immigrants were estimated to contribute £2.5 billion a year more in taxes than what they consume in public spending, and contribute skills in shortage in the existing population, especially in the public services. The Home Office claims that only between 5000 to 13,000 would be added to the annual inflow, although Migration Watch UK forecasts the figure as 40,000 a year.[139] The British government is aware of the potential effects on its social welfare system; it has denied access to housing and welfare benefits for at least two years to job-seekers from the new accession countries unless they are legally employed in Britain, set up an obligatory work-permit system for them in order to monitor illegal workers and tax evaders, and reduced quotas for low-skilled seasonal workers in the agricultural sector.

In human terms the old Commonwealth of the white Dominions 'is virtually invisible in Britain, its members merging into the background almost without trace ... its scions who come to Britain to work and study tend to be regarded as part not so much of the post-war Commonwealth as of the white English-speaking world'.[140] What Britain's policy towards the EU's expansion shows is that, despite all the caveats, white Christian European immigrants are obviously more easily assimilated, and the biggest immigrant community in Britain by far continues to be that of the Irish with about two million residents.

The Round Table in an editorial by Peter Lyon in 1986 declared,

> The biggest change in Britain's identity for four hundred years has occurred in the past twenty years. It is the change from an imperial into a post-imperial state. Overall, it has been much more multifaceted and radical than is usually appreciated, involving not only obvious changes of sovereignty and jurisdiction over many overseas territories but the cultural, economic and educational life of the British people themselves. ... Much more than is generally appreciated it has also brought about profound changes in British society, not least in attitudes to foreigners and immigrants, so that in some matters ... the British have become unprecedentedly cosmopolitan, in others (such as in attitudes to immigrants) they are stubbornly insular, even zenophobic.[141]

The question of race and colour has become a domestic problem from the 1960s onwards and accounted for why Rhodesia mattered then, and Zimbabwe does now.

3
Some Other 'Commonwealths'

The OIF, the CPLP, the OEI and the Dutch

Organisation Internationale de la Francophonie [OIF] (The Organization of La Francophonie)

After the Second World War the cost of Empire was as insupportable for France as for Britain. France's great power pretensions were called in question and subjected to ridicule, and for reasons of national prestige, the reassertion of its imperial authority abroad became as important as economic reconstruction at home. The existence of its colonies was one of the few cards France could play in making any claim for great power status, and in 1945 France had become a permanent member of the UN Security Council largely because of its sphere of overseas influence, much more so than due to its military or economic capabilities. Accordingly the French authorities were prepared to confront the nationalist movements in Indo-China and later in Algeria.

Somewhat like the diversity of Britain's dominions, colonies, dependencies, trust territories, protectorates and mandates, France by its 1946 constitution had created a Union in which their colonies were (1) Departments like Algeria, (2) Associated States such as Indo-China, (3) Protected States like Morocco and Tunisia, (4) Overseas Territories such as the African colonies and Madagascar, (5) Associated Territories like Togo and Cameroon and (6) League of Nations mandates. Departments were parts of France; Associated and Protected States were to move to independence and Overseas and Associated Territories remained under French administration pending clarification of their status at some time in the future. The Union was intended to integrate colonies into the French state by granting them equality of status gradually. This principle could not be realized through democratic participation in the constitutional organs of France because any representation by population would have meant a colonial domination of the motherland. France wanted to continue its tutelage, and so independence was not on offer, but the Union allowed African representatives to participate in French politics through electoral colleges. Such measures were intended to strengthen French influence and sideline the nationalists. The Union was not based on any principle of equality between the French Republic and its overseas territories, and even the framers of the Union seemed unclear as to whether the eventual goal would be for total assimilation and integration, or for the territories only to achieve greater autonomy. Certainly, to be a citizen of the Union was not the same as being a French citizen, and the territorial Assemblies were given few powers and remained under the control of the French governors. At the very fag-end of the Fourth Republic, reforms were enacted in 1956 and 1957 that would give the equivalent of Dominion status, but by then it was too late; the French Community proposed by de Gaulle in 1958 was rejected by Guinea, the grand vision crumbled, and France was already otherwise engaged in building a new multinational community in Europe.

In Indo-China, France had fought to defend its imperial status, but the region became, like Korea after 1950, a Cold War struggle fronted by the Americans which continued for 20 years after 1954. In 1949 the advent of the People's Republic of China changed the Indo-Chinese war's character. In 1950 the Soviet Union recognized the Vietminh while the United States acknowledged the puppet Bao Dai. In the same year North Korea invaded the South. The United States did not come to France's aid when French troops were besieged and defeated at Dien Bien Phu in 1954. Liberation movements in North Africa took heart from Vietnam, but the lesson was lost on the political circles in Paris who decided to fight the next colonial war, in Algeria, with even greater vigour and determination.

The loss of French dependencies began early. Syria and Lebanon were independent members of the United Nations in 1945. In 1951–54, France lost their Indian provinces. Cambodia and Laos were independent in 1953–54, and in 1956 Morocco and Tunisia became independent. Guinea opposed de Gaulle's Community in 1958, upon which all the French expatriates and military left the colony immediately, signalling France's disapproval. In accordance with the provisions of the new constitution, most French African colonies became independent from 1960 onwards although France retained military bases and concluded bilateral commercial and cultural agreements. Whereas for Britain, the biggest hurdle in terms of emotional impact, namely India, had been handled at the very start, French decolonization went on from the late 1940s to 1962, with the most emotional case coming at the very end of the process. The Algerian crisis brought about the end of the Fourth Republic and the start of the Fifth, and the French were able to chart a new course after 1960, which was to be towards Europe.

France, like Britain and Portugal, abstained on the UN General Assembly resolution 1514 (XV) 1960 on decolonization, though by then decolonization was well on the way to becoming the official policy of both Britain and France, though not yet of Portugal. Each European colonial Empire developed its own style of a continuing association with its former colonies. France was willing to use considerable economic assistance, and sometimes even military involvement, to retain influence, depending on the former colony's acquiescence with French policy.

Algeria

Algeria was the largest French possession, and integrated with France as a Department. During the Second World War, Algeria had been home to the resistance and had one million settlers in 1950. After its Vietnam experience, the French army smarted with humiliation and was determined to suppress the nationalist uprising by draconian means. The widespread use of torture resulted in international opprobrium and domestic unease in France. The army and the settlers wanted to induct de Gaulle into office to keep Algeria French, but de Gaulle in his turn used the army to gain power and then showed the generals that they could not challenge him. At first there was an attempt to retain Algeria as a domicile for the settlers and expatriates withdrawn from Indo-China, but after the revolt by the army was put down, de Gaulle decided on Algerian independence, and the 1961 referendum gave him the power to deal with Algeria on that basis. In 1962, after independence, about a million settlers departed from Algeria, and the Organisation Armée Secrète (OAS) launched a campaign of terror and assassinations. De Gaulle had finally cut loose from Algeria, bolstered by the prestige of nuclear capability developed since the 1960 test, but in France the end of Empire culminating in the loss of Algeria was keenly felt. In searching for a new world image, it was firmly believed both by the leadership and the public that France had a special global mission as the champion of freedom and spiritual values, and assistance to the Third World and defence of the French language became the new platform for French self-esteem.

Language

When UN formalities were being discussed at San Francisco, only English, Spanish and Russian were originally proposed as the working languages for the new international organization, and French was only accepted after energetic debate and a majority vote of one.[1] French is spoken by over one hundred million people as a first language, and the use of French is a strong unifying factor in the world. In Belgium and Canada it is the symbol of resistance to other groups. But compared to only a hundred million French speakers, there are 350 million English, 220 million Portuguese, 200 million Spanish, and 120 million Arabic. Almost 53 per cent of all Europeans now learn English as a second language, and in 1990, French was placed only twelfth among languages spoken in the world,[2] but apart from English it is the most widely dispersed across the continents, and has made something of a revival in that it is still the most commonly taught language after English. Yet in no country, other than in France, is it possible for French speakers to avoid contact with other main languages, and Senegal's President Léopold Senghor himself estimated that there were only 8 to 10 per cent French speakers in francophone black Africa.[3] But France itself comprises over 50 per cent of all French speakers, apart from being economically the strongest country in the Francophonie. Thus the rest of the protagonists of a French-speaking community of nations and peoples had inevitably to wait on the French government's readiness to accept the leadership of the Francophone grouping. For some critics though, Francophonie is 'nothing more than the last battle being waged by the French using African troops to protect their own language'.[4]

Early days

On the laborious road to the Organisation Internationale de la Francophonie (OIF), francophone civil society contacts had long preceded government involvement. At first there were various non-governmental activities like meetings of journalists, sociologists and universities, and after the 1958 constitution with its Community, when African countries were able to take the option of independence, the way was clear for closer cooperation in la Francophonie. Momentum built up after 1958 and various multi-tier concepts were considered, such as those countries with the closest links to France meeting each other more regularly. But the French government strongly preferred the route of bilateralism with its former dependencies to secure its various objectives of creating the Franc Zone, ensuring its raw material supplies, and concluding defence agreements and technical cooperation accords. Rather than encourage la Francophonie, France preferred instead to concentrate its attention on Europe.

At the official level, gatherings of ministers of education, youth and sports from French Africa and France took place from 1960 onwards, and francophone politicians started meeting at the initiative of Léopold Senghor in 1967. The Organization of the African and Malagasy Community (OCAM) took up the cause of a francophone organization with France at its centre, but the French government still remained inscrutable and discreetly silent. The impetus for la Francophonie was indeed never to come from the motherland France, but from Senghor of Senegal in 1965, seconded by Presidents Hamani Diori of Niger, Felix Houphouët Boigny of the Ivory Coast and Habib Bourguiba of Tunisia. Both Bourguiba and Senghor were at pains to deny that la Francophonie would be a vehicle for neo-colonialism and saw no contradiction between la Francophonie and the projection of black identity. Senghor's original proposal was shaped by the Commonwealth but his idea was based on cultural harmony, combining negritude with French civilization and culture and francophone solidarity. His concept was of an association that would lead to a great community of peoples sharing the same ideals and interests while having their own particular interests and civilizations preserved. No leader in British Africa had come forward with any similar philosophical vision.

The Agence de Coopération Culturelle et Technique (ACCT) was established at Niamey in 1970 during the second conference of French-speaking countries to promote education, cultural, scientific and technical cooperation through the use of French. Jean-Marc Leger from Quebec was the first secretary-general. It had a General Conference of Ministers every two years, a Bureau, and a staff of about one hundred. The ACCT was later to develop into the Agence Intergouvernmentale de la Francophonie (AIF), the main organ of the OIF.

Senghor in the mid-1970s continued to press for a Francophone summit to discuss the setting up of a new international organization, but this proposal lay in limbo due to Canada's dispute with Quebec on the latter's participation in the ACCT without Ottawa's clearance. This played into the hands of the French authorities since they were in favour of ambiguity and delay. France was reluctant because it already had excellent bilateral ties with its former colonies and by virtue of the EEC, a multilateral framework as well, within which to relate to them. De Gaulle feared a Commonwealth-type organization might weaken rather than strengthen France's international position. He was even sceptical about the term 'Francophonie', and apparently used it only once, in 1968, on the death of the Quebec Prime Minister Daniel Johnson.[5]

It took a long time for the French leadership to assess that the benefits to France might outweigh the costs. French colonialism was unusual in the prominence it gave to culture and language, and even today, France places more emphasis on language teaching in its aid programmes than do the other donors. Paris is much concerned with the status of the French language and is willing to spend large resources to maintain French educational activities. President François Mitterand's personal interest in cultural matters, together with the burdensome cost of supporting several African economies all by itself, eventually induced some rethinking in Paris. French language and culture were feared to be in retreat, and it was thought that multilateralism with a broader agenda and diversity might benefit France, and that promoting French internationally could not only support cultural contacts but a broader range of political and economic objectives as well.

Links to Africa: France and la Francophonie

Africa is essential to France's assumed role as a world power. Many African countries, apart from the dominance of their French-speaking elite classes, have laws, institutions, higher education and government systems that are firmly francophone in origin and character. France's relations with its former colonies were essentially bilateral and not organizational. When de Gaulle returned to power, there were hopes that French Africa would settle for internal self-government, or if independent, would remain somehow collectively associated with France. But the 1958 Community provided by the constitution was short-lived, and when Algeria became independent in 1962, the formal end of the French Empire was in sight. Only some overseas departments were left, scattered, small and isolated or of strategic importance, and integrated with France. The Community transformed itself into the Franc Zone and bilateral agreements between France and its former African colonies were the order of the day. The Francophone currency harmonization backed by France in Africa was the result of the dirigiste French policy and large sums were set aside for development aid. French protégés were created, and by the early 1960s, French political and economic ties with Africa were so strong that the need for any formal colonial-style control had become irrelevant.

Apart from the two notable exceptions of Vietnam and Algeria, French decolonization was relatively peaceful. The French maintained a strong presence in their former colonies and when the Community came to nothing, they created a network of formal multifaceted linkages. After 1973 they also conducted Franco-African summits. France set itself up as the leader of the European–African dialogue and preferences given by France to its colonies were reworked in the EEC system to include all EEC members. Members of the French Community by the Treaty of Rome gained access to the EEC and its development funds, and the Franc Zone guarantees the convertibility of currencies of several African countries, giving them a financial stability they would not otherwise enjoy.

France's readiness to send teachers and troops led to the perception in the African colonies of France as a reliable friend. Even the former Belgian colonies turned to France, since Belgium was unwilling and unable to provide comparable aid. About four dozen military interventions by France in former colonies from 1960 onwards, the latest being in Côte d'Ivoire and the Central African Republic, showed the French government's willingness to involve itself directly and to play the arbiter and peacemaker in its erstwhile dependencies, where its current role reflects much of the domination and dependence of earlier times.

The British, by comparison with the French, did not craft such durable ties within each country before independence, but envisaged the Commonwealth as the main conduit for providing desirable links and retaining influence after independence. Britain had a much more arms-length relationship with its ex-colonies than France. The Commonwealth is an innocuous club compared to la Francophonie, which is designed and utilized to give France considerable leverage. By the 1980s, when La Francophonie came into being, the British people were no longer nostalgic about the Commonwealth/Empire, not even on the part of its greatest former enthusiasts. But the French government does not by any means rely only on la Francophonie to provide linkages; it regards its former colonies as a valuable resource which, if properly used, could garner France political credit and economic power. Thus the Francophone summits are intended to underpin French cultural and diplomatic interests, and France is the prime mover, not just another member. La Francophonie summits ensure that the French viewpoint in international affairs is projected and its effect on the members evaluated. Though the French President is not the titular head of la Francophonie, it is precisely this French preponderance that makes participation attractive to the many countries that do not have a significant French-speaking population. La Francophonie is one of the few international organizations where cultural goals are held as paramount. No Arab country is in the Commonwealth though several are in

La Francophonie, because a linguistic and cultural union makes for easier affiliation, and France is seen as an effective promoter of Arab interests in Europe. While France goes along with the organization's appeals for democracy and human rights, it may not in practice attempt to implement any such agenda; its own purpose being more to do with the protection and promotion of French culture.

La Francophonie is by no means convulsed by racial questions. The organization is not disposed to criticize France; even France's relations with racist South Africa were never opened up for debate. No country has yet left la Francophonie, or been suspended or expelled. Links between France and political figures in the former colonies are very strong and many politicians in Africa have homes in France. Many first-generation colonial leaders had been members of the government in the Fourth Republic – in contrast to the case of Malta, which wanted to be part of Britain and enjoy the privilege of elected members in the House of Commons, but was rebuffed by Whitehall. France is strongly supported by large numbers of the members of its former Empire whereas Britain gives the impression that it would rather forget about its colonial inheritance, which it regards as a historic burden and an occasional embarrassment.

For France, there was always a strong post-war priority to maintain a separate identity in a significant world role; otherwise it felt it would suffer decline and its cultural distinctiveness would be eroded. La Francophonie places France at the centre of an organized geo-political organization, though ambiguity remains about its objectives. 'Francophonie is a changing concept ... not yet clearly understood nor yet itself clear on its purposes'.[6] Until the 1993 Mauritius summit, the definition of la Francophonie was that members had the use of French in common, but this was then changed to 'sharing french', a wider definition and admitting of some diversity, nicknamed by some purists the 'francopolyphonie'.[7] Up to 1993, the summits spent most of their time discussing the role of the French language and identity, and in the early summits, the Canadian and French representatives debated the purpose of la Francophonie itself. French was the starting point and still is a preoccupation, but currently there is greater emphasis on multilateral co-operation in various fields. But underlying most activities is the question of French pride, grandeur, Paris's great power concerns, and the special mission inherent to the French. The recent trends away from concentration on the French language, civilization and culture reflect the priorities of developing countries, the competing influence of the Canadians, and France consciously projecting itself as the third world's champion, as it did when it hosted the G8 summit at Evian in 2003.

Francophone civil society

Non-Governmental Organizations – women, parliamentarians, journalists, mayors, physicians, teachers, third world groups, Sahel groups and so on – continue and flourish in La Francophonie though they do not constitute any widespread popular movement as such. As in the Commonwealth, there is a lack of *inter se* cooperation, common purpose and clarity among these NGOs. In 1974 and again in 1998, committees were set up to coordinate and extend official recognition to such groupings – the same definitional problems that exist in the Commonwealth also exist in la Francophonie.

Press

La Francophonie enjoys multiparty support in France, but the French media give little or no attention to the association, and regard the summits as talk-shop occasions for dialogue but not action; the main discussions are seen as being on marginal matters such as on internal organization and the distant potential for better economic relations. This indifference by the media reflects the general disappointment among the French public at the lack of democratic norms in la Francophonie. The *Canard Enchaîné* sarcastically dubbed the enthusiasts of la Francophonie, as the 'francofaunes'.[8]

Economic

Commercial cooperation between France and the other members is not a strong factor in la Francophonie, and is not even as advanced as it is in the Commonwealth in defining any economic role for itself. France is the main economic partner of many African members and the Franc Zone is controlled and backed by the French, even after the introduction of the European common currency. Francophone trade is not that important to France – it imports 11 per cent and exports 15 per cent of its total trade turn-over with other members of the OIF,[9] and the two neighbouring countries of Belgium and Luxembourg are by far and away its main Francophone trade partners. Private business in France takes little notice of la Francophonie as an economic facilitator, a lack of attention that is shared by the member-states themselves.

Anti-Americanism

The French Union was regarded by the United States as hypocritical and too close to the resumption of colonialism, and the French smarted from bitterness at the perceived lack of American support in Indo-China. Therefore when it came to deliberations with the former African colonies on La Francophonie, there was not unsurprisingly an underlying anti-American tinge to the subject as well. European powers like France were intimidated into thinking that US economic power made the dominance of the American cultural model inevitable and France's acute concerns about the fragility of its cultural heritage became a strong impulse towards the ACCT being set up in 1970 in the modest beginnings which eventually led to the more structured organization of the OIF in 1997.

Evolution of the OIF and the Canadian-French rivalry

A full-fledged French replica Commonwealth was originally suggested by Senghor who had spoken in 1962 of 'A Commonwealth à la Française', but disputes between Canada and France over Quebec postponed a Francophone summit until 1986 in Paris which worked on this proposal. At the second summit in 1987 in Quebec there was still rivalry between Canada and France, Paris being concerned at Canada's growing role, which it looked upon as an American Trojan Horse[10] among the French-speaking nations. The third summit was at Dakar in 1989, and Jean-Louis Roy of Quebec – again a Canadian – was appointed secretary-general of ACCT, though France would have preferred some other candidate. At the fourth summit in Paris in 1991, France and Canada tried to link overseas aid to democratization efforts, and voted for sanctions against the military coup in Haiti. But friction continued between Canada and France, and France accused the ACCT of promoting Canadian interests rather than Francophone ones. At the fifth summit in Mauritius in 1993, Roy's term was extended by four years. The sixth summit 1995 at Cotonou dealt with economic matters including the use of the French language on the internet. At the important seventh summit in 1997 in Hanoi, the leaders decided to establish a Secretariat and an official organization of the Francophonie, to be called the OIF, with Boutros Boutros-Ghali of Egypt elected as its first secretary-general. The eighth summit was at Monckton in 1999, and the ninth at Beirut in 2002 when former President Abdou Diouf of Senegal was appointed secretary-general, the first black African to hold the post despite the original proposers of the organization having been leaders from black Africa way back in the 1960s. At the tenth summit at Ouagadougou in 2004 a 10-year strategic plan was formulated, French-inspired UN-backed peace proposals for the Ivory Coast were strongly endorsed and sanctions threatened against the Ivory Coast government unless it came to terms with the rebel-held north of the country. The Conference pledged to take initiatives to help crisis-torn Haiti, and supported a

Canadian move for greater use of humanitarian intervention with the proviso that it be undertaken under the auspices of the United Nations. A few years earlier, in 2000 at Bamako, the OIF, under the influence of Boutros-Ghali, responded to current world trends with a Declaration on democracy, human rights and freedoms which rejected the taking of political power by force, thereby echoing the Commonwealth's Harare and Millbrook pronouncements of 1991 and 1995 on similar issues.

In 2004 the OIF comprised 53 full members and 10 observers. Despite initial French government reluctance, but thanks to the composition of its membership, La Francophonie has slowly become a substantive forum with a broad agenda, with the result that summits now discuss political matters. Culture and language, originally the substance of the association, are now the support mechanisms. France's cultural priority is acknowledged, but Canada always competes for influence. Part of the price France has had to pay for its acceptance of la Francophonie has been discussion of Canadian concerns like fishing rights on the Atlantic coast. Rivalry continues between Canada and France, if not for outright leadership, then at least for agenda setting. These two countries enjoy a preponderant position in the organization; they had contributed as much as 85 per cent of the ACCT budget and little of the money available for consultancy goes to any country other than France and Canada. The Canadian government, inspired by the Commonwealth Fund for Technical Cooperation (CFTC), proposed a development programme for ACCT in 1975. Ottawa wanted to use la Francophonie as a means to extend its influence in Africa and in north–south matters, and to consolidate its position in the G7, and so it campaigned for expanding the organization's mandate beyond language and culture. First it promoted development issues, then political ones, having nothing to lose and something to gain in that it felt that La Francophonie made a contribution to Canada's national unity. The French leadership, on the other hand, distrusted Canada's sponsorship of development, thinking EEC's structures were more appropriate. Paris is equally suspicious of the Canadian government's desire to create links between the Commonwealth and la Francophonie and bi-lingualism. On the political side, the French authorities greatly prefer the forum of the Franco-African summits, where they are the dominant influence and their leadership is beyond challenge or competition.

Comunidade dos Países de Língua Portuguesa [CPLP] (The Community of Portuguese-speaking countries)

The Portuguese African colonies were integrated into Portuguese territory in 1951 as overseas provinces, and in 1972 they became overseas regions.

These colonies were never groomed for independence despite the military burden they represented. In 1954 the Portuguese lost their Indian outposts of Dadra Nagar-Haveli and in 1961 they surrendered Goa, Daman and Diu. Only after the 1974 coup in Lisbon did the process of decolonization start and then it was a total scuttle. Frente de Libertação de Moçambique (FRELIMO) was the only party in Mozambique negotiated with, though it never repudiated its dependence on the Soviet Union. In Angola, civil war broke out between the three freedom movements before independence. Movimento Popular de Libertação de Angola (MPLA), supported by the Soviet Union and Cuba, won out after Lisbon unilaterally suspended the Alvar Agreement of 1975 with União Nacional para a Independência Total de Angola (UNITA), MPLA and Frente Nacional de Libertação de Angola (FLNA) and decided to hand over power to MPLA alone. In Macao the Portuguese government came to an understanding with the Chinese, and in East Timor, the Indonesians annexed the territory in 1975 at a time when Portugal was advocating immediate independence despite the existence of three contending groups; Timor Democratic Union (UDT) which was pro-west, Timorese Popular Democratic Association (APODOTI) pro-Indonesian, and Revolutionary Front of Independent East Timor (FRETILIN) pro-left. In no case were the decolonized people consulted, and cultural, religious and racial links received no protection to safeguard their continuity.

The CPLP was conditioned by, but was not a product of, decolonization, since it came on the scene long after the decolonization process had been completed, and 174 years after Brazil had achieved its independence. There was some influence from the Commonwealth's example, although, as noted by one sceptical Portuguese observer, the Commonwealth had also been the inspiration for 'other, less fortuned [sic] adventures, such as the Union and Francophone Community and the Dutch–Indonesian Union'.[11]

There was an extremely slow and tortuous process of birth. The creation of such an association had first been suggested in the mid-1970s after accession to independence of the Portuguese African colonies, but was delayed due to the civil wars in Angola and Mozambique, and the indifference of Brazil, whose population represents 80 per cent of all Portuguese-speaking persons. Then the idea was revived in 1984 when the Portuguese foreign minister broached it in Cape Verde. In 1989 the Portuguese-speaking foreign ministers decided to form a Portuguese language institute in Cape Verde, and this pointed to the way ahead. After 1993 diplomatic representatives started to meet at the United Nations and in 1994 they began to draft a constitution in Brazil. Eventually the decision to proceed was made in Brussels in 1994, but further delay was caused by the President of Brazil not being able to attend a proposed inaugural summit in Lisbon in 1994, and a chain reaction followed, with Angola, Guinea Bissau, Mozambique and São Tomé Príncipe also pulling out. Then there was civil war in Angola, and disputes on funding delayed further progress until mid-1995.

The CPLP was finally set up in Lisbon in 1996 to promote concerted political and diplomatic action between seven members, Angola, Brazil, Cape Verde, Guinea Bissau, Mozambique, Portugal and São Tomé Príncipe, with the aim of strengthing cooperation in cultural, social, economic, scientific and legal areas and to help members to expand their influence in international organizations. East Timor was one of the Portuguese Community's early preoccupations and it joined as the eighth member in 2002. Since it is an association of states, Goa and Macao are not eligible. Decisions are taken by consensus with a summit every two years; foreign ministers are to meet each year, and a Secretariat was established with an executive secretary and a deputy appointed by alphabetical rotation. M.J.C Moco from Angola was the first executive secretary, and Luis de Matos Monteiro da Fonseca of Cape Verde is now in charge. The various organs of the Community to be set up are to be sited in different countries to avoid excessive concentration on Lisbon.

CPLP has the promotion of the Portuguese language as an objective, and members must have Portuguese as an official language according to the founding statutes. One of the pillars of the association is accordingly the dissemination of Portuguese, the 'shared house of lusophonie', as Nobel Prize novelist José Saramago has put it.

The CPLP has a development cooperation fund financed by voluntary contributions. It has engaged in democratic institution building, with help to East Timor's justice and public administration, election observer missions, and contact groups to help in stabilizing the situation in the wake of the civil war in Guinea Bissau in 1998, and after the coup in São Tomé Príncipe in 2003. The organization's official internet website briefing comes to a pithy and pertinent conclusion: 'It would be useless and counterproductive to prepare megalomaniac constructions in theory which, due to lack of resources, could never be put into practice.'

Organización de Estados Iberoamericanos [OEI] para la Educación, la Ciencia y la Cultura (Organization of Iberian-American States for Education, Science and Culture)

At the end of the Second World War, Spain, like Portugal, was not at first inclined to liberate its few remaining colonies, and the OEI as an intergovernmental organization guided by summits of heads of state/government took a considerable time to evolve. The organization began in 1949 as the Office of Latin American Education and in 1954 became an inter-governmental organization of sovereign states. In 1985 it adhered to the same name as before but expanded its objectives and approved new Statutes of Association, which include the objectives of promoting Spanish and Portuguese. The first summit was held in 1991 at Guadalajara and the body now has 21 members, including Spain and Portugal, and two observers, Puerto Rico and Equatorial Guinea. The preponderance of the two European countries in the association is fully accepted and is evidenced by the fact that the thirteenth summit in Bolivia in 2003 was attended both by the Spanish king and the prime minister, and by the Portuguese president and the prime minister, but only by the presidents of each of the other members. At the fourteenth summit in 2004 in Costa Rica all four European leaders were again expected, and while the King of Spain and the Spanish prime minister were both present, the Portuguese president was ill and the prime minister was unable to attend. Although the OEI's original project may have been to concentrate on non-political cooperation, including the dissemination of Spanish and Portuguese, the character of the association naturally changed once the heads of government started to meet annually. In the 2004 summit, while an important appeal was made to international financial organizations to allow developing countries to pay part of their debt burdens by expanding government spending on education at home, political issues like terrorism, opposition to the US Helms-Burton Act that punishes foreign companies doing business in Cuba, UN peace-keeping operations in Haiti, the Falklands, and economic relations between the European Union and Latin America especially in the context of opposition to EU agricultural subsidies that damage Latin American economies, came up for discussion and are noted in the final documents of the meeting.

Spain and Portugal prompted the elevation of this association to intergovernmental cooperation at summit level once they were established in the EEC, and with an eye to the French example, have used the organization to enhance their weight in the European Union. For their part, the developing members of the body have used the presence of the two European members to promote and protect their interests in the European Union.

The Netherlands Empire

The Netherlands Fundamental law, revised in 1922, pronounced that the Kingdom of the Netherlands comprised the territory of the

Netherlands, the Netherlands Indies, Surinam and Curaçao. In 1941, referring to her country and Indonesia, Queen Wilhelmina said in a radio broadcast, 'I feel convinced that after the war it will be possible to reconstruct the Kingdom on the solid foundation of a complete partnership ... I imagine that they will tend towards a Commonwealth in which the Netherlands, the East Indies, Surinam, Curaçao will parti- cipate and in which ... they will show the fullest willingness to render mutual assistance to each other'.[12] The Dutch public, like their Queen, thought that the masses in the third world were ignorant and indiffer- ent to politics, and that after the Second World War, the Dutch East Indies would be part of a revitalized and Dutch-dominated Kingdom.

Japan invaded Indonesia in 1942. Queen Wilhelmina in exile in London, with an eye towards Washington, launched her plan for a post-war Commonwealth of the Netherlands, the Dutch East Indies, Surinam and Netherlands Antilles. Roosevelt had prodded 'Minnie' for self-government to the Dutch East Indies, but she was not particularly responsive. She could envisage, she said, Java as being independent in 15 to 50 years, but for more backward regions, she was not even willing to speculate on a time-frame.[13] But she gave assurances of future reform as a pledge against promises by the United Kingdom and United States that the Dutch East Indies would be restored, and after the Japanese capitulation, the Potsdam conference in 1945 gave jurisdiction of Indonesia back to the Netherlands via the South East Asia Command. Like her people, the Queen believed in a divine and self-righteous mis- sion for the Dutch to bring the East Indies up to western standards by virtue of Dutch tutelage, and decolonization was not a matter for debate. The Netherlands could not, unaided, recover its far-flung terri- tories, and its prestige had collapsed with Japan's rapid advance into Indonesia. The old order had expired but no new order had been firmly established. The Dutch attempt to reestablish their rule was rejected by the Indonesians; and British, and even Japanese, troops tried in 1945 to protect the Dutch civilians from their colonial subjects seeking retribu- tion. Indonesian nationalists took advantage of the vacuum by pro- claiming a Republic unilaterally in August 1945.

After the war, there were those in the Netherlands who wanted a confederation of independent states or a Dutch Commonwealth of Nations in which Indonesia would have a kind of dominion status. But there were a large number of settlers (circa 300,000) and ethnic minor- ities like Arabs and Chinese, and it was argued by the Dutch political establishment that any local government comprising an Indonesian majority would only ruin the country. The growing strength of nationalism was systematically denied, and colonial policy was based on preserving Dutch control. A state of anarchy in Java and rampant terrorism led to the Dutch saying a 'Republic of Indonesia' would not be a matter for discussion – though they had reluctantly to concede that the spirit of nationalism was indeed stirring. But they still refused to negotiate as equals with the Indonesian leaders on independence or autonomy, and in 1946 they were not prepared to recognize the Republic. The Dutch leadership regarded the Republic as a Japanese fabrication and as a negation of democracy in Java and Sumatra, only owing its existence to terrorism practised by an extremist minority. Nationalist leaders like Sukarno, who had collaborated with the Japanese, were not to be forgiven by the Dutch on any account – in contrast to the British authorities' dealings with Aung San.

By the end of 1946 the last British soldier had left Java and Sumatra, and the British government, impressed by the strength of the independence movement after the battle of Surabaya, pressed for negotiations between the Dutch and the Republic. The Dutch government set up a three-man group under former Prime Minister Wim Schermerhorn to negotiate under UK mediation. Taking a cue from the French Union, the Dutch tried to interest the Indonesians in the concept of a federation of Indonesian states, and an agreement at Linggadjati in 1947 on an armistice and the formation of a federal state was reached. The Republic was to be recognized and both parties would work for a United States of Indonesia, though some nationalities outside Java, Sumatra and Madura could claim special status. The target date was 1 January 1949 and the objective was a Dutch–Indonesian Union under the Dutch Crown. But neither side was sincere. The Dutch Parliament passed the agreement with 'interpretations' that were rejected by the Republic. The Dutch proposals had been accepted only as a basis for negotiation by President Sukarno and Prime Minister Sutan Sharir, who were not willing to repudiate the dominant role of the Republic and wanted recognition of its authority over the whole of Indonesia, while the Dutch agenda was to persuade the Republic to accept some form of colonial sovereignty in the shape of the Union to enable Dutch forces to exterminate the anti-colonial elements. Dutch public opinion was exercised by tales of woe from compatriot-refugees from Republic-controlled areas. The military and former internees under the Japanese took extremely hard-line positions, and the Dutch military in Indonesia was reinforced. By November 1946 there were 47,000 troops in Indonesia.

A conference called by Lieutenant Governor-General Hubertus van Mook in Celebes rejected the Republican claim for a unitary constitution that would ensure Javan ascendancy, and the prevailing official line was for sovereignty linked with the Netherlands within a United States of Indonesia, and till then, the *status quo*. The self-perception of the Dutch was strongly imbued by feelings of ethnic and cultural superiority. They were desirous of settling the issue by force of arms and to reoccupy the whole of Indonesia under the guise of maintaining law and order, especially since the Republic could apparently neither control the local extremists nor the army. The Dutch wanted to counterbalance the existence of the Republic, which controlled Java and Sumatra, by using the federal concept and thwarting the Republic's domination over the rest of Indonesia. Separate governments were formed in islands other than Java and Sumatra, and with the approval of the Parliament in The Hague, the Dutch took 'police action' in July 1947 to implement federalism.

The United Nations Security Council in 1947 set up a Committee of Good Offices in Indonesia (UNGOC). UN good offices produced the Renville agreement in 1948, but it was bitterly unpopular in the Republic, with the national leaders accused of compromising too much. A second 'police action' took place in late 1948 with the Dutch trying again to enforce federation and seeking to eliminate the Republic as a political factor. These police actions resulted in some military success and the capture of Republican land, but in December 1948 the UN Security Council called for a ceasefire, Dutch withdrawal and the release of Republican leaders, and refused a hearing to Indonesian representatives other than those from the Republic. In January 1949 the Security Council went further and called for the transfer of sovereignty to the United States of Indonesia by 1950. The Netherlands for its part maintained that UN involvement was *ultra vires* in a matter of domestic jurisdiction, and claimed that the United Nations and its local presence, the UNGOC, condoned the Republic's excesses.

Meanwhile the United States came to believe that Dutch persistence in trying to defeat the Republic would lead to a weakening of Holland in Europe, apart from providing an opportunity for the advance of Indonesian communism. The American government accordingly vetoed any Dutch attempt to re-impose colonial rule and threatened to cancel Marshall Plan aid. Whereas in Indo-China the British had agreed to the reassertion of colonial control, Whitehall this time also decided not to help the Dutch to oppose the growing tide of Indonesian nationalism. The conviction that the Dutch had a specially ordained mission to fulfill in Indonesia was a firm belief with the leadership and public in Holland and this led to domestic frustration and humiliation, diehard opposition to Indonesian nationalism, and a gross underestimation of the

United States, Britain and the United Nations. The Dutch government had never taken the Atlantic Charter seriously, and felt that the British had shamefully 'abandoned' India in 1947.

The Dutch Cabinet then designated a diplomat, Herman van Royen, to negotiate. The presence of 100,000 conscripts in Indonesia was taking its financial toll, but the Republic's leaders were also under strain, despite having the United Nations' sympathy. Separate Dutch-sponsored governments in Java and Sumatra still existed, and fanatical Islamic extremism grew with Dar ul Islam and Masjumi. A conference was proposed, with the Dutch agreeing to return Jakarta to the Republic in return for a ceasefire and the presence of the federal governments at The Hague: the Dutch aim still was a United States of Indonesia with the Republic as only one of many components. The van Royen–Rum (representing Sukarno and Hatta) agreement paved the way to The Hague Round Table Conference and an agreement in November 1949. At The Hague, it was not possible for the Dutch to play off the confederalists and the traditional rulers against the Republic since they had come to some prior agreement, and sovereignty was transferred to the federal United States of Indonesia – the Republic and fifteen much smaller units – in December 1949. The UN Commission on Indonesia (UNCI), comprising an American, Australian and a Belgian, was at The Hague process and eased the way. The Indonesian nationalists claimed they would need help from the Netherlands in all things, including military. There was to be a Union with various mixed commissions with advisory power, and Queen Juliana as the head of it. No provision was made for the smaller regions that wanted to retain a special tie with the Dutch.

Most Indonesians were bitterly unhappy with the terms of their independence, for they considered that federation was only another form of divide and rule. Another misguided military adventure was to be decisive. In 1950, Bandung was occupied for a brief period by Raymond Westerling, a renegade Dutch captain, with deserters from the Indonesian army and federal units, who planned to depose the government in Jakarta. The defeat of this revolt led to a new constitution and the proclamation of a Unitary Republic of Indonesia in August 1950.

Between 1946 and 1949, the two so-called police actions or military campaigns resulted in 100,000 Indonesian and 6000 Dutch deaths – though half the Dutch casualties may not have been combat-related. Holland was politically isolated as well as near economic bankruptcy but the patronizing imperial mind-set had not changed. Indonesian independence was only reluctantly conceded in December 1949 and there was no Dutch development aid to Indonesia between 1951 and 1967. This period of Dutch colonial history is still highly sensitive; the Dutch repatriates and war veterans continued to have some enduring political influence; and it constitutes 'a collective blind spot in the Dutch psyche'.[14] As for the Indonesians, the majority of them are barely aware of their historical links with Holland because the Dutch left so little of their cultural heritage behind. In 1995, when Queen Beatrix visited Indonesia on an official visit, her trip was preceded by a bitter domestic debate on whether or not she should apologize for 350 years of Dutch rule and exploitation. Indonesian memories also continue to be long; in 2003 Yusri Ihza Mahendra, the Indonesian justice minister, referring to the atrocities committed by Westerling in the South Celebes, declared, 'I am not against the Netherlands. I am against injustice. Because they are unjust, I hate them.'[15]

West New Guinea

The Dutch government took the position that West New Guinea was a completely separate entity from Indonesia, and the Round Table conference had left the matter unresolved; it said West New Guinea should maintain the *status quo* for one year pending negotiations between the Netherlands and Indonesia. Dutch business interests were in favour of conceding Indonesian claims to West New Guinea in order to safeguard their assets in the rest of the Republic but the authorities in The Hague wanted to stand firm, and Australia, which in the United Nations and UNCI had always sided with the Republic, was strongly opposed to the handing over of West New Guinea to Indonesia. The stalemate between Indonesia and the Dutch on this question and continuing Dutch control of West New Guinea led to the collapse of the Dutch–Indonesian Union in 1954, expropriation of Dutch economic interests other than Shell, a third wave of Dutch repatriates in 1957 following the earlier migrations after the war, and the break of diplomatic relations in 1960. The Netherlands–Indonesian Union, a so-called working partnership, therefore ended in failure. In 1962 the Dutch transferred West New Guinea to the United Nations, and the UN Secretary-General called on the United States to mediate. Ellsworth Bunker, the mediator, proposed a plan to transfer sovereignty to a UN organ to prepare the population for self-determination. Indonesia was to receive the transfer of administration from the United Nations in 1963 and the United Nations was to supervise a free choice by 1969. In 1969 West New Guinea became part of Indonesia by virtue of a controversial vote of the Papuan people.

Dutch West Indies

In early 1948 the first Round Table Conference took place at The Hague, with Surinam and the Antilles present. This envisaged a 'tripartite kingdom', and in the following year Surinam was granted self-government in domestic affairs. In 1954 the Kingdom Charter gave Surinam and the islands equal partnership and autonomy in all matters except in 'kingdom affairs' such as foreign affairs and defence. Surinam achieved full independence in 1975, a decision expedited and strongly encouraged by the Labour government of Prime Minister Joop den Uyl and approved by a majority of one in the Paramaribo Assembly. The establishment of six independent Antillan states (Aruba, Curaçao, Bonaire, St Maarten, St Eustace and Saba) is not considered practical, nor even the formation of a single state due to inter-island rivalry, though Aruba became separately autonomous in 1986. The Dutch view the Antilles as a somewhat awkward colonial legacy, and their remaining West Indies possessions have an uneasy hybrid constitutional position between the British solution – full independence – and the French – full integration.

Some observations

The Commonwealth traditionally is held by its enthusiasts to be unique. This persistent claim was reiterated by Secretary-General Don McKinnon, at the Abuja summit in 2003, when he declared that 'the Commonwealth is a unique organization which has a unique role to play in today's world'.[16] The Commonwealth, wrote L.C. Green less extravagantly, 'is more a historic than a formal organization ... Its links are emotional, historical and psychological and despite the existence of the Secretariat, it lacks any of the characteristics of an international organization. ... It is the result of a historic evolution that defies imitation.'[17] It is self-evident that historical analogies are never perfect, but the Commonwealth did variously inspire the architects of the French Union, the Dutch–Indonesian Union, the OIF and the CPLP, and undoubtedly shares several characteristics with the associations mentioned in this chapter. So its claims to uniqueness have necessarily to be treated with considerable caution.

Each European colonial Empire had been largely self-contained, though among their common features were a protected market for investment and trade, a common language, legal and administrative systems, educational methods and migration both to and from the dependencies. It is true that Britain did not have to escape from authoritarianism like Portugal or be traumatized by the return of expatriates in large numbers to complicate domestic politics, like France and the Netherlands.

The general lack of bitterness attending the British transfers of power was in stark contrast with many colonial endings in Africa and Asia of other European Empires. There was comparatively little armed conflict or displacement of expatriate settlers – the Malaysian emergency and the Mau Mau were exceptions to the rule. But the Commonwealth may nevertheless be compared to other post-colonial European organizations, such as the OIF, the CPLP and the OEI, and some similarities can inevitably be discerned.

Transfer of sovereignty did not terminate European ambitions for a role in the former colonies. Like Britain, France sought a means of advantageous association with its colonies after the Second World War, although the adverse climate in the international arena, metropolitan weakness and nationalism in the colonies all militated against the re-imposition of colonial rule and of unreformed colonialism in particular. The colonies and the widespread sphere of influence they represented for the metropolitan country were for both nations one of the few trump cards they could play for international leverage, economically and militarily exhausted as they were after the war. The colonies were one of their main credentials to advance their claims to permanent seats on the Security Council.

In the eventual post-colonial organizations that were established, some major ex-colonies did not participate. In the Commonwealth, Ireland and Burma have stayed away, while in the OIF, Algeria and Syria are not present. There was more than a whiff of anti-Americanism in the first stirrings of both the modern Commonwealth and the OIF. Britain continued with a Sterling Area for some decades after the War, and France has introduced and sustained a Franc Zone with 15 countries in Africa. The Commonwealth was the inspiration for Senghor's initiative to suggest a Francophone organization, though his vision of its objectives was very different from the British concept. In both organizations, the creation of the Secretariats under a secretary-general took some time to evolve; in the Commonwealth in 1965, in the OIF in 1997. The main architects of both bodies at first considered several formulae to give the more weighty members a predominant role – an inner core and a periphery – before abandoning such ideas in favour of notional equality. Both hold a summit every two years. Both organizations have a multitude of non-governmental activity, which appears uncoordinated and haphazard and frequently somewhat removed from the realities of the strengths and weaknesses and even the directions, of the inter-governmental associations. Since 1993 civil society organizations accredited to the Commonwealth have arranged events in the margins of the association's summit meetings. In 2004, three hundred francophone civil society representatives assembled at Ouagadougou some weeks before the tenth OIF summit and agreed to convene before every future summit. Both organizations enjoy domestic multiparty lip-service, but the bodies are not rated highly by the press or public in either metropolitan country, who are disillusioned by the lack of democracy in many parts of the former Empire; nor by the private or public business circles, which see little of genuine value to themselves from the economic activities of the bodies. Both organizations mark an annual day in March as a festival for celebration.

There are as many dissimilarities, of course. The Union and the Community both perished but the Commonwealth has survived. While Britain initially relied on the Commonwealth to provide links with former colonies, the OIF was only incidental to France; most of the erstwhile colonies are more closely bound to France by various treaty obligations. There are strong bonds between the politicians of France and those in their ex-colonies; many had served together in the French institutions of the Union. The precursors of the OIF, namely the ACCT and AIF, began at around the time when Britain had shed all its remaining nostalgia for the Empire and Commonwealth. In contrast with the British, the French were poor colonizers, but effective post-colonial managers. Britain tackled the hardest emotional issue – India – first, in a parting of ways with little rancour,[18] whereas Algeria was handled last and with great animosity, by France. There is no doubt at all that the British conceived the Commonwealth, whereas the initiative for the OIF came not from France, but from the leaders of francophone black Africa. The French enterprise began slowly, with cultural, linguistic and technical linkages, then moved very cautiously to a political agenda; the Commonwealth began with political consultations, and only later came to structured development cooperation after 1971. And it has never dealt as such with civilizational issues such as culture or the promotion of the English language.

Britain faced no catastrophic colonial wars as in Indo-China or Algeria – though it had its own problems in India before partition in 1947, Palestine before 1948, Malaya (1948–60), Kenya (1952–56), the Canal Zone and Suez (1952–56), Cyprus (1955–59), Aden (1960–63), North Borneo (1962–66), Ireland and the Falklands (1982). Nor did it confront any domestic political and constitutional upheaval like France in 1958.

France showed more interest in the ACCT/AIF/OIF after its construction of a united new Europe along with West Germany; the Commonwealth was a delaying and negative factor in Britain's entry to the EEC. France, after Vietnam, is the largest country in population in the OIF; Britain lies only in fifth place in the Commonwealth – but both have the largest number of persons speaking the official language and by far the largest economies in the respective organizations. Whereas the OIF sees Canada continuously barking at France's heels for access to influence, Britain has no such rival in the Commonwealth. The OIF is not disposed to criticize French policy whereas members of the Commonwealth seek to use the organization to influence and at times to condemn British policy. France did not get embroiled like Britain in any heated discussion of colonial problems since the OIF was founded well after major colonial issues like the Vietnam and Algerian conflicts had been resolved. By contrast the Commonwealth Secretariat might not have come into being, or so soon, had it not been for the British–African clash over Rhodesia. Unlike the Commonwealth, no country has left the OIF, been suspended or expelled.

In contrast to the Commonwealth, the CPLP was a long time in the conception – a full 23 years after Portugal's escape from the authoritarian rule that enabled the colonies to achieve their independence. Unlike India under Nehru, the biggest country by far in the CPLP, Brazil, was at first cool to the concept of any association. The Portuguese set up the post-colonial organization after its EEC membership, not least with a view to enhancing their prestige in Europe. While its officials claim Commonwealth inspiration, and it holds summits every two years, the organization places great emphasis on the promotion of the common Portuguese language.

The OEI had an even more languorous start, having begun as an educational body in 1949. It evolved slowly into an intergovernmental body and then an organization under the leadership of heads of state and government in 1991. It now meets at the summit annually, with a predominant position held by Spain and Portugal, who use the organization to raise their profile in Europe while defending the interests of the Latin American members in the European Union. Apart from discussing a wide-ranging agenda, including political issues, the body has as a firm objective the promotion of the Spanish and Portuguese languages. Like the Commonwealth and the OIF, the OEI took many years and several summit meetings to establish a proper Secretariat. An office began in Madrid in 1949 to deal with Education, Science and Culture. A new machinery for Ibero–Latin American cooperation was started in the 1990s, and the latest version, a 'General Secretariat' with a wide mandate, had its statutes formally approved at Costa Rica in 2004.

There could never have been an Anglophone community, nor any Commonwealth agenda to promote English. The nearly worldwide adoption of English today is not inspired by any Commonwealth member but by the United States. The largest and most influential wholly English-speaking country is neither the United Kingdom nor India, but the United States, which was never in the Commonwealth. There could therefore never be an Anglophone movement which would not be totally dominated by the United States.

4
Nobody's Commonwealth?

The position of the Crown

Paradoxically, Ireland was the oldest of all the colonies of settlement but the last of them to be granted 'responsible self-government'.[1] The Irish nationalists had never wanted Dominion status and looked upon the Crown as a symbol of alien rule. From 1936 to 1949, in the Irish view, Ireland owed no allegiance to the Crown and was not a member of the Commonwealth, though it was 'in association' with the Commonwealth as symbolized by the King's signature on Letters of Appointment for Irish representatives abroad. In 1948 Ireland decided to repeal the External Relations Act that constituted the last remaining link with the British Crown, albeit confining its role to empty diplomatic formalities. With the repeal of this legislation came Ireland's decision to leave the Commonwealth, whereupon the British government confirmed, in a curiously unique anomaly, that it would not place Ireland in the category of a foreign state or treat its citizens as foreigners.

In 1947 London declined to allow Burma to become a republic and seek membership of the Commonwealth, and in 1948–49 no attempt was made to persuade Eire to remain in the Commonwealth. But after such a determined attachment to the concept of common allegiance to the Crown for a quarter of a century, especially in regard to Ireland, the British government nonetheless relaxed the requirements remarkably quickly when confronted with India's intention to become a republic. When Nehru was found willing to accept the idea of a non-constitutional head of the Commonwealth, the traditional theory and practice of allegiance were quietly set aside. The Foreign Office was opposed to repeating for India the Irish experience of first a Dominion, and then a republic 'in association' with the British Commonwealth; and Attlee wanted to arrive at a formula that enabled the greatest number of future independent territories to accede to the Commonwealth.[2] In the end, it was just the search for a form of words, and not a debate on the functions of the Crown in the Commonwealth, which was at issue. Such function as the headship embodies is only to represent a symbol, and there is no doubt that there is no function at all that can be attributed to the title of Head of the Commonwealth. The 1949 London Declaration's formula provided the King with no authority and no allegiance as Head of the Commonwealth, and it released the King from even token responsibility for any future Indian policy which it was feared might prove to be sharply different from the other Commonwealth members. Enoch Powell, taking a purist approach, found this status for the Crown 'constitutionally inexplicable and indefensible' and declared that 'this formula "Head of the Commonwealth" and the declaration in which it is inscribed are essentially a sham. They are essentially something which we have invented to blind ourselves to the reality of the position'.[3]

An Act of 1953 altered the Royal Style and Titles to describe the King's successor, Queen Elizabeth II, as Head of the Commonwealth. The coronation of Elizabeth II in 1953 was a strikingly imperial occasion, attended by all the Commonwealth Prime Ministers. The ceremony provoked euphoria in the British media regarding the Commonwealth. Newspapers reported that prominent in the pageant were colonial rulers in four open carriages and a procession of Prime Ministers, with contingents of naval, military, air and police units from all the self-governing Dominions and the colonies, dependencies, protectorates and territories which made up the British Empire. 'Fealty' and 'loyalty' were words liberally used in the press to describe the celebrations held in the white Dominions and far-flung realms, and 'enthusiasm' was also reported from India, Pakistan and Ceylon. *The Times* on that day wrote, 'Yet of all the links that bind the members together none is more open, more precious or more real than the link with the Crown.'[4] That was a period which was still anglo-centric and monarchical, but was soon to pass into history.

The British monarchy and the Empire had been united to the great benefit of the former's prestige and popularity. The emphasis placed on the new modern Commonwealth, and the tributes paid to it, were in part an attempt to compensate the world's only international monarch for the inevitability of the loss of the old Empire. Efforts were made to project the Commonwealth as a half-imaginary federation, whose purpose was as vague as its allegiance, but which would retain some lingering mystique of the old order. The editor of *The Times* wrote in 1984, 'in thirty two years as Head of the Commonwealth, the Queen's stature had increased enormously. ... Crown and Commonwealth are in my view indivisible ... It is no wonder then that the Palace properly cherishes, and indeed cultivates, the Commonwealth connection, since it gives a vast extra dimension to the status of the British Crown compared to the other European monarchies'.[5] This piece was part of an excellent and continuing exercise in public relations: without the Commonwealth connection, the utility and cost of the monarchy to the British taxpayer would be more energetically questioned.[6] Britain is unlike the other European Empires, which also have a small remnant of overseas dependencies, because the Queen is both the Head of the Commonwealth and the Head of State of over a dozen independent countries that have become, in a fashion, the core states of the Commonwealth. The Crown has become more important in the perpetuation of the old sentimental links, which also means that Britain's outlook on the world is disposed to be less European than that of the other countries in Europe.[7]

The Crown as Head of State has a downside; it still carries the controversial connotations of the Empire. Even in the then royalist Australia, the 1975 constitutional crisis over the dismissal of Prime Minister Gough Whitlam by the Governor-General exposed a widespread fear that the monarchical connection somehow deprived that country of full independence. And in declaring his country ready to move to republican status after over 40 years as a realm, the Prime Minister of Jamaica, P.J. Paterson, said in September 2003 that 'the majority of people in Jamaica are ready to consign to history the last vestiges of colonialism'.[8]

But the Crown in its capacity as Head of the Commonwealth apparently carries for the Commonwealth membership no such connotations, despite the aspect of an outdated paternalism when the majority of the members of the association are sovereign republics. Commonwealth experts have long agreed that the British prime minister tenders advice to the Crown as Head of State of the United Kingdom, and the Crown is constitutionally obliged to accept that advice. But the prime minister cannot advise the Crown on how to act as Head of the Commonwealth. However, it appears that the Queen abided by Heath's advice not to attend the Singapore summit in 1971 though she seems to have overruled any misgivings that are reported to have been conveyed to her by the British government before she attended her first Commonwealth summit in any republican country, at Lusaka in 1979, and later at Abuja in 2003, at both of which the spectre of Rhodesia/Zimbabwe loomed over the conference.

It has been questioned if the headship of the Commonwealth is a hereditary function, an issue understandably skirted by Secretaries-General Emeka Anyaoku and McKinnon, but given some credence by a Commonwealth Report on Membership Criteria approved in 1997 though without any discussion of this sensitive subject. Nehru in the Indian Parliament had made it clear that the 1949 London Declaration referred only to King George VI specifically and not to the Crown – in distinct contrast to the Statute of Westminster doctrine which had prescribed that Commonwealth members were 'united by a common allegiance to the Crown'.[9] Nevertheless, it was Nehru himself, who was certainly no monarchist, who on the death of George VI had sent a telegram to Queen Elizabeth, then on safari in Kenya, felicitating her on her accession to the Throne and describing her as Head of the Commonwealth, thereby finessing the issue of the King's successor's connection with the Commonwealth even before the Commonwealth prime ministers formally assembled a year later to consider the implications of the King's death. Now, there is no one with the authority of Nehru to foreclose a debate on this issue when the time for it arrives. The headship of the Commonwealth was a stratagem to replace the concept of allegiance to meet the challenge of Indian republicanism. Such difficulties have long since ceased to exist, and the association could therefore quite easily dispense with the idea and fall in line with other international bodies which make do without any 'Head', symbolic or ceremonial or otherwise.

The headship of the Commonwealth is fortified by symbols, and an ingenuous effort on the part of some Commonwealth commentators to broaden the role of the Crown. A Commonwealth Mace, a ceremonial symbol of authority, was presented to the Queen on the fortieth anniversary of her accession to the throne by the Royal Anniversary Trust, a British-based charity, and 'in consultation with Buckingham Palace, a protocol has been developed governing the use of the Commonwealth Mace ... The Mace is used in the presence of the Sovereign or an immediate member of the Royal Family representing the Head of the Commonwealth'.[10] And both Anyaoku and McKinnon since 1997 have sought, without comment or contradiction, to give greater salience to the Crown's position by inviting the Queen to participate in the opening session of the summits, though the function of the headship of the association unquestionably still remains without any substance.

Garner held the opinion that without an acknowledged head, the Commonwealth would be less visible and comprehensible.[11] When a premises in London for the Commonwealth was being considered by the British government, Norman Brook wrote to Macmillan, 'it would certainly strike the public imagination if the Queen as Head of the Commonwealth, were to make it [Marlborough House] available as a Commonwealth centre'.[12] The Queen agreed to the proposal in 1958. But hardly anyone knows or cares about it nowadays. Nevertheless, it is true to say that the Commonwealth is taken by the British public to be integrally linked to the duties of the Queen. Little or no effort has been made to dispel this view, for it suits the Queen, the British government and the public alike, and is assiduously propagated by a few partisans in Commonwealth circles. The Director-General of the Royal Commonwealth Society in *The Times* of 22 July 2003 referred to the 'unifying role which the Queen has undertaken over the last 50 years. That role has at times been decisive in holding together a diverse association in times of crisis ... There is no groundswell in the Commonwealth to diminish the role of its head: indeed, the opposite is the case'.

Predictably, the Queen's golden jubilee of her year of accession produced some characteristic contributions to Commonwealth hyperbole, an example of which is cited below. It was an opportunity, said a correspondent in *The Round Table*,

> for the nation and the Commonwealth to thank her for fifty years of service ... The Jubilee Year has served to bring home to people in this country, as in other member countries, that the Commonwealth is an increasingly relevant and positive factor in national domestic concerns, as society becomes more diverse, ethnically and culturally ... our partners will assuredly take note of the profound effect the Year has had both on the British perception of the Commonwealth, and on the perception, not only elsewhere in the Commonwealth, but also internationally, of what the Commonwealth means to Britain ... The most striking feature of the Commonwealth is The Queen's unwavering commitment to it ... It has suffused the character and development of the Commonwealth. As a result of it, the Commonwealth is centrifugal rather than centripetal: it is for us all to absorb and reflect.[13]

Domestic and public opinion

For three centuries Britain's role in international affairs had largely stemmed from its position as a colonial power, so much so that in the late Victorian years, Prime Minister Lord Salisbury regarded the defence of the Empire as the prime aim of the United Kingdom's foreign policy.[14] Queen Victoria herself had been largely indifferent to the Empire until the Indian uprising, an event which however transformed the Empire for her into a passionate fascination. Her diamond jubilee in 1897 was celebrated as the festival of an Empire comprising a quarter of the world's land area and population, 'a heady outlet for the imagination of a people ... there was no denying its stimulation to the national spirit ... the nation talked Empire, thought Empire, dreamed Empire'.[15] And Empire and Britain's colonial and imperial role did much to forge a common identity across internal differences. They consolidated Britain's national *persona* and 'welded England, Scotland and Wales together as one people, and gave the British a powerful sense of natural superiority over others'.[16] Many British people had family members or friends who had migrated to, or had served in, the Empire, which became an integral feature of popular culture and imagination. The white settler colonies had never been short of enthusiasm for the imperial connection; loyalty to the Crown and the mother country were intangible but very strong emotional bonds. Queen Victoria's birthday, 24 May, was celebrated as Empire Day, and was declared a public holiday in Canada, Australia, New Zealand and South Africa even before Britain in 1916. The instruction about the Empire in schools, the Imperial Institute, broadcasts by the BBC, Empire Day, Empire Exhibitions, newsreels, promotions of the Empire and the monarch's Christmas broadcasts all 'contributed to a national and cross-party sense that the British Empire retained its influence and significance in the world and that it constituted an economic and political complex which the British themselves could ignore only at their peril'.[17] The Victorian Empire had generated strong sentiments of power and authority for the British people, though the basis of that prestige was fragile and the mythical status of the Empire was to have a short history. The Americans and Germans in the early twentieth century were catching up or even overtaking Britain in economic power, education and technical skills,[18] and the slump and unemployment of the 1930s saw a change in the popular mood. The end of the Second World War was regarded by many in Britain as a chance to make a fresh start without the illusions or trappings of grandeur. Britain was in debt, industrially crippled and strategically strained to breaking point. It no longer had the men, money, the energy or the will to sustain the Empire. As economist and adviser to the Treasury John Maynard Keynes put it in 1946, 'We cannot police half the world at our own expense when we have already gone into pawn to the other half.'[19] The mass of the British people were probably no longer attracted by notions of power and influence: 'except in the vague and satisfying abstract, except in matters of "prestige", the British cared little about their Empire and knew still less'.[20] A poll in 1947 revealed that three-quarters of the population did not know the difference between a dominion and a colony, that half could not name a single British possession, and that three per cent thought the United States was still a British colony.[21] After the loss of India, the Empire to the majority was only 'a vague irrelevance'.[22] There was little sense of pride left in the Empire; if Britain was to be influential and prosperous, it would have to be as a part of Europe. But that realization was yet to dawn in the future.

Though the biggest hurdle to decolonization in terms of emotional impact, the transfer of power to India, had been surmounted at the very start, 'the ideology of Empire was not experiencing a sudden and dramatic death',[23] and films portraying the Empire were made well into the 1960s to evoke feelings of patriotic pride and achievement, and racial and cultural superiority. The British public were given the sense of still participating in a worldwide enterprise that represented success, causing French statesman and intellectual André Malraux in his *Anti-Memoirs* to reflect that, 'The entire British Empire bears the stamp of English greatness.' Victory in the Second World War had given Britain great power status, which survived even the Suez catastrophe, and its public were given constant reassurances that world power would remain in substance even if the form of influence was modified, and that the Commonwealth would be part of a great British-centred diplomatic and economic world system. The association of the monarchy with this experiment strengthened its appeal. Support for the maintenance of British prestige and its role in the world won adherents from across the ideological spectrum. The pro-Americans cherished Britain's special voice in an increasingly US-dominated world and the pro-Europeans looked forward to British supremacy in Europe. As for the neo-imperialists, some of their later aversion to the Commonwealth derived from the fact that the Commonwealth proved to be no substitute for the Empire.[24] As Enoch Powell sarcastically put it, 'those whom the British permitted to speak for them, were compulsively, besottedly, gripped by the delusion that something called the Commonwealth was making them "mightier yet" '.[25]

Britain pioneered the way to dismantling an Empire, and the history of the Commonwealth was to prove an accurate reflection of the rise, the apogee and the decline of the Empire. 'It was always the intention of the British Government,' claimed the determinist view of history, 'that the territories of the Empire should advance to freedom on a steady path from dependent colonies through internal self-government to Dominion status and eventual independence'.[26] The decentralized Commonwealth was an experiment in 'a final version of Empire'[27] and 'softened the sharp edge of finality'.[28] There was a convenient belief, which turned out to be a self-deception, that continuity for the British role and influence was being maintained. The concept of the new Commonwealth initially met with public approval even as colonialism was increasingly regarded as a discredited relic of a remote past. But 'like other ideologies, that of the Commonwealth was partly myth ... It was an idea in which, by the 1950s, many of the British people and their governing class no longer believed'.[29] British governments had tried assiduously to rationalize the Commonwealth, but it was 'an oddity from the start, and was now a benevolent enigma'.[30] Nevertheless, no one was quite able to anticipate the sudden and complete collapse of British influence in the wake of the transfers of power. On the contrary, many thought the relationships with the former colonies would be revitalized after independence, but the Commonwealth proved to be not very different, let alone unique, in the contemporaneous world of inter-state relations.

In the early years of the modern Commonwealth, there were those member states hostile to communism and those who were neutral; those in military alliance with the United States and those who were non-aligned; and those which were dependent on economic aid and those considered advanced or developed. All members at first agreed that target dates should be set for the independence of the remaining dependencies that should take into account the actual state of prepared-ness of the particular dependency; which partly explains, for example, Nehru's tolerant attitude towards the British government's preparations for Malayan independence. The exceptions to this rule were the harsh criticisms of Britain from the new members over its policy in the settler colonies like Kenya and the Central African Federation. Voting in the United Nations on colonial questions saw a split between the white Dominions and the others, though the strongest criticism by the new members was reserved for other European colonial powers – France, Belgium and Portugal.[31] Nehru's criticisms and his non-alignment policy, in particular, stung the High Tories who preferred the 'realities' of the old Commonwealth to 'some new unreal evolution that would make the worst of both worlds'.[32]

In the 1950s and 1960s, Britain was constantly involved as the key country in the issues discussed by the Commonwealth, much more so than any other country. 'Britain gives more time and energy to the cul-tivation of the Commonwealth than any other member,' noted Miller in

1958.[33] By the late 1960s, the image of the Commonwealth to the British public was of a body 'asking too much and costing too much',[34] and during the negotiations to join the EEC, advocates of a pro-European orientation regarded the Commonwealth as an economic burden Britain had nobly sustained for too long and primarily for the benefit of others. Problems encountered by Britain in the process of decolonization, including immigration and defence, were dubbed 'Commonwealth matters', which served to give the association a bad name at home. Old trading partnerships were bound to give way to new, patterns of investment to alter, and military priorities and strategies to change. The Commonwealth had nothing sufficiently solid to put in their stead, and the public, earlier fed on a diet of politicians' optimism about the Commonwealth, was confused. 'Public opinion in Britain', wrote Eayrs in exasperation in *The Round Table* in 1967, 'has shown itself to be impervious to reasoned argument about the Commonwealth. Oscillating unsteadily between extravagant romanticism on the one hand and a no less extravagant excoriation on the other, even the attentive public experiences the greatest difficulty arriving at balanced and judicious appraisals'.[35]

British politicians had lagged behind public opinion. Beyond the closed inner circle of policy makers, the Empire had already become a matter of public indifference. British politicians nevertheless remained anxious to mask any reverse of British world power – it was a matter of national prestige; they should never be seen to capitulate. At the same time they were careful not to be seen to be exercising overseas authority with too heavy a hand. The younger generation's perception of the Empire as little more than an organized system of exploitation and theft and the confrontation in the Commonwealth over Rhodesia and South Africa both combined to undermine the organization. Televisual satires in the 1960s debunked imperial values and stereotypes rather as cartoonist David Low's walrus-moustached Colonel Blimp had done in the 1930s, and responding to the public mood, the term 'Colony' was gradually abandoned as politically incorrect in the 1970s, and replaced first by 'Dependent Territory' and subsequently by 'British Overseas Territory'.

British opinion at home became progressively less aware of the Empire. There was no residue of enthusiasm for it. There was a slow but marked process of declining interest on the part of the public; 'Perhaps the truth was that neither arch-imperialists nor dedicated anti-imperialists were typical of their countrymen. Except at moments of great crisis or high military adventure, the British people seem to have taken their

Empire for granted.'[36] When it became a nuisance financially, militarily, and in negotiations with the EEC, British opinion favoured dispensing with it as quietly and painlessly as possible, though imperial sentiment was to find later nostalgic echoes in the Falklands War, the handover of Hong Kong, the Queen Mother's death – the 'last Empress of India' – and the Queen's golden jubilee. The new multi-racial Commonwealth was far below the level of public consciousness compared to the erstwhile all-white association of Dominions, although there was never perceived to be a clear or clean break between the old and the new Commonwealth because the new post-Second World War model was initially projected as an extension of Empire and a vehicle for British influence. In the process of transition, culminating in the freedom and association of equal partners, the Commonwealth was the facilitator and the finishing line, and as such, eventually lost its *raison d'être*. For Britain as the benevolent trustee, the Commonwealth was a painkiller. Those who valued the association as the offspring of the Empire were among the most disillusioned; some politicians and a section of public opinion deluded themselves that the Commonwealth was the Empire in contemporary form – war-time Cabinet Minister Leo Amery thought it might prove to be the nucleus of a new world order. But in effect, the 'Commonwealth was the last opaque reflection of the grand illusion'[37] of imperial prestige. A seamless transition from Empire to the Commonwealth had been confidently predicted; gradual, firmly under British control, with many aspects of the imperial relationship perpetuated. Such expectations eased the trauma of the loss of the colonies and of power, but they endured long beyond the point of relevance to the real situation in the world, the Commonwealth, or Britain itself. When the Commonwealth came to be observed by the public to be in fact a very different sort of creature, it came as a shock to the British people.[38] Trenchant criticisms from the African and Asian Commonwealth from the time of the Rhodesian UDI onwards outraged the British public and pushed the Commonwealth's reputation to the outer margins, though the Commonwealth faded from consciousness not only because of Rhodesia and South Africa, but also due to the growing primacy of east-west relations and rapid developments in the unification of Europe.

Official attitudes in 1963, soon after de Gaulle's veto, obdurately stated that 'no single suggestion was made that it [the Commonwealth] had, in effect, fulfilled its usefulness and could be discarded',[39] but Whitehall's bid for European entry showed that the Commonwealth as an asset in trade and commerce was indeed less valuable than it had been estimated to be, though, as *The Round Table* put it, 'this intangible had for years been publicly clasped to the bosom of after-dinner orators, Ministers of the Crown, even the Monarch'.[40] The public regarded the Empire/Commonwealth as of little significance for the foundation of Britain as a world power, and as a process, decolonisation had become largely de-linked from the currents of domestic politics and society. Britain usually meant Whitehall, and Whitehall had learned from the Irish experience to try to keep colonial and domestic questions in separate compartments. Its future role in European integration turned out to be a far bigger obstacle for Britain to surmount than decolonization, since it impinged on how the British saw the future for themselves and their position in the world.

Domestic politics was not the fount of new ideas or initiatives on the Empire/Commonwealth and played no decisive role, though there was a significant measure of bi-partisanship. The absence of public controversy suggests how little colonial affairs impinged on society in Britain as a whole. British colonial policy was not disrupted by any dissent at home, except briefly at the time of Suez. Though the management of imperial interests remained a high foreign policy priority till the 1960s and had led to the summary dismissal of the prospects of the European Common Market in the 1950s, British politicians of all parties viewed the British retreat from the colonies with calm; and to many, it was an act of statesmanship about which they could feel justifiably proud. The British political establishment differed little on the decolonization process. It was a marginal political matter, and no general election featured it as a campaign issue. If the parties differed at all, it was only in terms of 'traditions, ideas and self-images'.[41] The only Cabinet-level resignation on post-war colonial policy was that in 1957 of Lord Salisbury, Leader of the House of Lords and Lord President of the Council, on Greek Cypriot leader Archbishop Makarios' release from detention. British politicians as the years went by forgot about the Empire and were apathetic about the Commonwealth.

The new institutions that made their periodic appearance – the Secretariat, the Commonwealth Foundation, the Commonwealth Fund for Technical Cooperation, the Commonwealth of Learning – did not quicken the pulse of public opinion. At the governmental level Britain felt let down by its fellow-members, including by the old Dominions, who were felt by Whitehall to be paying far too much court to Washington. There were louder complaints from Australia than any other country about the Commonwealth Immigration Act of 1962 with accusations that Britain was turning its back on family and old friends. As Garner put it, 'from a host of petty complaints and perhaps also from the inevitable fact of growing up and therefore to some extent growing apart, there came upon all Commonwealth countries a mood of disenchantment'.[42] Britain was increasingly regarded by the other members as putting its own interests first. While the Commonwealth could be projected as a body with shared values and a multi-racial and multi-purpose bridge between countries of differing interests and priorities, Britain was increasingly being cast as a member by default. *The Round Table* recorded in 1970, 'to many people in Britain the Commonwealth now seems a useless, indeed an inconvenient pretence. It is no longer a source of wealth and power'.[43]

Once the Conservatives had reconciled themselves to the independence of India, there was little difference in the attitudes to the Commonwealth among the major political parties. Only a few spokesmen opined on colonial affairs, inside or outside Parliament. After the war, senior Labour ministers, in the form of both Bevin and Aneurin Bevan, viewed Britain as a potential independent force in international affairs and the multi-racial Commonwealth was therefore highly congenial to Labour thinking. Through it, benevolent British influence could be disseminated, meeting third world development needs, and it could act as a junction between the east and west, north and south, earning for Britain the envy and respect of the Americans. After 1964, Labour support for the Commonwealth, and especially its sympathy for Africa, was put to a severe test, and with successive economic crises came the realization that only EEC membership could offer an escape route from the economic downslide. Britain's increasing powerlessness was shown by the Rhodesian UDI in November 1965, with attacks on Britain by the African Commonwealth, and the organization looked less of an international political advantage and became associated in the electorate's mind with undemocratic rule, human rights violations and non-white immigration. In January 1968, the announcement was made that after 1971 Britain would cease to maintain its forces in the Middle East and South East Asia. The global role was abandoned, and with it, one of the underlying assumptions regarding the Commonwealth; and the 'unique and valuable legacy of the Imperial Era'[44] fell from grace.

As for the Conservatives, they were nothing if not pragmatic. If there had been any domestic constituency to be exploited, Churchill doubtless would have publicly resisted the independence of India.[45] Such a constituency did not exist. The Tories concurred with Indian independence provided India would remain part of the proposed Commonwealth world system in which British influence would predominate, and accepted that it was the substance and not the form of Empire which really mattered.

Those who had reservations on decolonization could not come up with any realistic alternatives. There were the 'Preferentialists' who supported close economic integration in the Empire/Commonwealth in a ring-fenced imperial free trade area. They faded away by 1954. The 'Suez Group' opposed the 1954 agreement with Egypt.[46] But there was little drama attendant on the prolonged process of decolonization; on the contrary, there was an air of inevitability to it.

Macmillan's 1957 profit and loss exercise did not point unequivocally to any rapid colonial withdrawal. Only during the 1960s was there a widespread reaction against the Empire caused by the kith and kin factor, apprehensions of violence, and fears of a Congo-type chaotic situation. The African nationalists, unlike their early Asian counterparts, were not men with backgrounds familiar with the old school tie and the exclusive clubs of St. James'. In the transfer of power in Africa, wrote David Adamson, there was in general 'scant sympathy for, or understanding of, the problems of black leaders, often good and genuinely kindly men, but equally men of limited experience and raw sensitivities'.[47] There was little domestic resistance either to the scaling down of colonial commitments or the application to the EEC in 1961. Throughout the period from 1951 to 1964, the Conservatives supported turning the Empire into the Commonwealth to maintain great power status, and even at the end of this period, their hopes of projecting British influence could still be termed plausible, and the approach towards Europe could be portrayed as merely a course-correction or pragmatic adjustment. The development of the Commonwealth also helped Britain to come to terms with its new situation of dependent status on the United States for its defence and financial stability.

But any idea that Britain could use the Commonwealth to play a major role in economic, political and military terms turned out to be misconceived. In public perception, the Commonwealth was increasingly peripheral to British security and prosperity, and to be placed in the dock to be criticized by undemocratic regimes which could not bear scrutiny themselves created an aversion which only the hardiest enthusiast for the Commonwealth could endure. Nowadays, wrote David Dilks, the Commonwealth 'plays no part in our General Elections, and little part in our general consciousness'.[48] The Commonwealth segment of the FCO was always at a disadvantage since it had for years oversold the special quality of Commonwealth relations, while the rest of the FCO remained unconvinced and was more oriented towards Europe and the United States. It was soon to be apparent that the Commonwealth would not be a major focus of foreign policy. Foreign Secretary Geoffrey Howe,

speaking of the association in 1983, said it 'remains central to our foreign policy – in particular outside the Atlantic Area. The intense official
and public interest in Grenada has once again shown that clearly'.[49] But
Grenada was an unfortunate example; the association was deeply
divided on the question of American intervention, with even the membership from the Caribbean region lacking unanimity.[50]

The psychological trauma and transformation caused by the loss of
Empire were assuaged by the predominantly-held teleological view that
the goal had always been the peaceful transfer of power to new nation
states; an act of grace and favour – though Palestine had been a distress-
ingly negative example. The show of British dignity in retreat was
important to the British national interest; the British had to be seen to
be in control of events. Britain's lack of power was therefore to be concealed, and Britain shown to be strong enough to preside over the loose
ends of Empire without any appearance of weakness. It was highly for-
tuitous that so few of the colonies – Gibraltar (the nearest dependency,
though itself 1077 miles distant from Britain), Cyprus, Belize and Hong
Kong – were seriously threatened with takeover by any foreign power.
British Honduras was granted independence as Belize in 1981 after a
long period of menace and intimidation from Guatemala which laid
claim to the territory; and the invasion of the Falkland Islands and
South Georgia by Argentina in 1982 proved to be the only occasion
when a colony was actually seized and had to be liberated from the grasp
of another power. The urgings of Governor Chris Patten for democracy
in Hong Kong, even at the short-term cost of a set-back to Sino-British
relations, set the stage as the British public would like to have it, as
following a liberal and humanitarian tradition. The growing influence
of the European Union in everyday life refocused national identity,
especially among the youth, making the erstwhile, though recent, imperial role seem totally anachronistic. It could hardly have been otherwise.
The old vehicles for past idealism were no longer in vogue – patriotism,
the Church, the Monarchy, Parliament, the BBC – all have taken severe
knocks. The concept of Empire and nationhood had been forged on
notions of superiority now regarded as totally absurd. The British
retained no coherent idea of what exactly they were, other than that
they carried a bigger burden of history, expectation and perhaps derision
than most other people.

'Overall, Britain has slipped to a position as a middle-ranking power,'
declared the Parekh Report in 2001, '... and the country is tempted
to look back, nostalgically, to past glories'.[51] It is a modest legacy compared to what was envisaged in the 1940s, 1950s and even 1960s. Was

colonialism destroyed by the changes in British society and the faltering economy after 1945; or was it an incidental by-product of the antagonism between the two super powers; or was it due to the rise of local nationalism? Perhaps all the three, but the answer was not, initially at any rate, any political impulse to disengage or a liberal and humanitarian inclination to decolonize. Nor did the egalitarian, liberating and energizing effect that some observers thought decolonization would have on British society ever take place. 'Perhaps', concluded John Darwin, 'the most obvious reaction to the disappearance of Empire was, in fact, indifference'.[52]

Media comments through the years

In the light of the perceptibly diminishing British governmental and public interest in the Commonwealth over the decades, it is hardly surprising that articles of substance on this subject in the British press in the post-war period are a rare occurrence. Yet the articles that did appear are representative of an on-going, though sporadic, discourse on the virtues, failings and future of the organization. What is perhaps more surprising is that they are not uniformly negative in tone; through the years, it seems that the Commonwealth continued to have its adherents, and it is still a body capable of stimulating hope among its votaries.

In a pre-Suez editorial in *The Economist* on 7 April 1956, the writer said something of value is achieved by the efforts the prime ministers made to meet in person, but 'nobody cares to define the Commonwealth too closely ... the Commonwealth works, it is said, and that is enough'. New members would find it easier to grasp what it is not rather than what it stands for. 'What then, it may be asked, is the worth of so negative an association? For Britain the Commonwealth is a gentle let-down, a featherbed of fine phrases and outward forms, to ease the psychological impact of the loss – now approaching its last phase – of a powerful Empire. Yet the phrases and the forms can still symbolize something positive and valuable that can persist. The new ways of parting friends has portrayed Britain's influence in a way Holland might envy and France may soon really miss. It has given a short respite in which the adjustment can be made to the real loss of power, the consequences of which emerge nakedly from time to time ... It has preserved the friendship of former dependencies. And it has kept up Britain's stock in America.'

In *The Times* editorial of 4 April 1964, the writer was equally positive; 'the Commonwealth needs open debate ... with all its embarrassments and imperfections the Commonwealth is the greatest effort at a multi-racial society of nations the world has ever seen. Multi-racialism is mankind's only way ... to universal peace and on a world scale, the only way in which Britain leads'.

The Round Table in volume 71, number 284 of October 1981, carried a piece by Evan Charlton which commented on the different attitudes in the body politic towards the Commonwealth. 'It is true enough' he wrote, 'that important elements in Britain's political life are out of sympathy with the lines on which the Commonwealth has developed ... United Kingdom leaders have felt themselves pilloried by representatives of the "have-nots" and suggestions that more generous financial aid should be a natural part of Britain's conscience money for past colonial sins are bitterly resented ... Fortunately there is strong opposition to such views. This cuts right across party lines and sees in the Commonwealth a magnificent experiment in international cooperation'.

Despite its title of 'Once an Empire, now an embarrassment', John Simpson in *The Spectator* of 23 October 1993, also had good things to say: 'It was always Britain's links with South Africa, not those of other countries, which were to be blamed and punished.' From 1961 till the latest Commonwealth conference in 1991, Commonwealth politics had been almost exclusively about Britain's approach to the white regimes of Southern Africa. 'This week's Commonwealth conference is the first non-contentious occasion of its type since the days 30 years ago ...' The Commonwealth had built up a life of its own, which the great majority of countries were proud of. For old members, it was a link with the third world. It was a matter of prestige to be a member. For the Caribbean leaders, it was their only hope of any outside support; for Africa and Asia, a valuable tie to the wider world and an alternative to possible domination by some regional power. But 'there is today no political support for the Commonwealth at Westminster ... In the space of a few years the Empire we had once prided ourselves on had become a source of embarrassment and guilt to us'. Meanwhile, the Commonwealth's 'political and business leaders speak English and still, in spite of our consistent lack of interest, tend to look to Britain for their cultural and political links'. Britain did not ask the organization to protect its interests, and its colonial past was something we wished to forget, to the detriment of our national interest.

Then there were other writers who were agnostic, cautious about the Commonwealth and uncertain about its value, typified by a commentator on the Secretariat who was obliged in 1989 to admit that 'what the

Commonwealth actually adds up to has always been hard to define'.[53] *The Round Table* itself, in 1990, acknowledged that 'as an organization the Commonwealth cannot be said to have a common founding purpose'.[54]

On 13 November 1995, *The Daily Telegraph* ran an article by Philip Johnston titled 'The Commonwealth has open house for dictators', but the contents were in a rather different tone, referring factually to the Commonwealth summit at Auckland, where a mechanism was drawn up, none too soon according to Johnston, providing for the possible expulsion of countries who flouted the norms of the organization.

The same newspaper on 26 August 1997, revealed the findings of a Gallup poll in an article titled 'Fame of a once Proud Empire is fading fast.' Only 1000 persons were canvassed, but some conclusions were drawn; that the British were proud that Britain had possessed an Empire, might not know too much about it, but regretted that it had disappeared. More than 80 per cent believed that decolonization was inevitable and fewer than 20 per cent thought the Commonwealth was more important to Britain than were Europe or the United States. The majority felt the ex-colonies should be left to their own devices, and there was no further responsibility on the part of Britain to them. Most felt that the mother country had done more good than harm to the colonies, that the Empire had left few scars and that relations with the ex-colonies were either good or very good. The older generation knew far more about the Empire than their children or grandchildren. Many British people could not distinguish between an independent Commonwealth country and a colony: 47 per cent thought Australia to be a colony, about the same proportion that got the answer right.

Given the growing negativity from both officialdom and the general public about the Commonwealth, the number of important critical pieces was not surprisingly somewhat larger.

On 27 December 1958, *The Economist* marked the season of goodwill with a scathing and satirical three-page piece on the Commonwealth entitled 'Cwthmas'. This poured scorn on the reported decision taken by prime ministers that year to rename 'Empire Day' as 'Commonwealth Day'. Shall we even know what exactly we are celebrating?, asked the article rhetorically. 'There are some arcane mysteries whose high priests prefer not to expose them to the vulgar gaze.'

Less vitriolic, but more influential, was the widely reported article in *The Times* of 2 April 1964, by 'A Conservative', commonly believed to be Enoch Powell. He called for a revision of the Conservative Party's position on the Commonwealth, and claimed that both the non-European members and the old Dominions were less well disposed to Britain than they were to countries like China and Germany. 'For Britain, the absurdities it imposes on our laws and thought have already done more harm than enough.' He adduced many arguments – coloured immigration in the past decade, that common citizenship was an outworn fiction, Commonwealth preference was a 'hagridden' commercial policy, and the monarchy was reduced to playing 'an alien part as one of the characters in the Commonwealth charade'. Britain was a European power, and should renounce the relics of Empire, and withdraw its forces from South East Asia, the Middle East and Aden: this would avoid the taint of colonialism or neo-colonialism in the United Nations. He complained that 'the Labour Party has become the party of the Commonwealth ... Harold Wilson in Lord Beaverbrook's clothing'.

The Economist returned to the charge in the season of goodwill in 1968. On 21 December that year, ten years after its first savage attack on the Commonwealth, it carried a stinging review of the past decade of the Commonwealth in a two-page spoof called 'God rest ye merry, Cwthmen'.

There followed in *The Times* on 10 August 1970, a reasoned critique by Max Beloff. Asking 'Does Britain need the Commonwealth?', he deplored Trudeau's determination to play down the Soviet threat, and claimed that the Empire and the Commonwealth were not distinctions that were clear to the American mind, and that the Commonwealth led to doubts about Britain's European commitment and possible 'covert imperialism'. The lack of any separate treatment for the old Dominions in the matter of immigration had soured relations with Australia and New Zealand. Coloured immigrants did not identify with Britain, and could prove to be a pressure-group for the countries whence they came. The Commonwealth led to Britain getting involved in intra-Commonwealth disputes like Kashmir and Biafra. While Britain gained no strength from the Commonwealth, it had to expend energy on matters like Rhodesia. He argued for bilateral arrangements based on national self-interest replacing the Commonwealth connection.

On 22 November 1983, in advance of the Commonwealth summit scheduled to be convened in India, Enoch Powell in *The Daily Telegraph* wrote; 'Some time there will have to be an end to this make-believe. Some day the Queen's ministers will have to stop advising her to undertake another and yet another journey through the phantasmagoria of cheering crowds and empty ceremonies which mock the memory of a power that was but is no longer.'

The Economist on 23 September 1989, reporting Pakistan's rejoining as a member of the Commonwealth, which it had left in 1972 on Britain's recognition of Bangladesh, and anticipating the upcoming Commonwealth summit in Malaysia, said 'In Kuala Lumpur its leaders will add another nicely drafted declaration to the world surplus of good intentions ... but they are short of practical business ... the club is in danger of having nothing much to express but its members' mutual friendship – good news that is no news at all'.

In the *Sunday Telegraph* of 22 October 1989, Peregrine Worsthorne's piece was uncompromisingly titled 'Abolish the Commonwealth'. 'It was and is an undesirable institution,' he opined. 'Thanks to the Commonwealth, Britain is now a multi-racial society, the divisive consequences of which will be with us for ever.' This was the penance for the sins of Empire. A decisive majority in Britain did not want a multi-racial society. Among other disadvantages were the delay in joining Europe, and harbouring the non-aligned movement, the main pillar of anti-Americanism, of which the chief leaders came from the coloured Commonwealth. By inculcating British traditions of obedience in the army and civil services, the Commonwealth had helped in the establishment of one-party states in Africa, and Commonwealth scholarships only served to indoctrinate returning African students with socialist ideas. 'One party rule and socialism – these were the Commonwealth legacies for Africa.' There had been pressure on Britain to de-stabilize South Africa, and Britain was supposed to refrain from attacking Commonwealth members without reciprocity. 'That is the trouble with the Commonwealth – it encourages people, even the Queen, to live in a world of illusions.' Britain had to show due deference to the Commonwealth since the Queen was the head of it, and 'she is a satisfied customer'. In so far as the Commonwealth had any popular support, it was because the Queen was at its head. The writer sees the end of the Cold War as leading to the demise of the Commonwealth. '... and no part of the rubble would be less missed than the Commonwealth.'

The Daily Telegraph of 15 March 2002, speaking of Zimbabwe, called for its suspension from the Commonwealth. 'Failure to do so will expose it as a club to which scoundrels can belong with impunity. In that case, there would be little point in its continuing to exist.'

Michael Brown in *The Independent* on the same day was even less equivocal: 'Why we have tolerated this farce for so long beggars belief ... Frankly, from the moment that Britain joined Europe the purpose of the Commonwealth ceased to be anything other than a talking shop ... The time has come for Britain to issue its own ultimatum over membership of the Commonwealth ... Mr Blair should say we have had enough of this farce and that we will, ourselves, leave the organization.'

The Times on 22 July 2002, carried a piece by Simon Barnes on the Commonwealth Games in Manchester. 'It is deeply odd that the Commonwealth Games take place at all. They commemorate the British Empire, which these days is regarded as one of the great crimes of history ... Why do the old boys of this particular empire still meet for a ten-day festival? Why aren't there quadrennial games for the Spanish or the Portuguese or the French or the Germans or the Dutch former colonies?'

One encomium and one omission might also be worthy of mention. David Adamson in 1989 in his book *The Last Empire* asserted that the Commonwealth 'staunched a haemorrhage of pride and confidence, cleansed a poisonous sense of failure and in a way vindicated the country's history',[55] whereas in *A Fighting Retreat: The British Empire 1947–97*, by Robin Neillands, the index of 21 pages to a book of 560 pages makes no mention of the Commonwealth – though there are several references to the association in the text.

Knowledge of the modern Commonwealth

The demise of the Empire was not to be allowed to detract from British prestige and influence, and was given comfort by the Commonwealth. This organization was seen as the logical culmination of imperial achievement, and led to the renaming of several British establishments of high repute, including the Royal Empire Society, the Imperial Institute, and others. The public were made to feel satisfied that the Empire was in successful and controlled transition. The power and reputation and general knowledge of the Empire among the British public had been promoted by periodic exhibitions in the nineteenth and twentieth centuries. The Wembley Empire Exhibition in 1924 was visited by some 27 million people but still made a loss, unlike the pre-1914 exhibitions. As late as 1938, there was an Empire Exhibition in Glasgow (in which India did not participate), which attracted over 12 million people. But after Second World War, the first-ever Commonwealth Arts Festival took place in 1965, in four counties in the United Kingdom, and apparently after nine years of consideration.

As the decline in Britain's position in the Commonwealth and the world at large was progressively driven home, it came to be asked how far British national interests were served by membership in a scattered community of states in which Britain's pre-eminence was no longer even acknowledged. Fewer and fewer Commonwealth members chose to avail themselves of the Empire's ultimate tribunal, the Judicial

Committee of the Privy Council; the organization could do little about poverty or race, and Britain was increasingly a target for criticism as the focal point of an organization which many viewed as 'an anachronism, a device ... hurriedly fashioned after 1945 to help the British political class come to terms with the loss of empire'.[56] Over time, the new Commonwealth was seen to have little more in common with the United Kingdom than with the United States or even the Soviet Union. Only in the less significant ways was the connection apparently still meaningful; in various non-governmental contacts, team sports, military traditions, and the four-yearly Commonwealth Games which had been started in 1930. The rest of the world had moved on. In the Falklands War of 1982, Commonwealth voting in the United Nations was more supportive than not, but this did not restore the public's confidence in the association, and the main legacy of the Commonwealth was seen as the largely unwelcome minority community of coloured immigrants in the United Kingdom. Previously highly influential Commonwealth organs and societies such as *The Round Table*, the Royal Commonwealth Society and the Commonwealth Institute were reduced in importance and became publicists for an organization in which the British public had lost interest, and some suffered a suspension or curtailment of their activities.

By an Act of Parliament in 1958, the Imperial Institute founded in 1893 was reconstituted as the Commonwealth Institute, and funded by the United Kingdom government ostensibly to increase knowledge of the Commonwealth in Britain. Throughout the 1990s its future was in peril, when the Foreign and Commonwealth Office, which had provided 90 per cent of the Institute's funding from 1963 to 1995, decided to terminate its grant. The Edinburgh branch closed its doors in 1996. The House of Commons Foreign Affairs Committee Report of 1996 anticipated 'a real prospect of permanent closure', and warned that 'this must be avoided'.[57] But to no avail. A categorically final budget allocation was made by the FCO, and in 2003 a decision was taken that the Institute would be sold and some of the proceeds used to set up a Centre for Commonwealth Education in the Faculty of Education in Cambridge, which would mainly be involved in supporting primary and secondary education and teacher training. The proposed centre and its activities are likely to recede into invisibility, somewhat on the lines of the fate of the Commonwealth Collection, the former Royal Commonwealth Society Library, which was purchased through public donations for the Library of the University of Cambridge, only to languish as a neglected and under-utilized resource and become something of a white elephant.

At the end of 2004, the Commonwealth Institute in Kensington was a forlorn spectacle, its gates for more than a year firmly closed to the public but with its name-board still displayed outside the premises and the flags of the Commonwealth member countries torn and dirty on street-side flag-posts until someone belatedly remembered to take them down in the first weekend of November.

The main showpiece of the Empire and Commonwealth in the United Kingdom is now the British Empire and Commonwealth Museum at Bristol, established by private financing in 2002. Typically, the name of the museum created a vexed problem of political correctness, which reflected the *zeitgeist*. Patrons of the museum initially complained that the word 'Empire' itself would put off potential benefactors. The word 'British' disappeared temporarily, only to be restored. The word 'Commonwealth' which was not originally there, was subsequently inserted. The Commonwealth in practice has little salience in the exhibition when compared to the visual fascination of the glorious and infamous centuries of the Empire, and emerges as a less than picturesque afterthought of the imperial heyday.

Various public opinion polls on the Empire and Commonwealth held after the Second World War suggested that there was some residual nostalgia for the Empire among those who remembered it, but that the younger generations knew or cared little either for the Empire or the Commonwealth. *The Round Table* reported[58] the results of a poll of 946 persons in January 1969, which suggested that seven out of ten respondents rejected the idea that the Commonwealth be wound up or that the United Kingdom should leave it, and these views varied little between age, sex, or party affiliation. A Commonwealth Institute/ *New Society* poll in 1983 showed that Scotland was the most pro-Commonwealth region of the United Kingdom,[59] and a Commonwealth Institute policy review in 1986 found that an element of British opinion looked at the Commonwealth as a relic of the past with little or no contemporary value as a political association.[60] In 1995, 43 per cent of a sample of British 15–24 year olds responded 'don't know' to the question, 'what does the Commonwealth mean to you?'[61] In 1997, on the Queen's golden wedding anniversary, a poll by *The Daily Telegraph* reported that people under 50 knew little about their country's imperial past, and the British Empire seemed as remote as the Roman Empire.[62]

This lack of knowledge about the Commonwealth and its good works continually drives its supporters to despair. Through the late 1960s and 1970s, the Commonwealth had sought to promote in Rhodesia a transfer of power that would make it possible for democracy to prevail, but it received no credit from the British government or public. In exasperated vein, *The Round Table* asked despairingly in 1976, 'no doubt the Commonwealth is not fashionable ...Why is the moderating, constructive function of the Commonwealth not more widely understood?'[63] In 1983 the editor of *The Round Table* noted that

> The Commonwealth, especially since 1965, has become an unique post-imperial international organization ... It is still, however, remarkable and regrettable how little is generally known of the unofficial Commonwealth, or serious questions asked of its general purposes and potential ... Britain does have residual colonial responsibilities ... the Commonwealth connection here is an asset and a help to Britain ... much more than a hindrance or embarrassment.[64]

In 1990 *The Round Table*, in what seemed oddly like a revival of the outmoded doctrine of using the Commonwealth for greater leverage in Europe, lamented that

> one day British ministers and diplomats will no doubt awake again to the opportunities which so many of its other members have long seized – of using the Commonwealth to serve their own particular interests. Time was when Britain palpably used the Commonwealth to ease the trauma of losing an empire. ... the Commonwealth stands there to provide Britain with a culturally familiar, world-wide, inter-regional connection which if she will only use it, gives her a striking comparative advantage in relation to Europe's place ... over each and every one of her European partners.[65]

At least part of the problem in official circles and public perception may be traced to the ambiguities of the Commonwealth's mission and purpose, the needless exaggeration generated by its enthusiasts and the Secretariat, and the philosophical-intellectual jargon presented to justify its continued relevance. Commonwealth logic was always shrouded in imprecision and rhetoric. Rather than have the rules broken, it was asserted, the creators of the new Commonwealth did without rules.[66] The result was that in the end people were more confused than ever as to what the Commonwealth was all about. Insiders revelled in the hermetic nature of the Commonwealth. *The Times* on Coronation Day declared: 'There are days when the mysteries of the Commonwealth partnership almost cease to be mysteries and become, for a few glittering hours, as near to being explicit as they can ever be ... what are the bonds which in Burke's prophetic words, "though light as air are as strong as links of iron"?'[67] Mansergh wrote sardonically about the capacity of Commonwealth theologians to be impenetrable. 'The evident incapacity of foreigners to comprehend the structure, and still more the spirit, of the British Commonwealth of Nations was a source of abiding satisfaction to British constitutional experts who appeared to consider the infinite complexity of imperial relationships as evidence in themselves of a superior political wisdom.' He added that while there was no particular virtue in this complexity, it did display unique political wisdom in allowing such flexibility despite the innate predisposition of twentieth-century governments to organize.[68] To illustrate Mansergh's point, what is one to make of *The Round Table's* following description of the Commonwealth in 1974?

> It is only when we come to an understanding of the Commonwealth as the institutional expression of the working-out of a distinctive human tradition in a variety of complex relationships with other human traditions that we find ourselves better able to understand what the members … have in common and what is the source of the Commonwealth's vitality.[69]

There had long been influential Empire-related lobbies and sentiment – in 1932, the Dominions Secretary pointed out that there were 33 imperial and patriotic societies in existence – but the Commonwealth failed to attract similar grass-root affection and loyalty, especially after the 1960s and despite the existence of some five dozen 'accredited' civil society organizations. In Britain there exists no effective pro-Commonwealth lobby; and no one to succeed in the tradition of the old strident pro-Empire stalwarts. The same people, admirable though they are as individuals, have been discussing the same issues in the Commonwealth for so long that nobody pays them much attention. Yet, 'writers and speakers on the Commonwealth', wrote Miller, 'are perpetually being pleased with themselves'.[70] The people to whom the Commonwealth still has an appeal are those with past associations with Commonwealth countries, or those who feel it is in itself a good system and one that Britain should not give up. These observers tend vaguely to see the way ahead for a Commonwealth 'whose essence is a network of personal relationships and voluntary organizations which will prove more trustworthy and desirable than the quasi-political structure created by the Secretariat and the heads of government meetings'.[71] A recurring theme in *The Round Table* from the 1950s onwards was the profound value of 'the inter-relations of a cultural, professional and private kind'.[72] In a submission to the Foreign Affairs Committee of the House of Commons in 1995–96, a former British Governor on the Board of the Commonwealth Foundation noted that 'the enthusiasm of many people and the efforts they put into Commonwealth professional bodies and NGOs are far more than can be explained simply by sentiment. They are evidence of the strength and attractiveness of the Commonwealth spirit and values'.[73] And most of these professional, cultural, social and sporting bodies, he noted, are located in London. Many had been formed even before the origin of the modern Commonwealth. 'Volunteering is one of the Commonwealth's greatest assets,'[74] asserted David Steel, Speaker of the Scottish Parliament, and Katherine West wrote that the unofficial Commonwealth is widely known to contain an impressive and ever-increasing pool of knowledge and expertise whose extent and quality have implicitly been undervalued in what she described as the inappropriately hierarchical two-tier concept.[75]

Enthusiasts of the existing Commonwealth civil society linkages, perhaps despairing of the lack of effectiveness in, support from, and access to, the inter-governmental machinery, are inclined to propound a view that suggests that such linkages could prove the ultimate salvation of the Commonwealth and underpin both its survivability and efficacy. But at this time of declining fortunes in the Commonwealth, can such civil society bonds paradoxically strengthen and become more effective? In fact, could these civil society linkages outlive the possible demise of the Commonwealth as an inter-governmental organization and become a new version of an extinguished 'modern' Commonwealth? Realistically, is the Commonwealth's NGO community likely to grow in numbers, influence and effectiveness? The semi-official and non-official bodies that are accredited to the Commonwealth are rarely united in any common cause and are often to be seen acting at cross purposes with themselves and to the umbrella organization to which they are loosely affiliated and from which they take their name. The energies of those who had worked in the Empire, family links through diaspora, personal contacts between individuals who had fought in the Second World War or had studied in the British educational system, are all rapidly declining with retirements and deaths. In Britain and the old Dominions, in the past few decades and certainly in the decades to come, there has been and will be significant and increasing levels of immigration from non-Commonwealth countries. All this will lead to a lowering of Commonwealth awareness, and the feelings of commonality and the ties of sentiment are weakening with the aging of the generation that witnessed the birth of the new Commonwealth. And the challenge always continues of finding effective linkages between civil society groups and the apparatus of the state sector. Rob Jenkins endorses this view:

> a sort of forced earnestness surrounds discussions of the non-governmental aspect of the Commonwealth. It usually includes a ritual intonation to the effect that the Commonwealth of NGOs is 'the people's Commonwealth', and is as important as the Commonwealth of states, if not more so, ... but ... relations between states are of significantly greater importance in effecting policy objectives – globalization or no globalization.[76]

As a result of the full-cost 'economic' fees for overseas students from 1981, the numbers of Commonwealth students from overseas in Britain, who may have been expected to promote information and curiosity, if nothing else, for the Commonwealth bond, have fallen. Their number declined as a percentage of the whole from 50 per cent in 1979 to 35 per cent in 1992, while those from the European Union increased from 13 per cent to 34 per cent in the same period.[77] Commonwealth students coming to Britain now are mainly from the more affluent Commonwealth countries like Malaysia and Singapore. Significantly, of all Commonwealth students studying abroad, over 50 per cent are in the United States and only around 15 per cent in another Commonwealth country[78] – another crack in the edifice of Commonwealth unity and further evidence of America's unwitting contribution to such fissures. And the Commonwealth as a field of study is a notoriously disadvantaged area for attracting any funding, even from the very institutions which profess to carry and safeguard the flickering torch of the organization, and were established for that very purpose. These bodies evidently prefer to see their grants used for more fashionably relevant subjects.

The House of Commons Foreign Affairs Committee Report, 1995–96

In 1995–96 the members of the Foreign Affairs Committee of the House of Commons examined Britain's relations with the Commonwealth and the Commonwealth's role and potential in promoting good governance, trade, investment, aid and development. The committee's report was published on 27 March 1996.

The report said 'In the United Kingdom, it [the Commonwealth] has traditionally been seen by many people ... as a reflection of the country's imperial past ...[79] it was understandable for a few decades after the end of Empire that the Commonwealth was seen in the United Kingdom as a relic of an imperial past – a political albatross around the country's neck',[80] but the report also concluded that in the organization, Britain enjoyed both friends and opportunities.

The two issues that had soured relations between Britain and the rest of the Commonwealth for 30-odd years – Rhodesia and South Africa – were now settled, with some input from the Commonwealth. The Cold War that had spilled over into Commonwealth relations was a thing of the past. So a new start could be made. 'In an increasingly global trans-regional political system, we believe that the Commonwealth network has great potential future value.'[81] The report went on to say,

> The Commonwealth is acquiring a new significance in a rapidly transforming world ... United Kingdom policy makers should bring this major change to the forefront of their thinking. ... From being a 'club' of countries all too ready both to criticize and make demands on the former imperial power, the Commonwealth is rapidly metamorphosing into a network with quite different interests and ambitions ... within our own national administration, and certainly within the FCO, more minds should be focussed on our Commonwealth role.[82]

The report identified two positive benefits to Britain; the value of Commonwealth networks, and the emerging potential for trade and investment. On the former, it saw the advantages of the Commonwealth for Britain as English being a common language, similar legal systems, accountancy procedures, educational links and business practices; as a network and bridge; as a broking house; and all these factors co-existing in a useful and manageably-sized forum for discussions on global matters like debt relief and debt management. On the latter, the report identified some of the fastest growing economies as being in the Commonwealth, with some interesting non-British cross-linkages already at work – for example, Canada with Africa and South East Asia, and Malaysia with Africa. It noted that economic ties with Asia had currently assumed added importance due to that continent's recent high GDP growth rates. The Foreign Affairs Committee Report went on to state that the United Kingdom should defend Commonwealth interests in international groupings to which it belongs and Commonwealth countries should defend the United Kingdom's interests in regional organizations to which they belong.[83] This anglo-centric approach is hardly surprising since the report is a product of the British Parliament and reflects a persistently-held popular view that the Commonwealth is essentially a set of bilateral relationships, with the United Kingdom at the hub and each of its former dependencies along the periphery.

Foreign Secretary Malcolm Rifkind, appearing before the House committee, saw the Commonwealth as a unique opportunity for a dialogue between countries in different parts of the world.

> It [the Commonwealth] is not something we have 'inherited'; it is something which has been a consequence of our own history and has been brought about by a common belief, shared with all our former dependent territories and colonies, that there was a sufficient commonality of interest to justify this relationship continuing, even after they became sovereign states. I think it is certainly a tribute to the way in which the Empire developed into the Commonwealth ... The Commonwealth provides an opportunity for us to influence the policies of many governments around the world ... to extend our cultural, social and political contacts ... and, as a consequence, we have an ability to influence events.[84]

But there were clear limits to that ability to influence other countries, and he hastened to disabuse the committee of the notion that Britain could be a ringmaster. He went on to add, 'each country determines its foreign policy in the light of what it perceives to be its national interest[85] ... the idea that membership of the Commonwealth requires any individual member ... to agree with all the others on matters of foreign policy has never been ... put forward by anybody'.[86]

The oral and written submissions to the Foreign Affairs Committee made some interesting and varied observations. Viscount Waverly, putting forward arguments reminiscent of the 1950s, went on record as feeling very positive:

> Britain certainly derives many advantages from membership. Political credibility with European partners and North Atlantic allies is enhanced, and influence within the Commonwealth partly justifies our place on the United Nations Security Council. United platforms can be forged to address world issues, and coherent action pursued within the United Nations system.[87]

And the Commonwealth Trust, comprising the 'old guard' or guardians, the Royal Commonwealth Society and the Victoria League, wrote,

> The French, the Dutch and the Portuguese who have tried to build their own versions of the Commonwealth for reasons of economic and political self-interest, find it difficult to understand why Britain has not made more use of its much more extensive network of links. ... Here are 51 countries, encompassing a quarter of the world's population, spread across all continents, with which Britain has a special relationship, including some of the fastest growing economies in the world. All these countries share a common working language – English – and common systems at all levels – based on the British systems – which is of inestimable value to Britain, when seeking business opportunities or the promotion of policies in world affairs. ... This asset appears to have been neglected by the United Kingdom over the years and its potential for the promotion of British interests not appreciated.[88]

Others, like Robert Holland of the Institute of Commonwealth Studies, were more cautious and identified the association's frailties in the political sphere. Elaborating on the Institute's definition of the Commonwealth as 'a congenial association of member states',[89] he opined that the organization found it hard to pressurize or criticize member states and there were limits to what friendly persuasion could achieve.

> The Commonwealth perhaps can be a watchdog but it had better be very careful about biting too hard. ... The idea that the Commonwealth can put things to rights ... seems to me extremely questionable. Public opinion, yes; watch, yes; highlight, yes; discuss, yes, but the need to feel you can be decisive or should be decisive is misleading ... the Commonwealth is open to a lot of Commonwealth bashing and a lot of simplistic criticism because people say, 'Oh, it should be decisive, it should be acting'. It is asking the impossible ... Historians have debated and are still debating the popularity of the Empire in its heyday and the answer is that they do not think and talk and dream about the Commonwealth throughout the pubs and clubs of the country. That was even in the heyday of Empire. Do not expect them to do it about the Commonwealth. You cannot expect people at any mass level to have enthusiasm of that sort.[90]

Richard Bourne of the Commonwealth Policy Studies Unit declared, 'the Commonwealth may be seen as the prototype of a post-modern international nexus ... a fluid mix of the inter-governmental and non-governmental has potential advantages'. But he also went on to say, 'this is an association which suffers from and could be killed by amnesia'.[91] And Peter Marshall, chairman of the Joint Commonwealth Societies Council, in terms which might unintentionally suggest that the association's days of relevance were over, felt 'the Commonwealth has a role as a shock absorber ... [it] can be realistically regarded as "the after-sales service of the British Empire" '.[92]

The 'Commonwealth factor' in trade and economic relations

The 'shared experience of the Commonwealth business culture', wrote Katherine West in 1995 in a Chatham House paper, 'can facilitate and consolidate mutually beneficial bilateral economic relations across regional and other kinds of boundaries'.[93] After quoting West, the House of Commons Foreign Affairs Committee Report went on to note that it had to be of some advantage to Britain that it has had a presence in the other member countries for over 100 years, which ought to give it a comparative advantage available to few others. 'The common use of the English language, similar legal structures, a common business culture and educational links combine to assist intra-Commonwealth trade and investment. ... Commonwealth membership helped to facilitate initial contacts.'[94]

West noted that the balance of British trade was shifting away from the European Union towards China and the Pacific rim. She wrote,

> In these new economic circumstances, the Commonwealth has the vital advantage of being ... a 'global sub-system' with multi-regional membership crossing the boundaries of the Asian, African, American and European regional groupings. This gives it the potential to be of real economic benefit in facilitating and consolidating bilateral and multilateral trade and investment contacts between and among Commonwealth countries. ... In the ethnically heterogeneous Commonwealth, its common business culture is now widely considered to be the most positive legacy of the British Empire.

Besides a shared business culture and the English language in common, West claimed that the Commonwealth had a shared tradition of legal, commercial and accountancy practices and procedures, giving what a former Secretary of State for Commonwealth Relations Patrick Gordon Walker called a unique 'capacity to cooperate'.[95]

In 1997 the Commonwealth Business Council (CBC) was set up to publicize, promote and exploit Commonwealth trade and investment networks for the benefit of the member countries. Thirteen of the world's fastest growing economies were in the Commonwealth, according to a Commonwealth Business Council newsletter of 2003, and it was said to be up to 15 per cent cheaper for any Commonwealth company to outsource business processing to another Commonwealth country. Ford and Katwala[96] in 1999 poured some cold water on such optimism by suggesting that the low awareness of the Commonwealth, particularly among the general public of its member states, meant that companies which might benefit from the 'Commonwealth factor' (namely, that all other things being equal, it was 10 to 15 per cent cheaper to do business within the Commonwealth) were hardly aware of the existence of the Commonwealth, let alone the possible advantages of the 'Commonwealth factor'. Even Katherine West retreated a little from her earlier positivism when she wrote,

> Of course ... neither the old nor the new Commonwealth has ever been a tightly integrated economic and political unit ... In today's world, Commonwealth countries engage in bilateral trade and investment relationships based on tough-minded and case by case assessments of comparative economic return ... such economic relationships have not been influenced by generalized loyalty to the Commonwealth.[97]

Lundan and Jones[98] in 2001 asked some pertinent questions. Is there a high propensity for members to trade and invest with each other? Does the Commonwealth add economic value? Do similarities lower the cost of 'foreignness'? They concluded that the 'Commonwealth factor' was more pronounced in foreign direct investment than in trade, and in that context, also more pronounced for first-time investors or exporters than for others. Further, it was only the small and less developed members that had a higher propensity to trade within the Commonwealth. They added that the Commonwealth link was useful for reducing knowledge-acquisition costs and could particularly help multi-national companies from developing member countries. This view was endorsed by William Bostock, who pointed out that the absence of linguistic trade barriers, where separate language identities have an economic transaction and opportunity cost, would undoubtedly facilitate commercial exchanges.[99] But such language ties and other linkages and traditions which add value for the Commonwealth act in a similar manner, of course, for the OIF, the CPLP and the OEI. And the Americans, who dominate the trends towards globalization in language as well as in economics, finance, culture and communications, can hardly be expected not to benefit from the widespread use of English and British traditions in the Commonwealth. This considerably diminishes the uniqueness and potential of the advantage which is claimed for the 'Commonwealth factor'.

In the early twenty-first century, total Commonwealth trade was about 20 per cent of global trade, but direct trade in 2003 with the other Commonwealth countries was only 9 per cent of Britain's total trade. Even that level of inter-action cannot be attributable entirely or even mainly to Commonwealth mechanisms. The highest percentages of intra-Commonwealth imports and exports occur in the trade figures for the least developed member countries, and the lowest for highly developed economies like those of Canada and the United Kingdom. Aid flows are determined on a bilateral basis or through the international financial institutions; in 1993–94, the House of Commons Foreign Affairs Committee Report noted that British bilateral aid to the Commonwealth was 38.5 per cent, down from 46.4 per cent of the total in 1992–93, the fall being due to greater contributions through multilateral institutions and concentration on the world's poorest countries. In 2002–03 this figure had further fallen to 26.4 per cent.[100]

Perhaps, in searching for a 'Commonwealth factor', the greatest economic benefit in Commonwealth membership is to be found in the diaspora of various ethnic groups in the former Empire, and the British-oriented background of various professional classes like doctors, architects and engineers, whose familiarity with Britain could induce them to make use of British consultants and order British equipment – but this too is not dissimilar to the advantages enjoyed by the other European colonial powers in their former dependencies, and of course, the United States worldwide.[101]

A new agenda for the old Commonwealth

Australia, Canada and New Zealand, the three countries which were the self-governing colonies of white settlement, were described as 'Dominions' to differentiate them from the other dependencies and to place them on a higher plane of association with the mother country.

They had fought shoulder to shoulder, and had suffered casualties, along with British troops in the second Boer war, and the first and second World Wars. As pioneer practitioners of the concept of full internal autonomy and founder members of the Colonial Conferences, the Imperial Conferences, the League of Nations, the United Nations and the modern Commonwealth, they comfortably hold the upper ground in the post-1947 Commonwealth, not least because of their familial and intimate ties with Britain. They are considered to practice the values that are supposed to characterize the Commonwealth, and with their longer experience in managing their own affairs and their greater diplomatic and economic resources than is the norm among the Commonwealth developing-country membership, they exercised a strong influence in the conduct and character of the evolving Commonwealth after 1947, including providing two of the four secretaries-general of the organization.

But there were of course manifestations of particular nationalisms and distinctive local variations. The growth of United States influence, especially in the Pacific theatre, and its growing preponderance in global political, economic, military and cultural areas, influenced changes in the world outlook of the three countries, even as they asserted themselves as middle-level powers with specialized experience and specific interests in their own neighbourhoods – the Australians and New Zealanders in the Pacific and the Canadians in the Caribbean. With the withdrawal of the British military potential from Asia and after changes in their trading patterns and the development of non-white immigration policies, the attitudes and actions of the three countries were not always in conformity with Britain's thinking. Australia had the self-belief to assume a new role with emphasis on an Asian identity, while New Zealand's diplomatic, political and economic reach was increasingly recognized as an influential factor among the islands of the Pacific. Canada with its close connections with the defence strategy and economy of the United States remained outside the Sterling Area, was able to use innovative diplomacy to find an exit policy for Britain after the Suez intervention, was sympathetic from the start to African nationalism and anti-racialist attitudes, and gave support to the African initiatives in the mid 1960s to create a Commonwealth Secretariat. Australia and New Zealand, American allies in ANZUS, participated on the ground in the Vietnam War, and Canberra was among the fiercest of Britain's critics over Macmillan acquiescing in South Africa's enforced withdrawal from the Commonwealth, London's desire to accede to the EEC, over the Commonwealth Immigration Acts of the 1960s, and Whitehall's decision to withdraw its military forces from South East Asia. Along with India, Australia was the initiator of the Commonwealth Heads of Government Regional Meetings (CHOGRMs) from 1978 to 1984, which was an effort to develop Commonwealth Asian regional cooperation independently of Britain – an attempt that was to prove unsustainable. Canada's membership of the other large post-colonial organization, La Francophonie, came about as a consequence of the Quebec question and provides a neat counter-point to its role in the Commonwealth. Ottawa introduced into the Francophonie elements derived from the Commonwealth such as a technical assistance programme, but its attempts to forge closer links between the Commonwealth and La Francophonie were less successful because the respective nature of the two organizations imposes definite limits on the potential for such cooperation.

Enjoying high standards of prosperity and living standards, the three countries, along with Britain, provide the bulk of the funding for the Commonwealth's activities and a large number of the consultants and expert advisers assigned by the Secretariat. All three countries make significant voluntary contributions to the Commonwealth's technical assistance budgets, although they do not generally regard the Commonwealth as an appropriate forum in which to formulate new ideas or launch new initiatives in development or economic policy. The Commonwealth Expert Groups, in vogue especially during Ramphal's tenure, which were think-tank studies to prompt international cooperation to meet contemporary challenges, did not enjoy their strong interest or support. Nor have they responded to an appeal in 1995 to restore the level of their donations towards development assistance to that of 1991–92 in real terms, although the amounts contributed by them to the Commonwealth are a small fraction of the total sums that they pledge to multilateral assistance or which are set aside for bilateral aid. In the Commonwealth, they pursue a somewhat doctrinaire approach to assistance projects, entertaining doubts about the value of 'demand-driven' proposals, in other words, those activities requested from the Secretariat by the recipient countries themselves. They prefer instead to increase allocations to those sectors and programmes that are given priority in their own bilateral development assistance programmes. Withdrawal of support by Australia or Canada for any Commonwealth programme can have severe effects, and, for example, the cessation of support by Canada for the Commonwealth Science Programme hastened its early demise. Small states' preoccupations are given a high degree of attention by all three countries, which is only natural considering the priorities of their immediate neighbourhoods and their 'near-abroads', while the

Commonwealth connection is considered an useful point of contact to enlist the support of the smaller states at a high political level on issues of importance to the three governments, particularly on the democracy and good governance agenda.

From the 1990s, new management theories and accountability seemed to dominate the thinking of these three major donors to the Commonwealth budgets. They successfully pressed, in the face of a somewhat bemused silence from the third-world members, for extensive reforms to, and reviews of, the Secretariat. Thus in rapid succession, the Secretariat was confronted with demands for multiple reviews by independent, mainly western, consultants, resulting in a variety of innovations; programme budgeting, gender monitoring, management of change, and impact assessments. Staff numbers were sharply reduced and the measure of governmental involvement and supervision in the administration of the Secretariat reached levels of micro-management that could hardly be justified in terms of the Secretariat's staff strength or financial resources. In addition, the three countries engaged in their own sundry national reviews of multi-lateral activity that called for the attention, time and responses of the Secretariat.

Within the last 18 years, each of the three countries has hosted a Commonwealth heads of government meeting; Canada in 1987, New Zealand in 1995 and Australia in 2002. Each country invested considerable political capital, human resources and prestige in these summits, and each was unhappily to be dominated by events that were unforeseen and by adverse developments in Africa. Two days into the conference at Vancouver in Canada, Fiji, which had earlier suffered a coup, became a republic and like South Africa several decades earlier, lost its Commonwealth membership not on account of its republican status, but because of that country's policies of racial discrimination. At the Canada gathering, the gulf between British policy and that of the old Dominions on South Africa became all too evident as Mrs Thatcher entered four reservations in five paragraphs dealing with sanctions against the Pretoria regime. At Auckland in New Zealand in 1995, a series of French nuclear tests in the Pacific shortly before the conference revived the horrors of weapons of mass destruction, and the French action was condemned by the 'overwhelming majority', a euphemism to cover Britain's refusal to go along with the consensus opinion of the meeting and a formula designed to obviate the need for John Major to record a formal reservation. But the conference was hijacked by another African issue, this time the draconian suppression of Ogoni opposition by Nigerian military dictator Sani Abacha. While consultations had been taking place in advance on the text of a Commonwealth initiative to promote the observance of good governance and the rule of law among its membership, it is rather doubtful if its passage at the conference in the form of the Millbrook Commonwealth Action Programme would have been as smooth as it turned out to be, if it had not been for the summary executions of nine Ogoni dissident leaders just at the start of the conference. This led to a strong mood of outrage and revulsion and resulted in the prompt suspension of Nigeria from Commonwealth membership. The Australian Commonwealth summit in 2002 at Coolum took place in the shadow of the terrorist attacks on the United States in September 2001, and had been postponed by a few months due to that tragedy. The outcome of this delay, however, was that there was a disconnect between the convention of the Commonwealth civil society community at Brisbane, which had been meticulously planned and was too far advanced to be postponed, and the summit of Commonwealth leaders which took place at a different and more secure venue some months later. On this occasion, the African issue that dominated the conference was the widespread concern about the rule of law in Zimbabwe. Mugabe did not attend the meeting but received support from some countries in Southern Africa, and the question was remitted to a *troika* of the leaders of Australia, Nigeria and South Africa. An opportunity to subject the Commonwealth to a searching analysis was lost at this meeting. A review of the organization at high governmental level had been contemplated, but in the end a wordy and pedestrian report submitted by a committee of officials was all that remained of the exercise.

Along with their zeal in reforming and supervising the Secretariat, all three countries from 1991 onwards set great store on the promotion among Commonwealth members of the principles of human rights, good governance and the rule of law. All have been members of the Commonwealth Ministerial Action Group, which was set up pursuant to the Millbrook decision, and have devoted robust attention and energetic participation to the working of this group. They were active in seeking to expand the guidelines for the group's future interventions, though no action has yet been possible under the terms of the extended mandate. They regard this group as the focal point when it comes to the Commonwealth's political values, and have high expectations of it; but when they ceased to be members of the group due to the practice of rotation, their interest in the Commonwealth as a whole seemed to flag.

Republicanism is growing in Australia and New Zealand, though it is not much in evidence in Canada. This trend is not likely to have any consequence on the relations of the three countries with either Britain or the Commonwealth. Consultations on Commonwealth matters between the three countries and Britain are close, constant and exclusive, and there is considerable coordination of positions before each important meeting, occasionally to the resigned consternation of the rest of the membership. As Adamson was to say, the Commonwealth 'was and remains essentially a two-tier organization divided on racial lines'.[102] None of the three countries see the Commonwealth as a gateway to global influence or economic opportunity, but with the sole exception of the United Kingdom, they will be the last to abandon the Commonwealth due to the overhang of history and tradition. They will without any doubt have a considerable stake and strong say in the future evolution of the Commonwealth.

The Commonwealth today – and tomorrow

The Commonwealth today

The potential for joint action

There is much which causes disappointment about the Commonwealth in action. As de Castro remarked, the Commonwealth has 'done better than not [sic] united by a sense of special togetherness' but relied on a 'perpetuation of symbols' like the position of the Crown, the common citizenship and the *inter se* doctrine, and because of the weakening of these over time, started to experience 'a sense of lethargy'.[103] It is rare indeed to find the Commonwealth capable of joint action in a common cause that is of contemporary relevance. On the contrary, as Miller stated, 'the Commonwealth in action ... is seen in a number of unrelated, and sometimes panicky, joint reactions to events and circumstances which seem to threaten some result which all the members of the Commonwealth are united in hoping will not happen'.[104] The Secretariat's Agreed Memorandum of 1965 appeared to recognize the futility of seeking joint action when it admits, 'nor does it [the Commonwealth] require its members to seek collective decisions or to take united action ...'. Therefore the Commonwealth's objectives are very different to those of the United Nations. The Secretariat tried from the mid 1960s to shift the emphasis from the international politics of the early years of the association to cooperative endeavour in development and the social sectors, recognizing that there was no common understanding on how to build cohesion within the Commonwealth or on how to extend its external influence. The association consequently became more inward looking and less capable of acting swiftly or decisively in the international political arena. The informal and voluntary nature of the civil society linkages between Commonwealth member states is claimed to be one of its greatest strengths but can hardly be regarded as a recipe or an alternative for joint governmental action.

From the early 1990s, with the end of the Cold War and the imminence of majority rule in South Africa, the Commonwealth shifted gears once more, and tried at its Harare and Auckland summits of 1991 and 1995 to develop a platform of good governance and human rights which would be generated and enforced among its members through encouragement, penalties and peer pressure. But it has proved difficult for the Commonwealth to play any role of substance with this new agenda because the member states bring to various issues their different starting points, interests and capacities, resulting in the lowest common multiple of agreement. The consensus principle by which the Commonwealth reaches its decisions presupposes that peer-group pressure can be significant. But peer-group pressure was unavailing on Britain when it came to Rhodesia and South Africa, and equally ineffective on recalcitrant members like Fiji, Pakistan and Zimbabwe between 1999 and 2003. What the Commonwealth can actually do in the real world seems to make little difference. The Commonwealth thus falls well short of playing any noteworthy operational role in major matters of multilateral political, economic or diplomatic concern. Activities like election observation, good offices, and consensus building are useful but by no means unique, and the results have not been uniformly beneficial. *The Times of India* in March 2002 tried to diagnose the malaise:

> The Commonwealth is founded on a unique principle of identity without reference to the political or ideological compatibility of its members. The principle simply is one of a voluntary reconciliation between Britain and almost all its decolonized territories under the auspices of an institution for collective cooperation. What has now come under severe strain is this notion of a binding principle … it is time the organization turned the spotlight on meaningful economic cooperation as a priority if not as a possible insurance against any potential irrelevance.[105]

On Zimbabwe, the most implacable opponents of the Mugabe government are Britain and the old Commonwealth, thereby polarizing a division along racial lines. This highlights the danger of attempting to formalize a more interventionist role for the Commonwealth and of seeking to promote good governance and democracy without the enforcement machinery to do anything concrete about it. The former threatens to split the Commonwealth while the latter merely shows up its inefficacy. The Commonwealth has held together a disparate membership, notwithstanding a certain similarity of legacies, by virtue of informality and some degree of fudge. So as Virginia Crowe shrewdly observed, 'to turn the Commonwealth from being a club to wielding a club is not appropriate'.[106] It is obvious that the Commonwealth will never achieve consensus on any member's domestic situation, and especially when such issues are far from resolved in the international community at large. The governance agenda, therefore, inevitably brings with it the seeds of division. The Commonwealth is unsuited to solving contentious disputes or to impose binding settlements. At the same time, through default or inaction, it also runs the risk of becoming a pliant legitimizer of undemocratic and unaccountable regimes, and turning a blind eye where regional, economic or other considerations appear more important.

Good governance

There was nothing about the legacy of British colonialism which particularly espoused human rights, though it might be put forward as an arguable generalization that the longer the colonial experience lasted, the better has been the human rights protection in the post-colonial period. The Commonwealth developing countries have done only slightly better than the third world, broadly defined. For example, seven Commonwealth member countries are to be found among the 21 highest-graded nations in Transparency International's 2003 black list for corrupt practices.[107] Many countries outside the Commonwealth have democratic values and institutions while many within the Commonwealth do not. It was possible for *The Times* in 1953 to pronounce that 'the only certain threat to Commonwealth unity would arise if a member deliberately pursued a policy, either internal or external, that put her outside the traditions of civilized conduct',[108] but it soon became impossible to argue that parliamentary and other democratic institutions in themselves constituted a sufficiently strong bond to hold the Commonwealth together, or even less, that the existence of the Commonwealth by itself guaranteed a continuation of the common values shared among the governing classes of the old Dominions. It is equally impossible to assert that common values pervade the various societies of the Commonwealth membership, or to imagine that the degree of common culture that the much smaller Commonwealth displayed until the late 1950s could remain constant. In practice, laudable institutions such as a free press, a non-political civil service, the independence of the judiciary and parliamentary democracy will continue to exist in several former British colonies irrespective of their relations with Britain or the future of the Commonwealth.[109]

An effort by the Commonwealth after 1995 to create a mechanism to monitor compliance with the expected standards of the organization as set out in the Harare Commonwealth Declaration of 1991 has fallen short of expectations. After winning some early credibility and kudos with regard to Nigeria, Sierra Leone and The Gambia, the activities of the Commonwealth Ministerial Action Group fell away when trying to deal with violations of the Harare principles in Pakistan, Fiji, the Solomon Islands and Zimbabwe. Attempts to define what was meant by 'serious or persistent violations' of those principles led to confusion and the customary difficulties in taking united action. Several member countries with serious and persistent democratic deficits have escaped censure, being either too significant or too insignificant, or with influential protection within the organization. The Commonwealth has no powers of mandatory implementation, no peacekeeping or intervention operational capability, and the instruments at its disposal are limited and blunt.[110]

In performing its good offices role, the Commonwealth has again enjoyed only limited success. In the past few years, Lesotho has been a successful intervention, but the organization's resources in personnel and finances are over-stretched and it cannot work effectively over the long haul. Therefore if it is able to achieve some early successes in any particular situation, it needs to give way at the appropriate time to other organizations or member states to consolidate these gains. Its inability to secure such effective follow-up activity has led to mixed outcomes in Tanzania–Zanzibar, Swaziland, the Solomon Islands, Guyana, Antigua/Barbuda, and elsewhere. Some special envoys, such as the one to Fiji between 2000 and 2004, have expended a great deal of time and resources with little or nothing to show for it. The association's activities in election observation have drawn praise, but the conundrum remains about how to deal with states whose election results are pronounced free and fair, but where the results are not upheld; and states where the election results are pronounced to be unrepresentative of the electorate's wishes, but where the results are allowed to stand nonetheless. This problem is not unique to the Commonwealth. A more specific matter is the extent to which members of the Secretariat are able to influence the final assessment and conclusions of Commonwealth observer groups. In the matter of race relations, the Commonwealth achieved a consensus, with the exception of Britain, on issues relating to the exclusion and oppression of the black African majority by the white minority regimes of South Africa and Rhodesia, but was unable to forge or sustain a common position against racism when it affected other ethnic groups across the Commonwealth.

As a mechanism for dispensing aid, the Commonwealth is of some significance to the newest and smallest members, and this factor may have been at least partially responsible for their enthusiasm in applying for membership. Many of the poorest countries, in monetary terms, receive more than they contribute to the organization, and what they receive, often on a demand-driven basis, is in the form of a grant and free from repayment, administration charges or conditionality. This is the area in which the 'comparative advantage' of the Commonwealth is most clearly in evidence. However, an unwelcome element of implicit conditionality is now being introduced, due to the increasing reluctance of the major donors to the CFTC to accept demand-driven draw-downs from the budget, and their growing insistence on greater allocations to sectors in which they place importance in their own bilateral programmes of Official Development Assistance (ODA), thereby making Commonwealth assistance play a supportive role to their own activities in the development field. A significant feature of this effort are the increasing allocations from the CFTC in the recent period to politically-related sectors, which would not have been allowed in the early years of the CFTC when the 'integrity of funds' was a hallowed principle.

To most Commonwealth member countries, issues of poverty and the difficult international economic environment are of the greatest concern. But it is hard to assert that either the industrial or the developing countries take the association's developmental role as agenda-setting; they do not consider Commonwealth activities in areas like education, health, science, women's affairs or youth to be a platform for policy or additionality. Can the Commonwealth act as a kind of sub-committee on north–south relations? It has made a contribution to the third world debt debate, largely by adopting British government initiatives that the organization then developed as a theme for consultations and consensus building. It has also vigorously promoted, since 1983, the cause of the security, development and prosperity of small states, understandable as a priority considering the composition of the membership of the Commonwealth, but essentially a subsidiary issue in the context of the reality of the world's power-equations both in their political and economic dimensions.

Nowadays, the Secretariat is of diminishing profile and significance. But since the Commonwealth has been Secretariat-centred after Britain surrendered its leadership in the mid 1960s, this tendency has induced the organization to drift towards the shadows. The internal debates on staffing, financing and managing the Secretariat all beg the fundamental question of the future of the Commonwealth as an organization. The quartet of highly developed countries tend to look upon the Secretariat as a laboratory for testing their often questionable theories of modern management, accompanied by incessant reviews and introduction of ever more consultants and new methods, with the predictable end-result of an accretion of uncertainty and inefficiency.

Self-assessment

David McIntyre claimed that 'the expanding post-Britannic Commonwealth ... remains the most noticeable part of the Imperial legacy after the English language and cricket'[111] but the *raison d'être* of the organization has been challenged by those like Ford and Katwala who in 1999 decried the Commonwealth's propensity to congratulate itself on diversity for the sake of diversity, on the growing number of its members, and on the facility provided for an exchange of north–south viewpoints, which were all, they claimed, of little practical value.[112] The Commonwealth Secretary-General in his Report of 1999 asked, 'can the Commonwealth ... turn the forces of globalization to support human advance? I believe it can. The expectation is that it will, possessing as it does endowments and experiences that well equip it for such a role'.[113] The Secretary-General in 2003 was equally forthcoming in his expectations of the organization. At the opening session of the Abuja Summit Conference, he declared, 'the success of this summit will lie, not in the words it generates, but in the impact it will have on people's lives. That is our mission in the Commonwealth. That is my objective as Secretary-General. And that is how we measure our success'.[114] Such categorical assertions strain credulity and could prompt the retort that if such absolute standards were indeed to be used, it might be difficult to avoid some negative conclusions. It is understandable that in articulating the organization's self-assessments and defining its objectives, its spokespersons are prone to over-praise its potential in an attempt to reverse the trend of receding interest and attention, but perhaps the Commonwealth protagonists would do better to take a leaf out of the CPLP's book and adopt a more modest approach.[115] But this has never been the Commonwealth's style.

The Commonwealth tomorrow

Background

Commentators have described it as misleading and a distortion to regard the present-day Commonwealth as a successor to either the British Empire and/or the British Commonwealth. Nevertheless, there is a historical past that accounts for its existence, though these antecedents do not necessarily bestow it with a current rationale or a work-plan. The British government's emphasis was always on continuity; on the seamless carry-over from the Empire to the Commonwealth. For a period the Commonwealth and the Empire existed side by side, and it took several years before possessive British imperialist attitudes and references to 'our Commonwealth' disappeared.

Peter Lyon wrote in 1999,

> Despite a current Commonwealth Secretariat-sponsored orthodoxy, the modern Commonwealth was not fully founded in 1949 ... In this currently fashionable ancient and modern version of Commonwealth history, decolonization, de-dominionisation, multi-racialism, an end to British-ness, perhaps a revised sterling area, as well as acceptance of republicanism, are all said or thought to have flowed from a particularly pregnant five days of discussions in London in late April 1949. This is another prominent example of the predominantly Whiggish way in which Commonwealth history is written or believed in by its votaries.[116]

Lyon's exegesis has considerable validity. The Commonwealth Prime Ministers Meetings of the 1940s and 1950s had closer parallels to the Imperial conferences than to the Commonwealth Heads of Government Meetings after 1971. At first the Commonwealth was an instrument for Britain to wield continuing influence in the post-colonial period. Later it took up racism as a *cause célèbre*. At present it is without any clear role, suffering from an absence of leadership, from divisions and resentments, including some of a racial nature; and dealing with the leftovers from the debates at the United Nations and other high tables. 'By 2003', wrote Austin, 'the job [getting rid of Empire] was done, and it now looks as if the new Commonwealth does not know what to do.'[117]

Arnold Smith had asserted an activist political role as the Commonwealth's first secretary-general, though the British government originally accepted the Secretariat on the basis that it would only pool and disseminate information and would not be an executive policy-making body. But Britain realized that the Secretariat would be the first step in decoupling the Commonwealth from British leadership. The United Kingdom's government had initially sought leadership, but eventually failing in consolidating that, became lukewarm about the Commonwealth. By the early 1970s, as the number of members in the association grew ever-larger, the priority given to the body in

Whitehall's foreign policy diminished rapidly. The enlargement of the Commonwealth with the admission of several new members liberated the thinking and the attitudes and voices of the members from the developing countries, undermined the stock of largely British ideas that had dominated the politics of the organization, and reduced in a very obvious manner the much vaunted aspect of the common heritage. In the process, Britain was also liberated from the Commonwealth since it felt increasingly free to pursue its own interests as the burdens of sentiment and obligation were removed. With Britain refusing to be pressurized by the Commonwealth majority and forthrightly asserting its independence from the organization, the process of its loss of influence continued. Much less was made of the common inheritance and shared values, and the presumed reservoirs of understanding based on history and sentiment were as much hostage to mutual suspicions as to exaggerated expectations.[118] In Commonwealth councils, Britain became regarded as a past leader rather than a predominant contemporary influence. Nevertheless, most sections of the British political establishment continued to embrace many of the nostalgic illusions about the Commonwealth and about Britain's role. They did not attempt to lead but neither did they ever contemplate trying to terminate the relationship.

After the 1980s, a decade during which there was increasing British scepticism and misgivings regarding the Commonwealth, came the end of the Cold War and apartheid in South Africa, the arrival into office of British prime ministers with more conciliatory views than Mrs Thatcher, and a summit in Edinburgh in 1997 on the centenary of Victoria's diamond jubilee and the Second Colonial Conference. There was some evidence of more involvement by the British government with Commonwealth affairs. In 1993 Foreign Secretary Douglas Hurd declared that 'we will get the most from the organization by working with the non-coercive, non-confrontational grain of its character, rather than by trying to turn it into a different type of creature'.[119] But Britain was still prepared to defy the strong feelings of the Commonwealth consensus when it found that its interests lay elsewhere. In 1973, just after Britain had joined the EEC, the British government had resisted New Zealand's efforts to condemn French nuclear testing in the Pacific. It did exactly the same in 1995, and chose to stand aside from the 'overwhelming majority' in the Auckland summit's final communiqué.

Political parties

In opposition, the main British political parties tend to be more pro-Commonwealth than when in power. Thus, when out of office in the early 1990s, Labour showed more enthusiasm for the Commonwealth than the government, and so do the Conservatives today. The party in power tends to encounter the realistic difficulties of working within the constraints of this unwieldy association and becomes sceptical or cynical, while continuing to pay lip service to the utility of the organization.

The Conservative Party's Commission on the Commonwealth in 2001 concluded that 'our strong conviction is that increased British involvement in helping the Commonwealth to maintain its relevance, into the twenty-first century, would be welcomed ... Britain as a leading member ... is well placed to help shape the future of this very diverse group of nations'. It goes on to recommend that Britain as the organization's chief progenitor should make it clear that it expects the Commonwealth to stand up to fellow members who do not meet their obligations freely entered into, and that 'an iron fist should be placed in the velvet glove of the Commonwealth'.[120] Former Foreign Secretary Rifkind in 2003 saw a role for the Commonwealth in promoting Middle East peace, for which purpose Israel, Palestine, Jordan and the United States should be enlisted as new members,[121] and shadow Foreign Secretary Ancram in the same year at Chatham House invoked the hackneyed 'three crucial circles' of the Transatlantic Alliance, Europe and the Commonwealth, and advocated a Politburo or Directorate for the association. He felt the Commonwealth should inspire as much awe as affection, and recommended that a 'powerhouse' of states be set up for that purpose.[122] This is a difficult concept, hard to sell to those countries outside the proposed charmed circle. As France's Premier Raymond Barre once said, 'What we need in Europe is a Directorate, provided we never admitted it exists.'

Official distance and distaste

In the first two decades after the Second World War and upto the formation of the Commonwealth Secretariat, British civil servants at the highest level, like Cabinet Secretaries Norman Brook and Burke Trend, had been intimately associated with the making of Commonwealth policy. But erosion was taking place, and the creation of the Secretariat deprived British senior officials of the status and prominence they had wielded in the organization. 'Since the launching of the Commonwealth Secretariat', wrote Lyon, 'British officials have, on the whole, deliberately sought to play rather low-key roles, in part in order to emphasize the point that they are actually no longer running the Commonwealth, or even trying to do so'.[123] To Whitehall officialdom, the Commonwealth was increasingly regarded as obstructing British interests and Burke Trend in 1968 described 'a kind of creeping disillusionment with the concept of the Commonwealth itself, both among the general public and in Whitehall'.[124] In 1978 *The Round Table* recorded that 'the reality is that Britain's current role in the Commonwealth is a model of self-effacement'.[125] According to Garner, the retention of the word 'Commonwealth' in the title of the Foreign and Commonwealth Office was to bear witness to Britain's continuing commitment to the organization.[126] But all the evidence points to the contrary. The Foreign Office was, and the upper reaches of the FCO still tend to be, ambivalent about the Commonwealth. The FCO's attention was on the big powers and the Cold War, and the Commonwealth was not at the top of anyone's list of priorities. Many in the British diplomatic hierarchy see little value in the Commonwealth; friendly cooperation does not fit into the same testing mould as the United Nations, NATO or the European Union. In an organization where symbols are important, the Secretary of State had decided in 1961 that Britain should be called by that name in the association – after all, it was part of a long tradition; it had been the British Empire and then for a time the British Commonwealth. But in 1999, a Foreign and Commonwealth Office minister addressed the Secretariat indicating that thenceforward Britain should be called 'The United Kingdom', in keeping with its appellation in other international bodies. Another break from history and another derogation from the 'uniqueness' of the Commonwealth.

The Commonwealth became constitutionally diverse and with the increasing membership came more freedom for the United Kingdom to pursue its own interests irrespective of any Commonwealth consensus. British officials considered that 'convenience and a certain degree of mutual understanding are all that one can hope for in such circumstances'.[127] The British government's policy, as noted in *The Round Table* in 1980, was to avoid taking initiatives 'which might be misinterpreted as an inherited or inborn imperial desire to lead and to guide.'[128] This caution further diminished the importance of the Commonwealth connection for Britain. There is now little investment in the Commonwealth politically, financially or in public awareness, and British and other leaders do not think of it as a suitable network to respond to big challenges. For example, when the British were lobbying for support for their position in the United Nations before the attack on Iraq in 2003, they did not trouble themselves to consult the Commonwealth as a grouping. Manifestly, neither the foreign policy nor the security nor the prosperity of Britain is in any way dependent on the Commonwealth. It is thus operating on the margins of British interests, but no elected government wants to be seen as dismantling the historic and traditional links.[129] So the choice between high-level attention and minimal concern has been made in favour of the latter. Derek Ingram of the Gemini News Service gave it as his view to the Foreign Affairs Committee of the House of Commons in 1995 that, 'Historically the Commonwealth is Britain's greatest contribution to the international community ... [but] ... today the Commonwealth has become almost a non-subject at Westminster.'[130]

An end to it all?

The benefits to Britain from the Commonwealth are enumerated as: the unrivalled networking opportunities; the expenditure by Commonwealth countries in London; the selection of British experts and consultants and training facilities; the inward flow of businessmen, investors and tourists; and English-language related offshoots such as the media, literature and the entertainment industry. But would these assets have needed a Commonwealth? Stephen Chan turned K.C.Wheare's aphorism of the late 1940s on its head by stating that if the Commonwealth did not exist, there would be no international compulsion to invent or reinvent it.[131] Certainly there would be no national compulsion in Britain either. For the common man, the break up of the Commonwealth would hardly matter. London's relations with the other three old Commonwealth members are not conducted institutionally but bilaterally, and no differences in the Commonwealth will affect the quality of their mutual economic or political relations. Adamson has written that the Commonwealth 'is in a state of decline which would be regarded as terminal if it were not for the fact that in British institutional life no one ever pulls the plug'.[132] Another explanation has been offered by Miller: 'There is a great deal of difference between making up your mind to leave something because you are not getting much out of it, and making up your mind to join something when you are aware that you will get very little out of it. In the first case all the force of inertia is at work against leaving.'[133] Ironically, it could be said that diminishing expectations have made the survivability of the Commonwealth easier.

David Adamson wrote of Mrs Thatcher and the Commonwealth, 'Mrs Thatcher's attitude towards the Commonwealth has been ambivalent – an unusual attitude for her. It arouses no enthusiasm, but she does not want it to fall apart, a development which would lead to her being accused of casting away Britain's inheritance through neglect and narrowness of vision.'[134] It would be regarded by the otherwise indifferent public as tantamount to selling the old family silver or losing the Crown jewels. The Queen clearly would not countenance it, and the government would not wish to confront the monarch on an issue that would seem to lack consequence. 'Great Britain is hardly recognisable as the Imperial Power that emerged from the Second World War ...', wrote Neillands, 'but certain international pretensions still remain, not least in the corridors of Westminster and Whitehall'.[135] And obviously, also at Buckingham Palace.

But the musing about the Commonwealth continues even in very high quarters. John Major asked, 'But if we don't keep using it, we shall eventually lose it. The Commonwealth needs a focus and a *raison d'être*. What should it be?'[136] That has remained the pertinent question. Can the Commonwealth develop a common understanding of how the new complexity of increasing international interdependence after the Cold War affects member states, and can it act to reduce global insecurity since that interdependence has increased the range of threats? Those in Britain who ponder the future of the Commonwealth can hearken both to optimistic and pessimistic opinion, even if the former is often couched in the customary exaggeration.

Virginia Crowe asserts that the Commonwealth 'could be a precisely appropriate organization for the new age dawning, bridging the old world and the new, east and west, north and south, rich and poor',[137] and Lord Thompson of Montifieth in the House of Lords in 1997 said of the Commonwealth, 'Simply because of its voluntary, flexible character, based on history and political and cultural links, it has a special potential, perhaps second to none, for a creative, dynamic contribution to global governance both within itself and as part of other regional and global institutions.'[138]

The Commonwealth Secretary-General's Report in 1999 stated that 'Because it [the Commonwealth] represents a principle that transcends narrow interests and divisions; because it works to translate the concept of our common humanity into living reality; and because it works for a more just and equal world in which the security of the vulnerable and the poor is assured, it represents hope in the world.'[139]

The opposition benches are more crowded. 'The Commonwealth', said *The Round Table* in 1970, 'is thus made up of national communities which are separate but similar. Above all, they all use English'.[140] This was a modest achievement to record for the new Commonwealth after over 20 years of existence, a point which was cuttingly made by a later chronicler, Niall Ferguson: 'What was wrong with the Commonwealth was not so much its declining economic importance to Britain as its growing political impotence. ... its only obvious merit being that it saves money on professional translators.'[141]

David Dilks claimed that 'the Commonwealth has been a political liability for every Prime Minister at some phase or other of his or her tenure',[142] and in May 2002, the director of the London-based think-tank Demos suggested that the Queen should embark on a world tour to apologize for the past sins of the Empire as a first step to make the Commonwealth more effective and relevant.[143] This is unlikely to happen. 'Here is the proverbial body', declared Simon Jenkins damningly in *The Sunday Times* on 22 October 1990, 'whose sole purpose is to look for a purpose'. A historian sums it up thus: 'I don't move much in Commonwealth circles ... but whenever I am placed among such people, I feel that I have been transplanted to a stately home, once splendid, now peeling, in which a much-loved elderly relative is dying inch by inch.'[144] Every brand needs to have a clear focus, a manifest sense of purpose and a distinct reason for being, criteria which the Commonwealth as an inter-governmental organization has ceased to fulfill.

Britain at the centre

The Commonwealth is the only international organization shaped by the British experience and the experience that other nations have had of the British. The 'British influence in the Commonwealth is pervasive and variegated', wrote Miller, 'being expressed not only in the political sphere but also in business, culture, education, language and institutions'.[145] Author and editor H.V. Hodson, in 1995, asserted that 'British culture, which is paramount among those of other sources in a multi-cultural Commonwealth, has a pervading Christian strain, manifest in language, literature, law, art, music, legend, ritual and much else. That is a fact which everyone has to recognize'.[146] Britain gave team games, once thought elitist, through the Empire/Commonwealth to the rest of the world. Compared to any other member Britain has the greatest contacts and affinity with all the other Commonwealth countries. The British government at first tried hard to modify its position from imperial ruler to equal partner, but the change did not always seem convincing. There was little lateral consultation between Commonwealth countries other than through Britain, and Britain was the key to everything. This situation may have moderated somewhat over the years but there continues to this day to be what may be called Britain's identitive focus in the Commonwealth. This is the sense in which Britain has never joined the Commonwealth; the organization was the outcome of British policy and not that of any other member. Whereas Britain can refer to its relations 'with the Commonwealth', other members speak of their relations with 'other members of the Commonwealth'. From the start, a characteristic of the association had been the tendency of all its members to regard the United Kingdom as the lodestar, the central point of orientation. Britain was and is the common denominator. As Adamson reported, 'What New Zealand, Sierra Leone and Belize have in common are their links with Britain. Without Britain the Commonwealth falls apart at once.'[147]

When Zimbabwe withdrew from the Commonwealth in 2003, its Foreign Affairs Permanent Secretary Didymus Mutasa said his country had joined the organization after independence in 1980, 'as a mark of respect to the British'.[148] In India, repeated cries were heard over the years in Parliament and the press for its withdrawal from the Commonwealth, but invariably on the basis of the current state of relations between India and Britain, whether over Kashmir, Suez, Goa, the Indo-Pakistan war of 1965 or immigration. The same applied to Pakistan, which withdrew in 1972 over Britain's recognition of Bangladesh and not over any general or specific Commonwealth issue as such. The Malaysians, enraged in the early 1980s by increased students' fees in Britain and restrictions on airline landing rights at Heathrow, introduced a 'buy British last' policy, and let it be known that they were contemplating leaving the Commonwealth. In every issue threatening the future of the Commonwealth – the Suez crisis, UDI, Tanzania and Ghana breaking diplomatic relations with London, arms sales to South Africa, sanctions against South Africa, Pakistan's withdrawal, the 1986 Edinburgh Commonwealth Games, Zimbabwe under Mugabe's rule – Britain has been centrally involved, and in the minds of the Commonwealth and other world leaders, Britain remained inextricably linked with the Commonwealth.

The Commonwealth Heads of Government Regional Meetings, an attempt at Asia–Pacific Commonwealth regionalism, which excluded Britain, were sponsored by the unlikely combination of India and Australia from 1978, mainly to avoid the entanglements of African issues in the normal Commonwealth meetings. This experiment stuttered to a halt in 1984 after only four meetings, having garnered neither sufficient funds nor sufficient enthusiasm to keep on convening.[149] When the Russians after the break up of the Soviet Union were designing a new association called 'The Commonwealth of Independent States' to reassert their primacy in the 'near-abroad' and protect their strong existing ties with the component parts of the former Union, they consulted only London about the *modus operandi* of their proposal, and not any other Commonwealth member country.

In the past there was reliance on Britain in all fields, but the presumption of British power and pre-eminence outlived the reality, and British proprietorial pride diminished over the years till the British-ness of the Commonwealth was not especially self-evident. But British nationals still hold the largest proportion of the positions in the Commonwealth Secretariat's staff-list, and Britain retains substantial Commonwealth infrastructure, mainly because there is no one else prepared to pick up the torch and attempt to revitalize the Commonwealth. Britain may not want a bigger part in Commonwealth affairs, even though the association is obviously related to British history, but no member will accept any one else's leadership. This fundamental truth was signalled by an unexpected source. In a submission to the Foreign Affairs Committee of the House of Commons in 1995–96, the Commonwealth Nurses Federation remarked that 'Britain's role in Commonwealth affairs is central; a Commonwealth without Britain and the unifying role of the monarchy would lose its focus. Commonwealth countries and bodies look to Britain for Commonwealth initiatives and leadership. This role could not easily be assumed by any other country.'[150] By 1980 the Commonwealth had come to terms with Britain's abdication of leadership. Because it no longer plays a hub role, Britain has nothing to fear from a weakening, or even break up, of the Commonwealth; it is no longer engaged in disburdening itself of Empire. Would the British government view with alarm the withdrawal of some or many of the members from the Commonwealth? Perhaps not, though the public perception, to the limited extent that it exists, is that its government is nevertheless central to, and more concerned about, the Commonwealth than are the other individual members, that the organization represents a remarkable and complex bond composed of history, obligation, sentiment, and prestige,[151] and that membership of the former colonies in it constitutes a latent symbol of gratitude to, and acknowledgement of, the former imperial power and majesty.

Can Britain again assume the leadership?

The Commonwealth was the inspiration for the French Union and the Community, and later, the Organisation de la Francophonie. It was one of the models for the Dutch–Indonesian Union, and the prototype of the Community of Portuguese-speaking countries. It served as a bridge between the Empire and the post-colonial period and afforded the British leadership the conviction that their country remained a world power. To the British people it gave the satisfaction that decolonization was following a well-ordered and pre-ordained process under benevolent British tutelage. But all that was in the past. At present the organization receives intermittent and low-level attention from the British government and not even as much as that from the British public. Those who recall its glory days are senior citizens. Those who have high expectations of its continuing relevance are more often than not frustrated. The Foreign and Commonwealth Office seems a misnomer. The community of Commonwealth states is considered capable of achieving little in addressing the international challenges of today, whether in bringing members deficient in human rights to book, or in alleviating poverty, improving the environment, educating the illiterate, or making the world a safer place from disease, terrorism or conflict. The Commonwealth falls between two stools; it is neither global with a universal following; nor is it regional, buoyed by local loyalties and able to engage in focused consideration of specific issues.

But the organization cannot yet be abandoned, even if its inactivity and apparent irrelevance are an occasional embarrassment. It is part of Britain's relatively recent historical past and is too closely associated with tradition and the position of the British monarchy. When Queen Elizabeth II was crowned, the Empire was still largely intact, and of the independent Dominions, only India had become a republic. Burma and Ireland were the sole exceptions in declining to join the new Commonwealth. If there was not this link with the monarchy, and if the Queen was not present at the summits, it is highly unlikely that any British prime minister would make the effort to attend the meetings. Since the British government cannot rid itself of the Commonwealth, it should consider the option of making some use of it, in the manner of France, Portugal and Spain in their respective post-colonial organizations. But any activist policy would carry some associated risks and will have to await the Queen's successor, and the probable absence of such strong attachments as the Queen currently shows towards the Commonwealth.

A new approach would be predicated on the premise that the British policy-makers see Britain as having a role to play in today's world; as a custodian of the values of democracy, good governance and human rights, as a flag-bearer for a new and equitable global political and economic order, and as being ready to invest the time and energy to provide leadership for those willing to follow. The premise equally rests on the British government having the will and the desire to lead, holding the conviction that its beliefs and institutions remain of value to other Commonwealth countries. This approach would require Whitehall to adopt a more assertive attitude, and to reverse the self-denying diffidence towards the organization that it has shown since prior to European entry. There would be prestige and practical value in leading a coherent like-minded values-based organization with a shared historical past. There is no country other than Britain that could aspire to leadership of the Commonwealth without strenuous challenge: any such proposition by Australia, Canada, India, Malaysia, Nigeria or South Africa would be considered pretentious, if not ludicrous, and be short-lived. It needs to be quickly added that there is no evidence at all to suggest that any of these countries, or for that matter any other member, would make a bid for leadership. There would certainly be some countries that would express reservations at the prospect of Britain overtly seeking to reassume its leadership of this organization, especially after the recent differences over Zimbabwe. There would be mutterings about neo-colonialism. Some countries, including perhaps some of the influential participants, could well withdraw their membership, but this should be considered no loss if the diminished numbers serve to make the Commonwealth more uniform in belief in a global value-system. The supportive would stay; the reluctant would leave. The smaller and more cohesive grouping would be an improved vehicle for united action. While the pieces on the old chessboard are no longer on the same squares, a post-modern Commonwealth could yet make a comeback to impress the Americans and the Europeans. There could be a return to the old collegiate informality between leaders and to succinct and meaningful communiqués. It would, finally, become the true 'modern Commonwealth', in a real break from the imperial past. There would be less stress on nostalgia, sentiment, exaggeration and the old order. There should be no demur from the Commonwealth civil society community, whose attempts to close the gap between themselves and inter-governmental Commonwealth activity have usually been met with condescension, indifference or even hostility. Their situation and the opportunities for their objectives would improve and perhaps even prosper.

A resumption of British leadership would also necessitate the restoration to Whitehall of many of the initiatives and powers surrendered to the Secretariat after 1965. Britain and some other countries have on occasion been frustrated by Secretariat actions that have drawn the organization into avoidable friction both within and outside the Commonwealth.[152] A remodelled Secretariat under an executive secretary entrusted with the sole task of carrying out the decisions of the previous summit would be an improvement on the present situation which is bereft of high-level political interest or inspiration. No country is prepared to stake a proprietorial interest in the organization. It has become nobody's Commonwealth.

Would it be worth the trouble for the British government to reassert its leadership of the Commonwealth? Is it not easier to let the somnolent

Commonwealth dogs lie, even if their occasional barks disturb the silence of neglect? The task may not in fact require so great an effort. It is obvious that Commonwealth consensus as presently constituted does not provide the cutting edge of policy formulation and decision-making. The installation of a Directorate or cabal would be contentious and would not work. Strong leadership is the only answer to re-invigorate the organization, and Britain is the only member-country whose leadership will be acceptable, if not to all, at least to the majority. It is the only country with strong and multifaceted links to all the other members, it is the only permanent member of the UN Security Council, and it has the greatest access to the world's only hyper-power, the United States. It is an acknowledged supporter of the developing world in the lobbies of the European Union and the World Trade Organization (WTO). A Commonwealth reduced in number to a compatible fellowship would be better than the disharmony over matters of principle that prevails at present in the so-called 'club'. It would put the Commonwealth back into the FCO, though a change of name for the new grouping should be considered in order to distance it from the colonial period and its more recent loss of reputation. The Commonwealth clock has to be turned back if it is not slowly to wind down to a complete halt.

Realistically however, is this scenario likely to appeal to British policy-makers? A Britain divided on the intensity of its links with Europe and to a lesser extent on the Trans-Atlantic Alliance is not likely to wish to add to its difficult international agenda an unwelcome revival of memories of Empire-building or influence-boosting among the former dependencies. The probable departure from the Commonwealth of some members with whom Britain enjoys substantial bilateral contacts would create an unnecessary controversy and the FCO, already wrestling with the problems of Islamic radicalism, Zimbabwe's travails and the lack of good governance and development in much of the Commonwealth third world, would demur at the prospect of possible new and debilitating public disagreements with Commonwealth developing countries. Assertion of leadership in the Commonwealth, howsoever easily acquired, would not be seen to justify the effort required to be expended on an organization ever more incidental to Britain's leading national interests. Therefore it is far more likely that in common with its approach to other bodies that have had their day, the preference in Whitehall will be to allow the cobwebs to collect over the association, allowing the sands of time eventually to disable the machinery. In the meantime, as in the comparable cases of the anachronistic Non-Aligned Movement and the Western European Union, attention to the Commonwealth and its works will be increasingly confined only to those involved in organizing its meetings and participating in them, and the media in the countries where such meetings take place. The rest of the world will have moved on.

If on the other hand, the option is for euthanasia, the *coup de grâce* will be simple enough to administer. If Britain stops attending Commonwealth meetings at high political level, and if Whitehall decides it can no longer provide over 30 per cent of the budget but wishes to be assessed, like all the other members, according to the UN scale, the organization can be counted upon rapidly to disintegrate. In a few years time, there will be nobody left to mourn its passing.

Notes

1 The Nehru Commonwealth

1. Dilks, *Great Britain, the Commonwealth and the Wider World*, p. 10.
2. Dilks, *Great Britain, the Commonwealth and the Wider World*, pp. 3–5.
3. Garner, *The Commonwealth Office*, p. 263.
4. Goldsworthy, *The Conservative Government and the End of Empire*, p. xxv.
5. *The Round Table*, no. 144, September 1946, p. 312.
6. *The Times*, 15 November 2002 and Ferguson, *Empire. How Britain Made the Modern World*, p. 339.
7. Darwin, *The End of the British Empire*, p. 18.
8. Porter and Stockwell, *British Imperial Policy and Decolonization*, vol. 1, p. 57.
9. Dilks, *Curzon in India*, vol. 1, p. 113.
10. Darwin, *Britain and Decolonisation*, pp. 92 and 97.
11. Mayall and Payne, *The Fallacies of Hope*, p. 18.
12. McIntyre, *British Decolonization*, p. 26.
13. McIntyre, *India. Ireland and the Headship of the Commonwealth*, p. 399.
14. Brown, *Nehru*, p. 252.
15. *The Times*, editorial, 2 June 1953. At this time, India was still the only republic.
16. *The Round Table*, vol. 50, 1959–60, p. 371.
17. *The Round Table*, no. 150, March 1948, p. 623.
18. *The Round Table*, no. 153, December 1948, p. 11.
19. A fuller treatment of South Asia and the Commonwealth is found in Krishnan Srinivasan's 'Lost Opportunities in South Asia', *Centre of South Asian Studies, Cambridge*, Occasional paper 5, 2003.
20. Mansergh, *Survey of British Commonwealth Affairs*, vol. 2, pp. 245–6.
21. McIntyre, 'India, Ireland and the Headship of the Commonwealth', p. 400.
22. Darwin, *Britain and Decolonisation*, p. 101.
23. Hyam, *The Labour Government and the End of Empire, 1945–1951*, p. xxv.
24. McIntyre, *The Commonwealth of Nations, Origins and Impact*, p. 442.
25. Hyam, *The Labour Government and the End of Empire, 1945–1951*, p. xxix.
26. Darwin, *Britain and Decolonisation*, p. 108.
27. For the simplified purposes of this study, the generic terms 'colony' or 'dependency' are normally used.
28. *The Round Table*, no. 150, March 1948, p. 520.
29. Miller, *The Commonwealth in the World*, pp. 53 and 58.
30. Garner, *The Commonwealth Office*, p. 320.
31. *The Round Table*, no. 156, September 1949, p. 396.
32. Porter and Stockwell, *British Imperial Policy and Decolonization*, vol. 1, p. 59.
33. Austin, *The Commonwealth and Britain*, p. 20.
34. Mansergh, *The Commonwealth Experience*, vol. 2, p. 167.
35. Mansergh, *Survey of British Commonwealth Affairs*, vol. 2, p. 368.
36. *The Round Table*, no. 183, June 1956, p. 218.

37. *The Round Table*, vol. 50, 1959–60, p. 371.
38. Darwin, *Britain and Decolonisation*, p. 154.
39. McIntyre, 'India, Ireland and the Headship of the Commonwealth', p. 403.
40. Goldsworthy, *Losing the Blanket*, pp. 5 and 103.
41. Porter and Stockwell, *British Imperial Policy and Decolonization*, vol. 2, p. 66.
42. Lyon, 'The Commonwealth in the 1970s', p. 174.
43. Stockwell, *Ending the Empire*, pp. 24–5.
44. Mansergh, *The Commonwealth Experience*, vol. 2, p. 160.
45. Miller, *Britain and the Commonwealth*, p. 189.
46. *The Round Table*, vol. 50, 1959–60, p. 339.
47. *The Round Table*, no. 153, December 1948, p. 11.
48. Miller, *Survey of Commonwealth Affairs*, p. 14.
49. Miller, *The Commonwealth in the World*, p. 275.
50. Goldsworthy, *Losing the Blanket*, p. 105.
51. Miller, *The Commonwealth in the World*, pp. 113–17.
52. Miller, *The Commonwealth in the World*, p. 116.
53. Lyon, '1949–1999: Fifty Years of a Renewing Commonwealth', p. x.
54. McIntyre, *British Decolonization*, p. 8.
55. McIntyre, *The Significance of the Commonwealth*, p. 17.
56. Miller, *The Commonwealth in the World*, pp. 278–85.
57. Adamson, *The Last Empire*, p. 34.
58. Porter and Stockwell, *British Imperial Policy and Decolonization*, vol. 2, p. 8.
59. Garner, *The Commonwealth Office*, p. 280.
60. Mayall and Payne, *The Fallacies of Hope*, p. 20.
61. *The Round Table*, no. 180, September 1955, p. 383.
62. Dilks, *Great Britain, the Commonwealth and the Wider World*, p. 31.
63. Mansergh, *The Commonwealth Experience*, vol. 2, p. 173.
64. Miller, *Survey of Commonwealth Affairs*, pp. 17–18.
65. *The Round Table*, vol. 52, no. 206, March 1962, p. 172.
66. Darwin, *Britain and Decolonisation*, p. 222.
67. Darwin, *The End of the British Empire*, p. 108.
68. Goldsworthy, *Losing the Blanket*, p. 5.
69. *The Round Table*, vol. 50, 1959–60, p. 337.
70. Porter and Stockwell, *British Imperial Policy and Decolonization*, vol. 1, p. 62.
71. *The Round Table*, vol. 45, no. 177, December 1954, p. 11.
72. Goldsworthy, *Losing the Blanket*, p. 99.
73. Hyam and Louis, *The Conservative Government and the End of Empire, 1957–1964*, p. xxxvi.
74. *The Times*, editorial, 2 June 1953.
75. *The Round Table*, vol. 54, no. 213, December 1963, p. 13.
76. *The Round Table*, vol. 56, no. 221, December 1965, p. 3.
77. Hyam and Louis, *The Conservative Government and the End of Empire, 1957–1964*, pp. xli and xliv.
78. Miller, *Survey of Commonwealth Affairs*, p. 363.
79. 'Third, they respect the right of all peoples to choose the form of government under which they will live; and they wish to see sovereign rights and self-government restored to those who have been forcibly deprived of them.'
80. Darwin, *Britain and Decolonisation*, p. 145.
81. Ryan and Pungong, *The United States and Decolonization*, p. 147.

82. Frey, Pruessen and Tan, *The Transformation of South East Asia*, p. 228.
83. *The Round Table*, vol. 37, no. 146, March 1947, pp. 105–6.
84. Darwin, *The End of the British Empire*, p. 69.
85. Adamson, *The Last Empire*, p. 59.
86. Ryan and Pungong, *The United States and Decolonization*, p. 173.
87. *The Round Table*, vol. 50, 1959–60, p. 299.
88. Adamson, *The Last Empire*, p. 53.
89. *The Round Table*, vol. 55, 1964–65, p. 105.
90. Mansergh, *The Commonwealth Experience*, vol. 2, p. 176.
91. Hyam and Louis, *The Conservative Government and the End of Empire, 1957–1964*, p. lxi.
92. Porter and Stockwell, *British Imperial Policy and Decolonization*, vol. 2, p. 16.
93. Mansergh, *The Commonwealth Experience*, vol. 2, p. 171.
94. Eayrs, *The Commonwealth and Suez*, p. 15.
95. Mansergh, *The Commonwealth Experience*, vol. 2, p. 235.
96. Mansergh, *The Commonwealth Experience*, vol. 2, p. 172.
97. Darwin, *Britain and Decolonisation*, p. 227.
98. Morris, *Farewell the Trumpets*, p. 530.
99. *The Round Table*, vol. 63, no. 252, October 1973, p. 415.
100. Darwin, *The End of the British Empire*, pp. 121–2.
101. Heffer, *Like the Roman. The Life of Enoch Powell*, p. 249.
102. Darwin, *Britain and Decolonisation*, p. 217.
103. McIntyre, *British Decolonization*, p. 53.

2   The African Commonwealth

1. Darwin, *The End of the British Empire*, p. 87.
2. Lyon, 'The Commonwealth in the 1970s', p. 175.
3. *The Round Table*, vol. 72, no. 285, January 1983, p. 6.
4. McIntyre, *British Decolonization*, p. 36.
5. McIntyre, *British Decolonization*, p. 108.
6. *The Round Table*, vol. 43, December 1952 to September 1953, p. 360.
7. *The Round Table*, vol. 46, no. 181, December 1955, p. 26.
8. *The Round Table*, vol. 46, no. 183, June 1956, p. 219.
9. McIntyre, *The Commonwealth of Nations, Origins and Impact*, p. 442.
10. Hyam and Louis, *The Conservative Government and the End of Empire, 1957–1964*, pp. xxxiv–xxxv.
11. Darwin, *Britain and Decolonisation*, p. 189.
12. Hyam and Louis, *The Conservative Government and the End of Empire, 1957–1964*, p. xxviii.
13. Hyam and Louis, *The Conservative Government and the End of Empire, 1957–1964*, p. xlviii.
14. *The Round Table*, vol. 52, no. 206, March 1962, p. 173.
15. McIntyre, *Colonies into Commonwealth*, p. 251.
16. Miller, *Survey of Commonwealth Affairs*, p. 117.
17. Miller, *Survey of Commonwealth Affairs*, p. 123.
18. Garner, *The Commonwealth Office*, p. 375.
19. *The Round Table*, vol. 50, 1959–60, p. 299.

20. McIntyre, *British Decolonization*, p. 120.
21. Garner, *The Commonwealth Office*, p. 350.
22. Miller, *Survey of Commonwealth Affairs*, p. 158.
23. Mansergh, *The Commonwealth Experience*, vol. 2, p. 186.
24. *The Round Table*, vol. 51, no. 203, June 1961, p. 223.
25. Ashton and Louis, *East of Suez and the Commonwealth, 1964–1971*, p. xxxi.
26. Miller, *Survey of Commonwealth Affairs*, p. 164.
27. McIntyre, *Colonies into Commonwealth*, p. 323.
28. Adamson, *The Last Empire*, p. 2.
29. McIntyre, *The Significance of the Commonwealth*, p. 123.
30. McIntyre, *The Significance of the Commonwealth*, p. 122.
31. McIntyre, *The Significance of the Commonwealth*. p. 63.
32. Hyam and Louis, *The Conservative Government and the End of Empire, 1957–1964*, p. xxx.
33. *The Round Table*, vol. 43, December 1952 to September 1953, p. 228.
34. Southern Rhodesia was represented at the 1930 and 1937 Imperial Conferences, with its observer status in the latter slightly enhanced over the 1930 arrangements.
35. *The Round Table*, vol. 54, no. 216, September 1964, p. 324.
36. McIntyre, *A Guide to the Contemporary Commonwealth*, p. 23.
37. Kirkman, *Unscrambling the Empire*, p. 181.
38. Garner, *The Commonwealth Office*, p. 351.
39. Kirkman, *Unscrambling the Empire*, p. 185.
40. Garner, *The Commonwealth Office*, p. 390.
41. McIntyre, *A Guide to the Contemporary Commonwealth*, p. 36.
42. Miller, *Survey of Commonwealth Affairs*, p. 226.
43. McIntyre, *The Significance of the Commonwealth*, p. 29.
44. Miller, *Survey of Commonwealth Affairs*, p. 230.
45. Miller, *Survey of Commonwealth Affairs*, p. 237.
46. McIntyre, *The Significance of the Commonwealth*, p. 30.
47. McIntyre, *Colonies into Commonwealth*, p. 323.
48. Mansergh, *The Commonwealth Experience*, vol. 2, p. 194.
49. Darwin, *Britain and Decolonisation*, p. 317.
50. Ashton and Louis, *East of Suez and the Commonwealth, 1964–1971*, p. lxxx.
51. Darwin, *Britain and Decolonisation*, p. 322.
52. McIntyre, *A Guide to the Contemporary Commonwealth*, p. 37.
53. Mansergh, *The Commonwealth Experience*, vol. 2, p. 199.
54. Adamson, *The Last Empire*, p. 22.
55. *The Round Table*, vol. 71, no. 284, October 1981, p. 335.
56. Mansergh, *The Commonwealth Experience*, vol. 2, p. 176.
57. McIntyre, *The Commonwealth of Nations, Origins and Impact*, p. 444.
58. *The Round Table*, vol. 50, 1959–60, p. 337.
59. Miller, *Survey of Commonwealth Affairs*, p. 355.
60. Judd and Slinn, *The Evolution of the Modern Commonwealth*, p. 96.
61. Goldsworthy, *Losing the Blanket*, p. 111.
62. Lyon, 'The Commonwealth in the 1970s', p. 175.
63. Mansergh, *The Commonwealth Experience*, vol. 2, p. 194.
64. McIntyre, *A Guide to the Contemporary Commonwealth*, p. 70.
65. Garner, *The Commonwealth Office*, p. 340.

166 *Notes*

66. McIntyre, *British Decolonization*, p. 94.
high67. Darwin, *Britain and Decolonisation*, p. 334.
high68. *The Round Table*, vol. 57, 1967, p. 154.
high69. Brown and Louis, *Oxford History of the British Empire volume IV*, p. 330. The figures are unsound but the general argument is telling.
high70. Mansergh, *The Commonwealth Experience*, vol. 2, p. 254.
high71. Mansergh, *The Commonwealth Experience*, vol. 2, p. 188–9.
high72. *The Round Table*, vol. 64, no. 253, January 1974, p. 111.
high73. McIntyre, *Colonies into Commonwealth*, p. 345.
high74. *The Round Table*, vol. 57, no. 225, 1967, p. 48.
high75. Lyon, 'The Commonwealth in the 1970s', p. 179.
high76. *The Round Table*, vol. 59, 1969, p. 310.
high77. McIntyre, *The Commonwealth of Nations, Origins and Impact*, pp. 460 and 474.
high78. Oral History Interview, 30 June 1971. Harry S. Truman Library, Independence, Missouri.
high79. Miller, *Survey of Commonwealth Affairs*, p. 434.
high80. Holland, *The Decolonizing Metropole*, p. 65.
high81. Austin, *The Commonwealth and Britain*, p. 45.
high82. McIntyre, *Colonies into Commonwealth*, pp. 327–9.
high83. Miller, *The Commonwealth in the World*, p. 262.
high84. Darwin, *The End of the British Empire*, p. 43.
high85. Ferguson, *Empire. How Britain Made the Modern World*, p. 352.
high86. McIntyre, *Colonies into Commonwealth*, p. 330.
high87. Austin, *The Commonwealth and Britain*, p. 22.
high88. Darwin, *Britain and Decolonisation*, p. 129.
high89. Hyam, *The Labour Government and the End of Empire, 1945–1951*, p. xxiii.
high90. McIntyre, *British Decolonization*, p. 87.
high91. Ferguson, *Empire. How Britain Made the Modern World*, p. 354.
high92. Porter and Stockwell, *British Imperial Policy and Decolonization*, vol. 2, p. 32.
high93. Louis and Robinson, *The Imperialism of Decolonization*, p. 479.
high94. Mansergh, *The Commonwealth Experience*, vol. 2, p. 196.
high95. Goldsworthy, *Losing the Blanket*, p. 135.
high96. *The Round Table*, no. 340, October 1996, pp. 481 and 490.
high97. *The Round Table*, vol. 57, 1966–67, number 225, p. 18.
high98. McIntyre, *The Commonwealth of Nations, Origins and Impact*, p. 461.
high99. Ryan and Pungong, *The United States and Decolonization*, p. 126.
high100. *The Round Table*, vol. 53, December 1962–September 1963, p. 21; and vol. 56, December 1965–October 1966, p. 365.
high101. Miller, *Survey of Commonwealth Affairs*, p. 462.
high102. Darwin, *The End of the British Empire*, p. 50.
high103. Ashton and Louis, *East of Suez and the Commonwealth, 1964–1971*, p. lxv.
high104. *The Round Table*, vol. 61, no. 244, October 1971, p. 444.
high105. *The Round Table*, vol. 58, no. 229, 1968, p. 36.
high106. Ferguson, *Empire. How Britain Made the Modern World*, p. 354.
high107. Darwin, *Britain and Decolonisation*, p. 324.
high108. Darwin, *Britain and Decolonisation*, p. 308.
high109. Miller, *Survey of Commonwealth Affairs*, pp. 522 and 525.
high110. Darwin, *Britain and Decolonisation*, p. 234.
high111. Ashton and Louis, *East of Suez and the Commonwealth, 1964–1971*, p. xxxvi.

112. Darwin, *The End of the British Empire*, p. 81.
113. Lyon, 'Commonwealth Sense and Sentiment', p. 100.
114. Darwin, *Britain and Decolonisation*, p. 324.
115. Darwin, *Britain and Decolonisation*, pp. 299–302.
116. Darwin, *Britain and Decolonisation*, p. 324.
117. Mansergh, *The Commonwealth Experience*, vol. 2, p. 199.
118. Lyon, 'The Commonwealth in the 1970s', p. 182.
119. *The Round Table*, vol. 52, no. 207, June 1962, p. 227.
120. Statistics in this chapter draw *inter alia* on McIntyre, *Colonies into Commonwealth*, pp. 331–4;. Morris, *Farewell the Trumpets*, p. 24, Ferguson, *Empire. How Britain Made the Modern World*, p. 113; Parekh, *Report on the Future of Multi-Ethnic Britain*, p. 375 and Hitchcock, *The Struggle for Europe*, pp. 413–20.
121. Migration Watch UK internet website, briefing paper History number 6.2, 10 August 2001.
122. Bourne, *Britain in the Commonwealth*, p. 17.
123. Ward, *British Culture and the End of Empire*, p. 183.
124. Porter and Stockwell, *British Imperial Policy and Decolonization*, vol. 2, p. 76.
125. Porter and Stockwell, *British Imperial Policy and Decolonization*, vol. 2, p. 77.
126. Hitchcock, *The Struggle for Europe*, pp. 413–414.
127. Mansergh, *Survey of British Commonwealth Affairs*, vol. 2, p. 303.
128. McIntyre, *The Significance of the Commonwealth*, p. 89.
129. Porter and Stockwell, *British Imperial Policy and Decolonization*, vol. 2, p. 77.
130. *The Round Table*, number 206, March 1962, p. 120.
131. Garner, *The Commonwealth Office*, p. 322.
132. Heffer, *Like the Roman. The Life of Enoch Powell*, p. 451.
133. McIntyre, *The Commonwealth of Nations*, p. 467.
134. *The Round Table*, vol. 61, no. 242, April 1971, p. 291.
135. McIntyre, *The Significance of the Commonwealth*, p. 92.
136. Adamson, *The Last Empire*, p. 165.
137. *The Round Table*, no. 358, January 2001, p. 92.
138. Morris, *The Times*, 7 May 2002.
139. *The Times*, 17 August 2003.
140. Adamson, *The Last Empire*, p. 159. An astounding figure of 300,000 Australians working in Britain 'at any one time' according to the Australian High Commission quoted in *The Times* of 9 November 2004 is not a subject of debate or controversy.
141. *The Round Table*, vol. 75, no. 298, April 1986, p. 107.

3   Some Other 'Commonwealths'

1. Bostock, *Assessing the authenticity of a supra-national language-based movement – la Francophonie*, p. 3.
2. Therien, 'Cooperation and Conflict in la Francophonie', p. 497.
3. Bostock, *Assessing the authenticity of a supra-national language-based movement – la Francopohnie*, p. 14.
4. Ager, *Francophonie in the 1990s, Problems and Opportunities*, p. 61.
5. Bostock, *Assessing the authenticity of a supra-national language-based movement – la Francophonie*, p. 5.

6. Ager, *Francophonie in the 1990s, Problems and Opportunities*, p. 177.
7. Ager, *Francophonie in the 1990s, Problems and Opportunities*, pp. 73–5.
8. Bostock, *Francophonie; Organisation, Coordination, Evaluation*, p. 26.
9. Ager, *Francophonie in the 1990s, Problems and Opportunities*, p. 113.
10. Therien, 'Cooperation and Conflict in la Francophonie', p. 509.
11. de Castro, 'The Community of the Portuguese Speaking Countries', p. 123.
12. *The Round Table*, no. 142, March 1946, p. 161.
13. Ryan and Pungong, *The United States and Decolonization*, p. 125.
14. Doolan, 'Time for Dutch Courage in Indonesia', p. 3.
15. *Media Monitor*, 10 October 2003.
16. Commonwealth Secretariat Press Release 5 December 2003.
17. *Encyclopedia of Public International Law*, vol. 10, p. 35.
18. Heffer, *Like the Roman. The Life of Enoch Powell*, pp. 37 and 98. Powell called India 'the most striking frontispiece of Empire' ... 'a shared hallucination between the rulers and the ruled'.

4   Nobody's Commonwealth?

1. Ferguson, *Empire. How Britain Made the Modern World*, p. 249.
2. McIntyre, 'India, Ireland and the Headship of the Commonwealth', p. 400.
3. Heffer, *Like the Roman. The Life of Enoch Powell*, pp. 184 and 883.
4. *The Times*, editorial, 2 June 1953.
5. *The Round Table*, vol. 73, no. 292, October 1984, pp. 360–6.
6. Adamson, *The Last Empire*, p. 117.
7. Darwin, *Britain and Decolonisation*, p. 327.
8. BBC News internet website, 21 September 2003.
9. Mansergh, *Survey of British Commonwealth Affairs*, vol. 2, p. 252.
10. Coolum Commonwealth Heads of Government Meeting (Chogm), internet website, 2002.
11. Garner, *The Commonwealth Office*, p. 356.
12. McIntyre, *A Guide to the Contemporary Commonwealth*, p. 61.
13. *The Round Table*, no. 369, April 2003, pp. 221–33.
14. McIntyre, *Colonies into Commonwealth*, p. 5.
15. Morris, *Farewell the Trumpets*, pp. 24 and 29.
16. Parekh, *A Report on the Future of Multi-Ethnic Britain*, p. 21.
17. Brown and Louis, 'The Twentieth Century', p. 217.
18. Morris, *Farewell the Trumpets*, p. 30.
19. Louis and Robinson, 'The Imperialism of Decolonization', p. 464.
20. Morris, *Farewell the Trumpets*, p. 474.
21. Morris, *Farewell the Trumpets*, p. 474.
22. Morris, *Farewell the Trumpets*, p. 497.
23. Brown and Louis, 'The Twentieth Century', p. 225.
24. McIntyre, *The Commonwealth of Nations*, pp. 462–3.
25. Heffer, *Like the Roman. The Life of Enoch Powell*, p. 916.
26. Neillands, *A Fighting Retreat*, pp. 41–2.
27. Darwin, *The End of the British Empire*, pp. 51–3.
28. Mansergh, *The Commonwealth Experience*, vol. 2, p. 241.
29. Brown and Louis, 'The Twentieth Century', p. 252.

30. Morris, *Farewell the Trumpets*, p. 497.
31. Miller, *The Commonwealth in the World*, p. 249.
32. Porter and Stockwell, *British Imperial Policy and Decolonization*, vol. 2, p. 69.
33. Miller, *The Commonwealth in the World*, p. 252.
34. Miller, *Survey of Commonwealth Affairs*, p. 505.
35. *The Round Table*, vol. 57, no. 225, 1967, p. 55.
36. Judd and Slinn, *The Evolution of the Modern Commonwealth*, p. 13.
37. Morris, *Farewell the Trumpets*, p. 501.
38. Ward, *British Culture and the End of Empire*, pp. 51–3.
39. Miller, *Survey of Commonwealth Affairs*, p. 506.
40. *The Round Table*, vol. 63, no. 251, July 1973, p. 368.
41. McIntyre, *British Decolonization*, p. 81.
42. Garner, *The Commonwealth Office*, p. 343.
43. *The Round Table*, vol. 60, n. 240, October 1970, p. 379.
44. Darwin, *The End of the British Empire*, p. 29.
45. Holland, *The Decolonizing Metropole*, p. 66.
46. Darwin, *The End of the British Empire*, p. 31.
47. Adamson, *The Last Empire*, p. 17.
48. Dilks, *Communications, the Commonwealth and the Future*, p. 5.
49. *The Round Table*, vol. 73, no. 289, January 1984, p. 7.
50. Bahamas, Belize, Guyana and Trinidad and Tobago opposed US intervention, as did the United Kingdom. But Barbados, Jamaica and the Organization of Eastern Caribbean States supported it.
51. Parekh, *A Report on the Future of Multi-Ethnic Britain*, p. 24.
52. Darwin, *Britain and Decolonisation*, p. 328.
53. Doxey, *The Commonwealth Secretariat and the Contemporary Commonwealth*, p. 10.
54. *The Round Table*, vol. 79, no. 316, October 1990, p. 369.
55. Adamson, *The Last Empire*, p. 34.
56. James Mayall quoted in *Commonwealth and Comparative Politics*, vol. 39, no. 3, November 2001, p. 4.
57. House of Commons, *The Future Role of the Commonwealth*, vol. 1, p.xliii.
58. *The Round Table*, vol. 59, 1969, pp. 170–1.
59. Sir David Steel, Speaker of the Scottish Parliament, in his Commonwealth Day Lecture, 2001, half-jokingly said: 'there was no such thing as the British Empire; it was a Scottish Empire on to which the English attached themselves.'
60. McIntyre, *The Significance of the Commonwealth*, p. 22.
61. Bourne, *Britain in the Commonwealth*, p. 13.
62. See supra chapter 4, p. 123 and Ward, *British Culture and the End of Empire*, p. 128.
63. *The Round Table*, vol. 66, no. 262, April 1976, pp. 117–19.
64. *The Round Table*, vol. 72, no. 285, January 1983, pp. 3–5.
65. *The Round Table*, vol. 79, no. 315, July 1990, p. 264.
66. Morris, *Farewell the Trumpets*, p. 500.
67. *The Times*, editorial, 2 June 1953.
68. *The Round Table*, vol. 84, no. 334, April 1995, p. 191.
69. *The Round Table*, vol. 64, no. 256, October 1974, p. 366.
70. Miller, *The Commonwealth in the World*, p. 303.
71. Adamson, *The Last Empire*, p. 130.
72. *The Round Table*, no. 183, June 1956, p. 220.

73. House of Commons, *The Future Role of the Commonwealth*, vol. 11, p. 204, Dr John Wood's submission.
74. Steel, Commonwealth Day Lecture, 2001.
75. West, *Economic Opportunities for Britain and the Commonwealth*, p. 9.
76. Jenkins, 'Reassessing the Commonwealth', p. 22.
77. House of Commons, *The Future Role of the Commonwealth*, vol. 1, p. xxxvi.
78. Dilks, *Communications, the Commonwealth and the Future*, p. 11.
79. House of Commons, *The Future Role of the Commonwealth*, vol. 1, p. v.
80. House of Commons, *The Future Role of the Commonwealth*, vol. 1, p. lxi.
81. House of Commons, *The Future Role of the Commonwealth*, vol. 1, p. xviii.
82. House of Commons, *The Future Role of the Commonwealth*, vol. 1, pp. lx–lxi.
83. House of Commons, *The Future Role of the Commonwealth*, vol. 1, p. lxi.
84. House of Commons, *The Future Role of the Commonwealth*, Minutes of Evidence, pp. 143–4.
85. House of Commons, *The Future Role of the Commonwealth*, vol. 1, p. v.
86. House of Commons, *The Future Role of the Commonwealth*, Minutes of Evidence, p. 145.
87. House of Commons, *The Future Role of the Commonwealth*, vol. II, p. 292.
88. House of Commons, *The Future Role of the Commonwealth*, vol. II, pp. 88–91.
89. House of Commons, *The Future Role of the Commonwealth*, vol. II, p. 124.
90. House of Commons, *The Future Role of the Commonwealth*, vol. II, pp. 127–31.
91. House of Commons, *The Future Role of the Commonwealth*, vol. II, pp. 181–2.
92. House of Commons, *The Future Role of the Commonwealth*, vol. II, pp. 265–6.
93. House of Commons, *The Future Role of the Commonwealth*, vol. 1, p. xxiv; and West, *Economic Opportunities for Britain and the Commonwealth*, p. 39.
94. House of Commons, *The Future Role of the Commonwealth*, vol. 1, p. xxvii.
95. West, *Economic Opportunities for Britain and the Commonwealth*, pp. 22, 27, 39.
96. Ford and Katwala, 'Reinventing the Commonwealth', p. 10.
97. West, *Economic Opportunities for Britain and the Commonwealth*, p. 25.
98. Lundan and Jones, 'The Commonwealth Effect', pp. 102–16.
99. Bostock, *Francophonie: Organisation, Coordination, Evaluation*, p. 108.
100. House of Commons, *The Future Role of the Commonwealth*, vol. 1, pp. xxviii–xxix; and the internet website of the Department for International Development.
101. Miller, *Britain and the Commonwealth*, p. 200.
102. Adamson, *The Last Empire*, p. 53.
103. de Castro, 'The Community of the Portuguese Speaking Countries', pp. 268 and 294.
104. Miller, *The Commonwealth in the World*, p. 255.
105. *The Times of India*, editorial, 27 March 2002.
106. Crowe, 'The Commonwealth in a Changing World', p. 23.
107. Transparency International's internet website.
108. *The Times*, editorial, 2 June 1953.
109. Miller, *The Commonwealth in the World*, pp. 260–1.
110. A more detailed treatment of this subject is found in Krishnan Srinivasan's 'Complaisance or Compliance with Commonwealth Principles?', *The Commonwealth and Comparative Politics*, vol. 41, no. 3, November 2003.
111. Brown and Louis, 'The Twentieth Century', p. 702.

112. Ford and Katwala, 'Reinventing the Commonwealth', pp. 2–3.
113. Commonwealth Secretary-General's Report, 1999, p. 21.
114. Commonwealth Secretariat Press Release, 5 December 2003.
115. See supra chapter 3, p. 95.
116. Lyon, '1949–1999: Fifty Years of a Renewing Commonwealth', editorial, *The Round Table*, no. 350, April 1999, p. i.
117. Austin, *The Round Table*, no. 376, September 2004, p. 620.
118. Austin, 'The Commonwealth and Britain', p. 16.
119. *The Round Table*, vol. 83, no. 329, January 1994, p. 21.
120. Cluff, *A Future for the Commonwealth*, pp. 2 and 7.
121. *The Times*, 11 April 2003.
122. Ancram, 'After Zimbabwe, has the Commonwealth still got a purpose?', Chatham House lecture, 5 February 2003.
123. Lyon, 'Commonwealth Sense and Sentiment', p. 100.
124. Garner, *The Commonwealth Office*, p. 373.
125. *The Round Table*, vol. 68, no. 271, July 1978, p. 270.
126. Garner, *The Commonwealth Office*, p. 430.
127. Miller, *The Commonwealth in the World*, p. 303.
128. *The Round Table*, vol. 70, no. 277, January 1980, p. 14.
129. Austin, 'The Commonwealth and Britain', p. 47.
130. House of Commons, *The Future Role of the Commonwealth*, vol. II, pp. 243–5.
131. McIntyre, *The Significance of the Commonwealth*, p. 22.
132. Adamson, *The Last Empire*, p. 1.
133. Miller, *The Commonwealth in the World*, p. 284.
134. *The Round Table*, vol. 79, no. 313, January 1990, p. 5.
135. Neillands, *A Fighting Retreat*, p. 559.
136. West, *Economic Opportunities for Britain and the Commonwealth*, epigraph.
137. Crowe, 'The Commonwealth in a Changing World', p. 1.
138. Steel, Commonwealth Day Lecture, 2001.
139. Commonwealth Secretary-General's Report, 1999, p. 24.
140. *The Round Table*, vol. 60, no. 240, October 1970, p. 377.
141. Ferguson, *Empire. How Britain Made the Modern World*, pp. 354–5.
142. Dilks, *Communications, the Commonwealth and the Future*, p. 6.
143. Ferguson, *Empire. How Britain Made the Modern World*, p. xiii.
144. Dilks, correspondence with the author, October 2004.
145. Miller, *The Commonwealth in the World*, p. 299.
146. *The Round Table*, vol. 84, no. 333, January 1995, p. 91.
147. Adamson, *The Last Empire*, p. 1.
148. BBC News, internet Online, 10 December 2003.
149. CHOGRMs, Sydney: 13–16 February 1978; New Delhi: 4–8 September 1980; Suva: 14–18 October 1982; and Port Morseby: 8 August 1984.
150. House of Commons, *The Future Role of the Commonwealth*, vol. II, p. 191.
151. Adamson, *The Last Empire*, p. 175.
152. In 2003, for example, the BBC World Service reported that the United Kingdom had criticized Secretariat officials as being 'unhelpful' by instigating developing countries to adopt protectionist and anti-free market policies, apparently in connection with negotiations in the WTO. The Commonwealth Secretary-General was quoted as riposting that the Commonwealth was no longer Britain-centred and claimed that he had

the freedom to act and employ such persons as he chose. Another rift was reported in *The Times* of 18 October 2004 when the secretary-general was said to rebuff a British government suggestion of a joint meeting between the British Prime Minister, the French President and the secretaries-general of the Commonwealth and la Francophonie. And in a press release on 20 July 2005, the secretary-general condemned the British government's unwillingness to facilitate the commercial sale of the defunct Commonwealth Institute as 'selfish imperialism' and 'a betrayal'.

Bibliography

Adamson, David, *The Last Empire: Britain and the Commonwealth*, I.B. Tauris, 1989.
Ager, Dennis, *Francophonie in the 1990s: Problems and Opportunities*, Cleveland Multilingual Matters, 1996.
Ancram, M., 'After Zimbabwe, has the Commonwealth still got a purpose?', Chatham House Lecture, Royal Institute of International Affairs, 5 February 2003.
Anyaoku, E., *The Inside Story of the Modern Commonwealth*, Evans Brothers, 2004.
Anyaoku, E., *The Missing Headlines: Selected Speeches*, Liverpool University, 1997.
Ashton, S.R. and Louis, WM.R., *East of Suez and the Commonwealth 1964–1971*, Part 1, H.M. Stationery Office, 2005.
Austin, Dennis, 'The Commonwealth and Britain', Chatham House paper 41, 1988.
Bostock, W.W., *Assessing the authenticity of a supra-national language-based movement – la Francophonie*, Edinburgh University, 1986.
Bostock, W.W., *Francophonie: Organisation, Coordination, Evaluation*, Sheffield University, 1986.
Bourne, R., *Britain in the Commonwealth*, Royal Commonwealth Society, 1997.
Bourne, R., *The Case for a Commonwealth Policy Studies Unit*, Institute of Commonwealth Studies, 1998.
Bourne, R., *Where Next for the Group of 54?* Commonwealth Policy Studies Unit, 2001.
Brown, J.M., *Nehru: A Political Life*, Yale University, 2003.
Brown, J.M. and Louis, WM.R., 'The Twentieth Century', *Oxford History of the British Empire*, vol. IV, OUP, 1999.
'Canada and La Francophonie', Reference Series No. 53, Department of External Affairs, Ottawa, 1982.
Cluff, A., *A Future for the Commonwealth*. Commission on the Commonwealth, 2001.
Commonwealth and Comparative Politics, vol. 39, 2001.
'Commonwealth and La Francophonie', Report of a Seminar 2002, Franco-British Council British Section.
Commonwealth Business Council, News Letter, Jan/Feb 2003.
Commonwealth Secretary-General, Biennial Reports. Commonwealth Secreteriat.
Cline, Ray S., 'Trouble in Paradise', *Antillan Review*, June 1985.
Cribb, Robert, *Historical Atlas of Indonesia*, Hawaii University, 2000.
Crowe, V., 'The Commonwealth in a Changing World: New Relationships and New Dimensions,' Wilton Park Paper no. 129, 1997.
Dahm, Bernhard, *History of Indonesia in the Twentieth Century*, Pall Mall Press, 1971.
Darwin, John, *Britain and Decolonisation*, St. Martin's, 1988.
Darwin, John, 'Decolonisation and the End of Empire', *Oxford History of the British Empire*, vol. 5, OUP, 1999.
Darwin, John, *The End of the British Empire: The Historical Debate*, Blackwell, 1991.

Dasgupta, C., *War and Diplomacy in Kashmir 1947–48*, Sage, 2002.

de Castro, P.C., 'The Community of the Portuguese Speaking Countries', *Verfassung und Recht in Übersee*, nos 2 and 3, 1998.

De Jong, L., *The Collapse of a Colonial Society*, KITLV Leiden, 2002.

De La Serre, F., Leruez, J. and Wallace, Helen, *French and British Foreign Policies in Transition*, Chatham House,1990.

Dewar, D., Commonwealth Day Lecture, Edinburgh, March 2000.

Dilks, D., *Communications, the Commonwealth and the Future*, Hull University, 1994.

Dilks, D., *Curzon in India*, 2 vols, Taplinger, 1969.

Dilks, D., *Great Britain, the Commonwealth and the Wider World, 1939–45*, Hull University, 1998.

Dilks, D., *Youth Exchanges in the Commonwealth*, Royal Society of Arts, August 1973.

Dilks, D. and Manley, R., *Commonwealth Youth Exchange Council*, Royal Commonwealth Society, 1971.

Dimier, Veronique, 'The French Union, 1945–58', *ECPR Copenhagen*, 2000.

Doolan, Paul, 'Time for Dutch Courage in Indonesia', *History Today*, vol. 3, Issue 47, 1997.

Doxey, Margaret P., *The Commonwealth Secretariat and the Contemporary Commonwealth*, Macmillan, 1989.

Eayrs, James, *The Commonwealth and Suez*, OUP, 1964.

Encyclopedia of Public International Law, vol. 10, Max Planck Institute, 1987.

Ferguson, Niall, *Empire. How Britain Made the Modern World*, Allen Lane, 2003.

Ford, K. and Katwala, S., 'Reinventing the Commonwealth'. Foreign Policy Centre, 1999.

'*Francophonie*, testing time for democracy', *West Africa*, Issue 4080, 1996.

Frey, Marc, 'European Development Policy in South East Asia', *Contemporary European History*, CUP, 2003.

Frey, Marc, 'The US and colonialism in South East Asia, 1940–45', *American Studies*, vol. 48, no. 3, 2003.

Frey, M., Pruessen, R.W. and Tan, Y.T., *The Transformation of South East Asia*, Armonk, ME Sharpe, 2003.

Gallagher, J., *The Decline, Revival and Fall of the British Empire*, CUP, 1982.

Garner, Joe, *The Commonwealth Office 1925–68*, Heinemann, 1978.

Goldsworthy, David, *Losing the Blanket*, Melbourne University, 2002.

Goldsworthy, David, *The Conservative Government and the End of Empire, 1951–1957*, Part 1, H.M. Stationery Office, 1994.

Goslinga, Cornelis C.A., *Short History of the Netherlands Antilles and Surinam*, Martinus Nijhoff, 1979.

Gunthorp, D. (ed.), *Commonwealth Trade and Investment Almanac*, Hanson Cooke, 1997.

Hall, H.D., *Commonwealth. A History of the British Commonwealth of Nations*, Van Nostrand Reinhold, 1971.

Heffer, S., *Like the Roman. The Life of Enoch Powell*, Orion, 1999.

Hendrickson, E., 'Surinam and the Antilles', *The World Today*, June 1984.

Hitchcock, W.I., *The Struggle for Europe*, Doubleday, 2003.

Holland, R., 'The Decolonizing Metropole: British Experience From India to Hong Kong 1947–1997', *European Review*, vol. 8, no. 1, 2000.

House of Commons Foreign Affairs Committee, *The Future Role of the Commonwealth*, vols 1 and 2, H.M. Stationery Office, 1996.

Howard, M. and Louis, WM.R., *The Oxford History of the Twentieth Century*, OUP, 1998.

Hyam, R., *The Labour Government and the End of Empire, 1945–1951*, Part 1, H.M. Stationery Office, 1992.

Hyam, R. and Louis, WM.R., *The Conservative Government and the End of Empire, 1957–1964*, Part 1, H.M. Stationery Office, 2000.

Jenkins, R., 'Reassessing the Commonwealth', Chatham House paper, Royal Institute of International Affairs, 1997.

Judd, D. and Slinn, P., *The Evolution of the Modern Commonwealth 1902–80*, Macmillan, 1982.

Kempthorne, M., 'Status of Member Countries', Institute of Commonwealth Studies, 2001.

Kirkman, W.P., *Unscrambling an Empire*, Chatto and Windus, 1966.

Louis, WM.R. and Robinson, R., 'The Imperialism of Decolonization', *Journal of Imperial and Commonwealth History*, vol. 22, no. 3, 1994.

Lundan, Sarianna M. and Jones, G., 'The "Commonwealth Effect" and the Process of Internationalisation', *World Economy*, vol. 24, no. 1, January 2001.

Lyon, Peter H., 'Commonwealth Sense and Sentiment', *The Listener*, 26 July 1979.

Lyon, Peter H., '1949–99: Fifty Years of a Renewing Commonwealth', *The Round Table*, no. 350, April 1999.

Lyon, Peter H., 'The Commonwealth in the 1970s', *The World Today*, April 1971.

Mansergh, N., *Survey of British Commonwealth Affairs, 1939–1952*, vol. 2, OUP, 1958.

Mansergh, N., *The Commonwealth Experience*, vol. 2, Toronto University, 1982.

Mayall, James, *International Affairs*, vol. 74, Chatham House, RIIA, 1998.

Mayall, James and Payne, Anthony, *The Fallacies of Hope*, Manchester University, 1991.

McIntyre, W.D., *A Guide to the Contemporary Commonwealth*, Palgrave, 2001.

McIntyre, W.D., *British Decolonization 1946–1977*, St. Martin's, 1998.

McIntyre, W.D., *Colonies into Commonwealth*, Blandford, 1974.

McIntyre, W.D., 'India, Ireland and the Headship of the Commonwealth', *The Round Table*, no. 365, July 2002.

McIntyre, W.D., *The Commonwealth of Nations: Origins and Impact, 1869–1971*, Minnesota University, 1977.

McIntyre, W.D., *The Significance of the Commonwealth, 1965–1990*, Macmillan, 1991.

Media Monitor, Hugh Quigley (ed.), Den Haag.

Miller, J.D.B., *Britain and the Commonwealth*, Duke University reprint 33, 1970.

Miller, J.D.B., *Survey of Commonwealth Affairs. Problems of Expansion and Attrition 1953–69*, RIIA/OUP, 1974.

Miller, J.D.B., *The Commonwealth in the World*, Duckworth, 1958.

Moco, M., 'Four Years of Cooperation in Portuguese: the CPLP, a Mature Community', *NATO's Nations and Partners for Peace*, 2000, spl. pt 1.

Morris, Jan, *Farewell the Trumpets*: An Imperial Retreat, Faber, 1978.

Neillands, R., *A Fighting Retreat. The British Empire 1947–97*, Hodder and Stoughton, 1996.

Parekh, B., *Report on the Future of Multi-Ethnic Britain*, Profile Books, 2001.

Pluvier, J.M., *South East Asia From Colonialism to Independence*, OUP, 1974.

Political Handbook of the World 1997, Binghampton University, New York.

Porter, A.N. and Stockwell, A.J., *British Imperial Policy and Decolonization, 1938–1964*, 2 vols, Macmillan, 1987 and 1989.

Ryan, D. and Pungong, V., *The United States and Decolonization*, St. Martin's, 2000.

Schiavone, G., *International Organisations – A Directory*, Macmillan, 1997.

Smith, A. and Sanger, C., *Stitches in Time*, Andre Deutsch, 1981.

Steel, David, Commonwealth Lecture, Glasgow, 16 March 2001.

Stockwell, Tony, *Ending the British Empire*, London University, 1999.

Taylor, R.J and Hamilton, J., 'Canada in Action – the Commonwealth, La Francophonie', R/L Pub Consultants, 1994.

The Round Table, The Commonwealth Journal of International Affairs.

Therien, J.P., 'Cooperation and Conflict in La Francophonie', *International Journal Toronto*, no. 3, 1993.

Verrier, Anthony, *Through the Looking Glass: British Foreign Policy in the Age of Illusions*, J. Cape, 1983.

Ward, Stuart, *British Culture and the End of Empire*, Manchester University, 2001.

West, Katherine, *Economic Opportunities for Britain and the Commonwealth*, Royal Institute of International Affairs, 1995.

Index